Economic Foreign Policies of Industrial States

Economic Foreign Policies of Industrial States

Edited by
Wilfrid L. Kohl
Johns Hopkins University
Bologna Center

Lexington Books
D.C. Heath and Company
Lexington, Massachusetts
Toronto

Library of Congress Cataloging in Publication Data

Main entry under title:
Economic foreign policies of industrial states.

1. International economic relations—Addresses, essays, lectures. 2. Economic history—1945- —Addresses, essays, lectures. I. Kohl, Wilfrid L.
HF1411.F59 338.91'172'2 76-43584
ISBN 0-669-00958-x

Published simultaneously in Canada.

Printed in the United States of America.

International Standard Book Number: 0-669-00958-x

Library of Congress Catalog Card Number: 76-43584

Contents

Preface

Foreign policy in the 1970s is increasingly concerned with economic issues. The fading of the Cold War bipolar confrontation and the rise of détente have somewhat reduced our preoccupation with traditional security questions, allowing other issues to rise on foreign policy agendas. A further reason for the politicization of economic issues in international politics is the growing web of economic interdependence, as national economies become more and more interlocked through the expansion of trade and international investment, yielding a corollary reliance on some kind of stable exchange rate regime. This politicization has been further reinforced by the collapse of the Bretton Woods system and the need to negotiate a revised and extended international economic order to take its place. Ths result has been a blurring of the traditional distinction between "high" and "low" policies, as the international economy has become a much more active subsystem of world politics. As the title of this book is meant to suggest, the economic components of foreign policy can no longer be treated simply as an extension of domestic economic policy.

Several recent studies have noted the heightened importance of economic issues in international relations and the necessity that a new international economic system be created to take the place of the defunct Bretton Woods system.[a] Yet there are few studies of the relationship between economics and politics in the making of national economic foreign policies, subjects we need to understand better before an improved international economic order can be devised. This volume is intended as a contribution to our empirical knowledge of the economic foreign policies and policy-making processes of the advanced industrial states. Although most of the contributors are economists, the chapters have been written from a political economy perspective. This approach is facilitated by the fact that many of the authors have had policy experience as government officials or advisers.

The introductory chapter by C. Fred Bergsten sets the stage by reviewing the major features of the post-World War II international political-economic system as anchored in the institutions of Bretton Woods under a strong U.S. leadership. Bergsten analyzes the factors behind the collapse of the Bretton Woods system and discusses alternative approaches for creating a new order for international economic relations. Given the need for some kind of managed system to assure order and the impossibility of continued U.S. dominance due to changed circumstances, Bergsten argues for a system of collective multilateral

[a]See especially C. Fred Bergsten (ed.), *The Future of the International Economic Order* (Lexington, Mass.: Lexington Books, D.C. Heath and Company, 1975); C. Fred Bergsten and Lawrence B. Krause (eds.), *World Politics and International Economics* (Washington, D.C.: Brookings Institution, 1976); Hugh Corbet and Robert Jackson (eds.), *In Search of a New World Economic Order* (New York: John Wiley, 1974); Richard N. Cooper, *The Economics of Interdependence* (New York: McGraw-Hill, 1968).

management while pointing out the considerable obstacles that must be overcome to achieve it. He concludes by reviewing some of the policy issues that need to be addressed if new international regimes for trade, money, and investment are to be devised. Bergsten's chapter depicts the international context in which national economic foreign policies operate in the mid-1970s.

Seven "country" chapters follow, dealing with the economic foreign policies of the major economic powers of North America, Western Europe and Japan. Each of the authors of these essays was asked to discuss the economic resource base of his country and the major themes in its postwar foreign economic policy, while noting any particular national biases in the goals set for such policies and any tendencies to use economic policies for political purposes. The extent of each country's economic interdependence is also assessed. Moreover, the authors were requested to explain the political context and the policy-making processes of their countries as regards economic foreign policy. Finally, the impact of European Community membership on national foreign economic policies is addressed, along with the general attitude of most of the countries toward international economic institutions. Naturally, the authors were allowed some flexibility in formulating their chapters, and the results reflect to a considerable extent each contributor's major areas of interest and expertise.

In the chapter on the United States, Harald B. Malmgren reminds us that throughout most of the postwar period the American economy has been self-sufficient to a high degree, and that American foreign economic policy has traditionally been subordinated to domestic policy. Dissenting from revisionist interpretations, Malmgren sees no consistent pattern of U.S. use of its economic power to underpin designs for political hegemony over its allies. He argues inter alia that the Washington policy process has been and is too complex and arbitrary to allow the implementation of any one foreign economic policy vision. In the 1970s, however, Malmgren sees the era of separation of foreign political and foreign economic policy in the United States rapidly coming to a close, as exports have increased to over 7 percent of GNP, and with increasing vulnerability to oil and raw material shortages. External economic policy must now be related to national political objectives. He admonishes that the process of making American foreign economic policy, which can now be called economic foreign policy, needs improvement as a result.

Benjamin J. Cohen's essay on Great Britain focuses on the major shift in recent British foreign economic policy, the decision to join the European Community. Cohen shows how this shift can be explained primarily by external economic factors, especially the growth of British trade with the EC countries, and the diminishing importance of economic ties with the Commonwealth. A corollary political consideration by government policy-makers was the recognition that only through the EC could Britain hope to maintain global political influence. The implications of EC membership for Britain's future economic foreign policies are assessed.

French policies under General de Gaulle offer perhaps the clearest example of the use of foreign economic policy for political purposes, since the General used international monetary and other policies to support his foreign political objectives, especially to combat what he saw as increasing U.S. hegemony in Europe. But, as Edward L. Morse demonstrates, the increased openness of the French economy since 1969, along with changes in political leadership and continuing domestic political constraints, have made the conduct of a coherent French economic foreign policy more arduous. Morse examines shifts in French policy under Georges Pompidou and under Valéry Giscard d'Estaing.

It is well known that West Germany's recovery after World War II was spurred by export-led growth, and that the German economy today remains heavily reliant on exports. In his subtle analysis Wilhelm Hankel shows that there was no planned postwar German foreign economic policy, but that a free market approach naturally led German industry to seek foreign customers to replace earlier markets in other parts of the now divided nation. What developed out of this process, however, driven ostensibly by ideological liberalism, was a subtle neo-mercantilist policy that may leave West Germany potentially weaker in the long run, in spite of its present economic strength, because of its reliance on a fair weather international economy.

In his treatment of Italy, Marcello de Cecco stresses the profound economic transformation which that country has undergone since the war, the persisting gap in levels of development between the North and the South, and Italy's strong dependence on exports and imports of raw materials, energy, and agricultural products. Italy's growth has been assisted by a clear choice for free trade, West European economic integration, and the use of monetary policy. However, as de Cecco explains, domestic political fragmentation has frequently prevented formation of a policy consensus, slowing economic reform and making the conduct of a coherent economic foreign policy difficult.

Like Italy, Japan is also heavily dependent on imports of raw materials, oil and primary commodities. Philip H. Trezise points out how this reliance on external supplies has increased markedly with Japan's spectacular economic growth, culminating in visible economic vulnerability in the energy and raw materials crises following 1973. Discussing the factors behind Japanese growth, Trezise challenges the "Japan Incorporated" argument that holds that a domestic consensus existed between big business, politicians, and civil servants on growth and the promotion of export trade as a primary objective. Trezise, nevertheless, stresses the weight of domestic interests that have slowed change in Japanese foreign economic policy and maintained, for a long period, a highly protectionist stance.

The essay by H. Edward English affirms that the Canadian economy is characterized by a high degree of economic interdependence because it has relied to a large extent on external, primarily American, capital for the development of domestic natural resources. In addition, Canada depends on external markets for the sale of many resource-based products. While on the one hand Canada has supported multilateral trade arrangements, strands of a protectionist policy can be found in several areas, for example on foreign investment, as a perceived necessity for political reasons to maintain Canadian national identity.

Two final chapters depart from the pattern of essays on particular countries. The chapter by Geoffrey Denton and Theo Peeters evaluates the extent to which the European Community has taken over national foreign economic policies and become an actor in the world political economy. The authors conclude that the EC's sovereignty is still very limited, since only in the trade area can it really conduct foreign relations. The role and positions of the community in the Tokyo Round of multilateral trade negotiations and in recent association agreements are evaluated in some detail. The prospects for extending the community's sovereignty to other areas of external economic policy, which could enable it to conduct a more effective economic foreign policy, are assessed.

A final chapter by Roger D. Hansen analyzes the perceptions of Third World countries of the Bretton Woods system as a system favoring the industrial countries and examines recent shifts in the political economy of North-South relations since 1973. In light of OPEC's oil diplomacy, the rise in commodity prices, and pressures in the United Nations for a "New International Economic Order," Hansen explores whether the developing countries have reached a turning point in their bargaining power vis-à-vis the industrial countries. He concludes that the developing countries will probably be unable to maintain the solidarity necessary to bargain successfully to change the rules of the international economic game, though some limited gains are possible in specific areas if OPEC takes the interests of the poorer countries seriously into account.

W.L.K.

Acknowledgments

Most of the essays in this book are revised and updated versions of lectures originally presented either to a graduate foreign policy seminar or to a faculty seminar on international political economy, both of which I chaired, at Columbia University under the sponsorship of the Institute on Western Europe during 1973-1975. The support of an NDEA European studies grant from the Office of Education for this political economy program, conducted jointly with the Center for European Studies at the City University of New York, is hereby acknowledged and deeply appreciated. This particular publication is very much a product of the Columbia Institute on Western Europe, of which I was associate director until 1976. The critical comments of members of the Columbia faculty seminar on international political economy and a number of graduate students were immensely helpful to me and to many of the contributing authors. I am especially grateful for support and advice at various stages from my former colleagues, Professors Donald J. Puchala, presently director of the Columbia Institute on Western Europe, and Joan E. Spero of the Institute's faculty.

It is particularly satisfying to me that it was possible to include in this volume an essay on Italy, written on relatively short notice by a new colleague, Professor Marcello de Cecco of the University of Siena and the Johns Hopkins University Bologna Center. In a small way Professor de Cecco's contribution provides a bridge to my own new assignment as director of the Bologna Center, where we hope to conduct further research over the next several years on some of the questions raised in this volume.

W.L.K.

Economic Foreign Policies of Industrial States

1 Introduction: The International Economy and World Politics in the Post-Postwar Era

C. Fred Bergsten

The international system that successfully governed economic relations among the non-Communist countries in the first postwar generation had three major component parts: an international monetary system based on fixed exchange rates and the dollar; a trade regime that focused on tariffs and relied on nondiscrimination among its members; and a network of foreign assistance arrangements that featured transfers of capital and technical assistance from richer to poorer countries. That system has almost totally collapsed, or become irrelevant in dealing with the major world economic problems of the second postwar generation. I will discuss the reasons for its demise and assess the outlook for the construction of a new international economic order, and then apply that framework to some of the current problems of international money, world trade, and foreign investment.

The Bases of the Postwar International Economic Order

Five features dominated the Bretton Woods system[a] as it developed in practice, and they made it a success for most of the postwar period.

First, it operated within the context of a rigid, bipolar international security system. It is always necessary to view international economic relations as a subsystem of world politics as a whole. And the dominant feature of world politics in the first postwar generation was, of course, a frigid cold war and confrontation between East and West, which remained intense through at least the early 1960s and dominated the entire international environment during that period.

This security context meant that economic issues that otherwise might have surfaced and created international tension tended to be submerged both by the leader of the anti-Communist coalition, the United States, and by the other members of the coalition—whether they were formal members of an alliance system, as in Western Europe, or simply dependent on the United States for

[a]The "Bretton Woods system," as used throughout this chapter, encompasses the rules and institutional arrangements of the International Monetary Fund and International Bank for Reconstruction and Development (developed at Bretton Woods, New Hampshire, in 1945), which largely governed international monetary and development relations, respectively, and the General Agreement on Tariffs and Trade, which governed international trade relations from 1949.

their security in a world perceived to be highly insecure, as in the "Third World" of developing countries.[b] All these countries had an overriding desire to avoid frictions that would upset the fundamental relationship, which was critical for the national security of each as they perceived it at the time.

Indeed, this security framework not only minimized economic conflict among the non-Communist countries. Virtually every positive U.S. initiative in the field of foreign economic policy—the Marshall Plan, Point IV, support for the creation and development of the Common Market, the Kennedy Round (and its predecessor trade negotiations), and even the creation of special drawing rights—was motivated largely by the overall U.S. foreign policy concern of strengthening the Atlantic and Pacific Alliances and the Third World, thereby repelling the threat of Communist advance. At the same time, the "security dilemma" of countries other than the United States induced them to submerge some economic problems that they otherwise might have attempted to surface.[c] Hence economic issues remained at a lower level of discourse than otherwise might have occurred, and they were handled largely in a "purely economic" context; countries seldom sought to politicize economic issues by linking them with noneconomic issues.[1]

Second, the international economic system of this period, like any political system, developed in a particular historical framework conditioned by contemporary perceptions of the relative saliency of different problems. In creating and maintaining the Bretton Woods system, the decision-makers of the 1940s and 1950s sought primarily to avoid a replication of the problems of the interwar period—particularly the breakdown of the international economy in the 1930s that deepened and broadened the depression, which in turn played a major role in the economic dislocation within particular major countries, especially in Europe, which in turn contributed significantly to the advent of totalitarian governments, which in turn brought on world war. Thus there was perceived, correctly so, a direct linkage between the breakdown of the international economic order and the breakdown of world peace. That view played a critical role, certainly among U.S. policy-makers, in the decisions to create and maintain for a generation the postwar economic system.

Some revisionist historians have challenged this view, claiming that the security issue was simply a cover for U.S. imperialism. And one certainly cannot prove definitively whether economic or security concerns dominated the motives of U.S. policy-makers, since one could describe the liberal international economic order that emerged as either "a bastion against totalitarianism" or "a

[b]"Third World" itself is a cold war term, which distinguished the developing countries from the "First World" of non-Communist industrialized countries and the "Second World" of Communist countries.

[c]It is interesting to note the same pattern of relationships within the Communist alliance systems. Because of their "security dilemmas," the countries of Eastern Europe remained largely subservient to the Soviet Union on economic issues during most of the first postwar generation.

world safe for American capitalism." However, it is highly instructive that the leading proponents of the revisionist approach never even mention Munich in over seven hundred pages of discussion of the first ten years of postwar U.S. foreign policy.[2] This telling omission indicates how the revisionists often fail to take into account the overriding importance of security concerns in postwar U.S. foreign policy, which in turn lent critical importance to the view that the breakdown of the international economy played a major role in the security problems that emerged.

So the historical framework within which the postwar economic system was developed and maintained was based, for many years, on a desire to avoid repeating the events of the 1930s: flexible exchange rates that facilitated competitive depreciations, import barriers, and export subsidies. The central objective of the postwar system was to avoid those developments via fixed exchange rates, trade liberalization, and international rules to check national efforts to export unemployment to other countries.

A third factor underlying both the creation and maintenance of the postwar system was the leadership of the United States. The United States maintained an economic umbrella over the world economic system very similar to the nuclear umbrella it maintained over the security system, and provided the basic leadership function.[3] It was willing, indeed eager, for the dollar to play the central role in the monetary system despite the increasingly adverse effects of that role on the U.S. economy.[d] It was willing to run balance-of-payments deficits, which enabled other countries to increase their reserves and run trade surpluses. It was willing to make "nonreciprocal" trade concessions to ensure that each succeeding round of international trade negotiations reached agreements.

Countries abroad accepted this U.S. leadership. In the early period they had little choice. Even when they became stronger, in the 1960s, they remained uncertain of their own strength and continued to receive very tangible benefits from the system in being able to meet their own economic objectives.

The United States viewed these developments as serving its own economic, as well as security, interests; its role was by no means wholly altruistic. The economic effects of running a dollar system and balance-of-payments deficits were perceived as at least marginally desirable from the U.S. standpoint, and freer world trade was viewed primarily as providing additional foreign markets for U.S. exports. World economic leadership was accepted in the United States

---

[d]The effects were adverse primarily because they deeply constrained the United States from adjusting its balance-of-payments disequilibria through devaluation, the only economically effective means of adjustment that was politically feasible for the United States, and thereby sharply increased both unemployment and protectionist trade pressures in the United States. For a discussion of the costs and benefits of the dollar's role to the United States, which demonstrates that security concerns must have dominated U.S. policy unless there were major errors of perception of the economic effects, see C. Fred Bergsten, *The Dilemmas of the Dollar: The Economics and Politics of U.S. International Monetary Policy* (New York: New York University Press, 1975).

through the 1950s because the United States was then the dominant world economy and did not have to worry too much about foreign competition, and through most of the 1960s because the U.S. economy was doing so well.[e] The systemic objective of maintaining an open world economic system as part of overall U.S. foreign policy was dominant, but the economics supported such an approach as well. Thus for a variety of reasons peculiar to the particular period, a U.S. leadership position was accepted both at home and abroad and provided an underpinning for continuing the Bretton Woods system.

The other two factors that underlay the Bretton Woods system were more economic in nature. The fourth was a high degree of consensus on the goals sought by the international economic system.[4] Again with the 1930s very much in mind, the primary objective was to avoid unemployment and to avoid individual countries' efforts to export their unemployment to others. These rather simple shared goals continued to dominate the economic objectives of most major countries into the 1960s. They were a crucial element in the effective functioning of the international economic system.

Fifth, tremendous prosperity in all the key national economies underlay the whole Bretton Woods success. There were no deep economic problems like those of the interwar period or, indeed, the pre-World War I period. It was a period of economic prosperity and growth unprecedented in all recorded history. In a sense, therefore, Bretton Woods was a fair weather system. Its underlying economic conditions were very favorable, not only in the industrialized world but also in the developing countries, most of which achieved dramatic growth rates in the 1960s and so shared in the overall prosperity.

These five factors were the basic underpinnings of the Bretton Woods system, both at its inception and in its continuing success. In the first half of the 1970s, however, each of those five factors changed dramatically. With those changes has gone the functioning of the previous international economic order.

The Collapse of the Postwar International Economic Order

First, the security blanket that smothered most international economic disputes has been largely nudged aside. Perceptions of possible East-West hostilities are greatly reduced. Perceptions of détente are widespread throughout the world. Military confrontation between the big powers is viewed as highly unlikely, and the superpowers are unable to make much political use of their military might either.[5] As a result, dependence on the United States by its allies has greatly diminished and the salience of the security issue has been greatly reduced.

[e]From 1960 through 1969, U.S. unemployment declined steadily and sharply to a post-Korean War low. Corporate profits rose to all-time highs in 1967 and remained at that high plateau for two more years.

Economic differences would thus rise toward the surface even if they had not increased in magnitude themselves. This in turn increasingly politicizes international economic relations, eroding the "two-track" system of the Bretton Woods period.

Second, history is easily forgotten. The generation of decision-makers who remember the problems of the 1930s from personal experience has largely passed from power. Indeed, it is the postwar record of booming economic success, not of depression and competitive depreciation, that informs the views of most current decision-makers, who believe that international economic issues are unlikely to get out of control and raise major difficulties.

The recent economic strains that have plagued virtually all countries have provided a reminder of the risks of international economic conflict. However, they are still largely viewed as an aberrant rather than a deep-seated structural problem. And their inflationary aspects appear to generate more concerns than their high rates of unemployment, further differentiating the phenomenon from the 1930s.

The third factor, U.S. leadership, has also changed from both the side of foreign acceptance and the side of domestic feasibility in the United States. It is quite clear that other countries have achieved international economic power positions very close to, if not greater than, that of the United States. Several European countries now virtually equal the United States in terms of per capita income. German monetary reserves alone are about double those of the United States; Europe as a whole has international reserves many times higher. Germany and Japan have run bigger trade surpluses than the United States has ever run. On a whole variety of indicators of international economic power, other countries—Japan, the European Community, even Germany alone—far exceed the United States. And even formerly "developing countries," most notably the oil producers but many others as well, also are achieving important levers of international economic power.[6]

Traditionally, the United States has been less open to international transactions than virtually any other non-Communist country and thus more able than most to avoid economic repercussions from abroad. However, the ratio of trade to GNP has doubled for the United States in the last decade and now exceeds 7 percent. Europe, by coalescing in the EEC, has reduced its trade dependence on the outside world to under 10 percent, and Japan has a similar ratio. So in these aggregate terms, the differences are not great. They narrow even further when one considers that U.S. firms, through their direct investment overseas, rely far more on foreign markets for their profits than do European and Japanese firms. If one adds nontrade factors to the trade ratios just mentioned, the difference between the United States on the one hand and Western Europe as a unit and Japan on the other hand is reduced even further.

Thus it is simply archaic to say that the United States, in the post-postwar era, can remain aloof to the world economy and therefore that it has much greater power than other countries. Others have indeed increased their power positions relative to the United States on a whole variety of concepts and therefore simply will not accept the U.S. dominance of the past.

Simultaneously, the United States is unwilling to play the kind of leadership role it did in the past for purely domestic reasons. Some aspects of that leadership role were costly for the United States: it did not have control over its exchange rate, which is crucial for domestic jobs and price levels; other countries could essentially determine the international adjustment process and set the level of world reserves; the welfare and anti-inflation benefits that the United States achieved through payments deficits had gradually come to be offset by the adverse employment effects in the United States of an overvalued exchange rate; unilateral trade concessions were totally unpalatable in a world of tough competition and severe economic problems at home. Internationalization of the costs of systemic leadership became too high for the United States to pay alone.

As a result, the nation that built and maintained the Bretton Woods system brought it down in August 1971, with the devaluation of the dollar, cessation of its convertibility into U.S. monetary reserves, and a temporary import surcharge. There remains a view that a collapse of the dollar overhang—the dollar balances held by other countries—forced the United States to devalue, but this is simply incorrect. Gold conversions were much smaller in 1970 and 1971 than they had been in some earlier years. The dollar had been de facto inconvertible from the advent of the two-tier gold system in 1968. Indeed, there was very little foreign pressure, either indirect or directly through efforts to convert dollar balances, to force the United States to act. The change in U.S. international economic policy was not forced by other countries.

What happened was that the United States decided that the existing exchange rate alignment, and the existing monetary system, no longer served its national interests. The Nixon administration concluded, with much justification, that the overvaluation of the dollar had come to cost half a million or so American jobs, a significant element in an unemployment rate that was close to 6 percent (particularly with a presidential election little more than a year away). The United States did not have control over its exchange rate, which was particularly crucial because exchange rate adjustments are the only effective balance-of-payments adjustment tool for the United States—since it simply cannot deflate its economy for external reasons (because trade is too small a part of its total economy) or maintain effective controls over its international transactions (because they are so large in absolute terms). So the United States had given up a key policy tool, with very adverse internal economic effects, which led it to conclude that the existing situation did not serve its internal interests and had to be changed.

These changes in U.S. policy were implemented in a very costly manner, with lasting adverse effects on overall U.S. foreign policy as well as U.S. economic relations.[7] But the underlying problems were very deep for the United

States, and the motivating factor—the internal disillusionment with the international economic system as it affected the United States—was quite understandable. For purely internal reasons, in addition to other countries' unwillingness to accept it in a world of relatively equal economic powers, U.S. leadership as we have known it is a thing of the past.

The two other, more economic, factors that supported the Bretton Woods system have also changed radically. As noted above, a key factor was the shared objective of most countries in fighting unemployment and in avoiding national efforts to export unemployment. That consensus has now given way to a growing multiplicity of policy objectives that range far beyond avoiding unemployment, and even beyond maintaining price stability as well; it now includes a variety of desiderata such as more equitable income and regional distribution, and environmental concerns.

The theory of economic policy, as developed by Tinbergen and others,[8] indicates that the number of policy instruments must equal the number of policy targets. Thus as the number of policy targets multiplies, as it has been doing in virtually every country, governments grope for more policy instruments. They devise new fiscal incentives and government expenditure policies, and ways of disaggregating monetary policies.

They also look to international economic policy to avoid disruption of their internal policy efforts, through such events as sharp increases in imports of goods that compete with domestic output or sharp decreases of imports of needed consumer goods (such as food) or industrial inputs (such as oil). And they seek to use foreign economic policies positively to help them achieve their internal targets. Regarding foreign investment, for example, country after country is manipulating the local subsidiaries of multinational enterprises to help backward regions, fight unemployment, provide foreign exchange earnings, and promote other domestic policy objectives in ways that will not undermine their decision-making sovereignty.[9]

As countries thus increasingly manipulate their foreign economic policies to try to cope with their increased number of economic and social policy targets, the whole international economic picture is complicated dramatically. This can be seen clearly within Europe. The Common Market is stagnating, indeed backsliding, in part because member countries now force it to consider regional policies and other complexities. Each national government is trying to achieve an increasing variety of objectives, and the difficulty rises exponentially when it moves onto the European stage. When the issues project onto the world stage, the reconciliation of these national complexities becomes even deeper. So the move from a relatively simple world of shared goals to a world of much more complex and often conflicting goals is a vital factor in the breakdown of the international economic system.

Finally, the fair weather world of the past is giving way to much more serious economic problems. The energy crisis has heightened those problems dramatically.[f] But even before its onset, the spread of rampant inflation throughout the industrialized world had become extremely serious, especially when it became coupled with deep worldwide recession in 1974.

Indeed, the advent of rapid inflation alone was already changing the whole nature of the international economic policy problem. For the last forty years or so, the basic objective of most countries' foreign economic policies was to avoid importing unemployment; countries would even try to export unemployment to each other if they thought they could get away with it. This meant that countries were basically trying to depreciate their exchange rates, or at least not let them appreciate. They would erect barriers to imports to protect domestic industries. And they would subsidize exports.

But once the basic national problem became inflation rather than unemployment, the objective of foreign economic policy was reversed. Countries no longer wanted to depreciate their exchange rates, but to appreciate them. During the early 1970s, in fact, numerous countries have explicitly upvalued or appreciated their exchange rates in order to fight internal inflation. They also removed barriers to capital inflows, to force their exchange rates up to help them fight inflation.

Japan sold over \$6 billion of its reserves during 1973 to keep its exchange rate *up*, in order to buy imports more cheaply and to stockpile commodities to hedge against both current inflation and future inflation, less than two years after it had intensely resisted massive pressure from abroad to move the yen higher. Some countries even revalued their exchange rates when they were not running balance-of-payments surpluses, a rather dramatic change from five years earlier when no country would revalue even when it was running heavy payments surpluses—what might be called "competitive exchange rate appreciation." The United States suddenly concluded in 1973 that the depreciation of the dollar had gone much too far, because it was exacerbating internal inflation, just months after it had been actively promoting such depreciation. But as soon as the dollar came back a bit, other countries intervened in the markets to stop its appreciation to avoid the inflationary consequences on themselves. Even France, after it dropped out of the "European joint float" in early 1974 because it felt the mark was pulling the franc too high, intervened massively to avoid further depreciation after the rate dropped a mere 5 percent.

The same change occurred in trade policies. In the early 1970s many people were very worried about a resurgence of protectionism of the traditional type, to

[f]See Edward R. Fried and Charles L. Schultz (eds.), *Higher Oil Prices and the World Economy* (Washington, D.C.: Brookings Institution, 1975). They conclude (p. 21) that higher oil prices cut real gross domestic product in 1974 by 2.5 percent in the United States, 2.7 percent in Western Europe, and 4.2 percent in Japan—accounting for 50 to 100 percent of the overall change in those countries from the pre-embargo outlook.

check imports.[10] The balance-of-payments problems kindled by the energy crisis deepened that concern in 1974. But country after country, both industrialized and developing, unilaterally reduced its barriers to imports in 1973-1974 because inflation had replaced unemployment as the key problem in most countries even after the advent of the energy crisis.

Even the historically most protectionist countries, Canada and Australia, unilaterally cut their tariffs across the board. The United States completely removed (or at least suspended) its import quotas on oil, steel, meat, sugar, and cheese. Japan, Germany, a number of oil-exporting countries such as Iran and Nigeria, and even many developing countries such as Colombia have done so. Even Italy, which resorted to import controls in 1974 because of its huge payments deficit, exempted a wide range of products from the outset and started liberalizing the system as soon as it was instituted.

This trend was particularly surprising because it occurred during a runup to an expected multilateral trade negotiation in which countries were planning, in the traditional way, to trade off import barriers against each other on a strictly reciprocal basis. In that kind of environment in the past, countries have always husbanded their existing import barriers to preserve their negotiating position in the coming reciprocal talks. Yet country after country unilaterally cut its import barriers instead.

Indeed, export controls for a time replaced import controls as the dominant issue of international trade policy. The United States has applied them on several foodstuffs and raw materials. The Arab oil embargoes are the clearest case, and the "new OPECs" are applying export quotas or taxes on numerous other primary products.[11] A number of other developing countries have done it on a number of their raw materials. There are strong signs that it will be done increasingly in manufactured products as well as in raw materials; the United States has seriously contemplated export quotas on a number of products that have been in short supply at home, and in several products where exports boomed because domestic price controls diverted output into foreign markets.[12]

These new trends, which stem from the advent of high levels of global inflation, raise the specter of beggar-thy-neighbor policies like those that occurred in the 1930s when the primary problem was unemployment—especially since no international economic framework now even exists through which to try to deal with these potential international conflicts. In the absence of such rules and institutional frameworks to deal with the problem of access to supplies, we will continue to see unilateral nationalist measures as countries seek to fend for themselves on the supply side just as they once did on the demand side. And if recession persists along with inflation, the world economy could experience countries trying to export *both* inflation and unemployment through controls, in different sectors, over both exports and imports.

Options for the Future

These dramatic changes in the international economic situation explain the breakdown of the old regime and point to the problems in creating a new one. What, in fact, could the new international economic order look like?

There are three broad options for managing any kind of international economic system. One is hegemony by an individual country with the power to exercise it. The successful systems of the past, of which there are only two, have in fact been based largely on national hegemony–the British before 1914, the United States for the first generation after World War II. But there is simply no candidate for that position now. No single country is in a position to dominate the world economy, either in terms of its domestic politics or foreign acceptance of such a regime. So this is not a viable option at present.

A second option is "nonmanagement," based on the principle of "letting the market do it." There would be no effort at concerted management, via a conscious decision not to take overt measures. Exchange rates would float freely, without government intervention. Trade and investment would be free.

There are some tendencies in that direction. The world has moved toward flexible exchange rates, although they are managed rather than purely market-determined floats. This is a major improvement in the international monetary system, though floating has already permitted competitive appreciation and always runs risks of competitive depreciation. Eurocurrency markets remain unfettered, though this provides an impetus to unstable evolution of a multiple key currency system. And there has been a renewed liberalization of imports through the market pressures exerted by inflation, after the renewed growth of import barriers after the completion of the Kennedy Round in 1967 through about 1971.

But in view of the multiplicity of national economic and social goals described above, and the deepening involvement of most countries in the world economy, it is highly unlikely that countries would agree to let the market fully work out such a critical price as the exchange rate and let trade flows–or even more so, investment flows–go unchecked. It in fact would be highly contradictory for countries–particularly those countries that depend much more on the world economy than the United States, but even the United States, whose involvement in the world economy has increased dramatically over the last twenty years–to increase the number and scope of their internal policy objectives, and hence policy instruments, and at the same time willing to give up all direct management of their international economic relations.

So the two options of hegemony by a dominant power and nonmanagement by "letting the market do it" appear unlikely, whether they are deemed desirable or not in principle. In that case we are left with the third possibility: joint management among several countries, particularly those with the greatest power in the world economic system. In a situation where goals often conflict, joint management among roughly equal powers is very difficult. It has never been accomplished effectively.

Europe is central to this whole question. A united Europe is probably an essential element to any new, jointly managed international economic order. But there are few signs that such a Europe is developing. Indeed, European integration has stagnated for the last few years and even been backsliding.[13] Europe can still coalesce negatively to block initiatives taken by others and avoid forward progress in international economic reform. But it seems unable to play a positive and constructive role in pushing forward the creation of new institutions, rules, and frameworks for a reconstructed international economic order. It thus appears dubious that Europe is going to be able to play the major role that is necessary to get the needed management, at least in the short run.

Indeed, the urgency of the issues suggests that it may prove impossible to wait for Europe to get together, and the United States may have to work more directly with Germany—which, alone among the other non-Communist countries, is an economic superpower. It should do so in a subtle way that minimizes the inevitable political problems, but in fact try to deal on a range of issues directly with Germany. In turn, the United States and Germany could then seek to bring along their own closest allies (e.g., Japan and the rest of the Common Market, respectively). Finally, decisions would be implemented through the existing international institutions with their broad national memberships. This approach, based on three concentric circles of decision-making, would be hierarchical but nevertheless broadly based with active participation by a wide range of countries. It might be one way to push ahead on the key monetary, trade, commodity, investment, and other issues that require early forward movement.[14]

These are the three broad options for creating a new international economic order. We turn now to a more detailed examination of three critical components of that order: international money, trade, and investment.

The International Monetary System

Economists divide the international monetary issue into two primary conceptual components: the adjustment process and the liquidity, or financial, problem. There was little progress on either during the negotiations of the Committee of Twenty and its inner group, the Committee of Five, during 1972-1974. They agreed to disagree in early 1973, and again in late 1975, and papered over the critical issues with calls for "a return to stable but adjustable exchange rates" with "floating permitted in particular circumstances." However, major evolutionary changes have been occurring on both parts of the monetary question.

In March 1973, the world moved to a system of unilaterally managed floating exchange rates. The adjective "managed" is necessary to indicate that it is not a system of *freely* flexible exchange rates, *à la* traditional theory, but one in which countries quite actively intervene in the markets. The "unilateral" is also important, because virtually all that intervention has been carried out by international monetary authorities acting alone, to pursue their own national objectives. As noted earlier, for example, Japan did so in 1973 to keep its exchange rate high to fight inflation.

The system of unilaterally managed floats has many merits. It is certainly superior to past efforts to try to shore up fixed exchange rates, which inevitably become indefensible as national economies progress at different rates and along different structural paths. The main problem is with its unilateral aspect, which raises the risk of inconsistent intervention by different monetary authorities—even intervention operating at cross purposes, leading to conflict in the exchange markets among national governments. We have not seen much of such conflict, though it could once more become a serious problem.

The central banks have been providing an important degree of leadership in evolving the new monetary system. Rather than continuing to talk about fixed parities or other ideas that are clearly not going to be implemented for some time, they have begun to work within the evolving flexible-rate system to develop procedures for joint intervention in the markets and at least some degree of consultation. It can be hoped that the system of unilaterally managed floats would now evolve into a system of multilaterally managed floats. "Managed" would not mean an effort to set parities or intervene in the markets frequently, but rather a surveillance system so that national authorities would know what their counterparts were doing, and have some rules and guidelines against which to judge whether such intervention were permissible or whether it could raise conflicts with other countries' goals. Agreement to systematize further the efforts already begun was reached at the "economic summit" meeting at Rambouillet in November 1975.

Such a system, with guidelines for floating, would be somewhat similar to a system of fixed exchange rates with guidelines to prompt frequent adjustments, perhaps with some international sanctions to back them up as discussed at length by the Committee of Twenty. Some observers argue, in fact, that there is no real difference between a floating-rate system over which there is multilateral surveillance of intervention and a fixed-rate system with rules prompting rapid adjustment of parities. Logically, that view may be right. The two approaches represent fairly proximate points in the middle of a spectrum ranging from freely flexible exchange rates at one end to rigidly fixed rates at the other.

In fact, however, there is a significant difference in the presumptions as to what would occur in practice under the two approaches. Under a floating system, even with much more multilateral surveillance than now exists, the presumption is that rates will move. Such a system should achieve more rapid adjustment of imbalances, and indeed to some extent prevent their occurring. Exchange rates in such a system would not provide easy targets for speculators.

This is quite different from the way an adjustable peg system would probably work in practice, given the continued predilection of many monetary authorities to return to fixed rates. If the world returned to a system of parities, even with the best intentions to adjust as soon as necessary when the guidelines indicated such a need, there would in fact be much of the rigidity that characterized the Bretton Woods system, which is untenable. Thus the U.S. government has been right to insist on a high degree of flexibility. Such flexibility is best achieved by the present system of managed floats, if amended to provide effective multilateral surveillance.

It is easy to understand why the United States now so strongly supports maximum flexibility of exchange rates, after insisting on fixity throughout the Bretton Woods period, by looking at two simple facts concerning its economic position. U.S. reserves, relative to the country's international transactions, have become virtually the lowest of any industrialized country (and lower than many developing countries), and foreign dollar accumulations are unlikely to provide the United States with nearly as much additional financing in the future as in the past. So the United States would be in the worst position of any major country to defend a fixed exchange rate, and hence quite naturally opts for a high degree of flexibility.[15]

In addition, the United States simply could not rely on internal inflation or deflation, adopted purely for balance-of-payments reasons, to achieve adjustment. Its foreign sector is still small enough that massive internal changes would be needed to achieve relatively small changes in the external balance. The fact that Europe (as a whole) and Japan are also relatively closed to the world economy suggests that exchange rate flexibility is right for them, too. Thus a high degree of flexibility of exchange rates is likely to permeate the international financial system for the indefinite future. The main need is to develop consultative procedures and surveillance mechanisms to avoid the risk of conflict in the exchange markets that might otherwise occur.

The international financial mechanism is also evolving from the dollar-based regime of the past into a multiple currency system. Some people have argued that the dollar has no real rivals, and will remain *the* key currency in the international financial system.[16] But the Deutsche mark has already far surpassed sterling as the second key currency in the world, both for reserve asset and private transactions purposes, and its use is growing rapidly. A portfolio adjustment is occurring out of the dollar into a series of other international currencies, particularly the Deutsche mark. Countries around the world—Brazil, several Arab countries, Israel, and many others—are increasingly holding Deutsche marks in their reserves, which reflects the rise of the Deutsche mark as a major force in international finance.

Indeed, a Deutsche mark zone has developed in Central Europe. The so-called snake in the tunnel is hardly a "European Community float," because three members of the Common Market (Britain, Italy, and Ireland) were never members and France also departed for a while in 1974-1975, all to float on their own. At the same time, at least four countries that are not members of the Common Market are part of the operation: Sweden, Norway, and Austria and Switzerland de facto. Thus it is not a Common Market operation because it excludes some Common Market members and includes some non-Common Market members.

In economic terms, it can be called only a Deutsche mark zone. What characterizes all the "member" countries is their high degree of dependence on the German economy, and its dominant role in their trade and therefore on their internal economies. Those countries have decided that pegging their currencies to the Deutsche mark is in their economic interest, as would be predicted by the theory of optimum currency areas.

Some of the members have had reservations about the arrangement from time to time. The French were hesitant when the Deutsche mark dragged up the French franc, and they lost a sizable share of their reserves in staying within the "snake" in September 1973; they subsequently left in early 1974. The mark has dragged up other currencies within the unit, and the Germans have in fact revalued twice to limit that effect. But the steady appreciation of the whole group of currencies, throughout the period since floating began in March 1973, has generally been welcomed by the others because of its anti-inflationary effect.

In fact, the widespread talk about the "depreciation of the dollar" in May-June 1973—which President Georges Pompidou called its "third devaluation"—was an incorrect characterization. The dollar was not depreciating against the Canadian dollar, the yen, the pound, the lira, or any of the other currencies around the world that account for the great bulk of U.S. trade and capital flows. It was only the Deutsche mark zone, then comprising nine different currencies, that was moving up against the dollar. Hence we were witnessing an appreciation of the Deutsche mark zone, not a depreciation of the dollar. This was one manifestation of the strength of the Deutsche mark and the attachment of these other currencies to it.

Like the advent of unilaterally managed floats, this trend raises some worrisome questions about the future. In the early 1960s, when analysis of international monetary reform was at an early stage, a number of observers considered very seriously the option of a multiple-reserve currency system.[17] One objective of such an approach, pursued by some U.S. government officials, was to legitimize the key currency roles of the dollar by bringing other currencies into a similar position; others involved had more cosmopolitan ideas in mind. But every single observer rejected the multiple-reserve currency system as the worst possible option because of its inherent instability: *à la* Gresham's law, there is increased risk of instability the more different types of assets that exist.

In addition, portfolio shifts among key currencies can produce exchange rate relationships that do not reflect the current competitive condition of the different national economies. Indeed, the decline in the key currency role of the dollar may produce its systemic undervaluation for some time to come just as the buildup in that role in the 1960s resulted in its systemic overvaluation. The result could be the export of unemployment from the United States to other countries and the acceleration of protectionist pressures there, the very same problems that developed earlier in the United States. Hence the continued evolution of a multiple key currency system can destabilize the functioning of the flexible exchange rates.[18] But the market is now creating such a system, as the dollar's relative role has declined as a result of the fundamental changes in the world economic and political situation described above.

Such changes always evolve with some time lags in the monetary area, because there is much inertia in it. Sterling retained a world role long beyond Britain's objective capability to support such a role for its currency, which was very costly for Britain. The same evolution is occurring with the dollar and it will continue despite the resurgence in relative U.S. strength due to the world food crisis and the lower U.S. dependence on oil imports.

Again, the question arises whether there should be international regulation to prevent the development of a multiple key currency system. It is quite feasible for different currencies to continue to be used for private transactions purposes. But all the national currencies that are in countries' monetary reserves should be consolidated in the IMF in return for special drawing rights, in an effort to make special drawing rights the dominant reserve asset of the future.

Thus the international monetary system is now moving toward unilaterally managed floating exchange rates and multiple key currencies. Both have very promising attributes. But both raise problems, because they are not operating within any system of international rules and institutional arrangements. It would be prudent to try to develop such arrangements, based on collective management by the major monetary powers, to avoid the risk of destabilizing economic trends and potential conflict among nations.

International Trade

Most observers in the early 1970s would have predicted the outbreak of massive bursts of protectionist import policies in the wake of a world recession as deep as occurred in 1974-1975 and the sharp deterioration in trade balances triggered for virtually all industrialized countries by the sharp increase in oil prices in 1973-1974. Yet no such outburst occurred. Indeed, by an overwhelming vote, the United States Congress in December 1974 authorized U.S. participation in the most ambitious trade-liberalizing negotiation in history.

There are two basic reasons why the international trading system has held up so well. First, as noted above, the continued presence of rapid inflation rates has deterred countries from raising barriers to imports, since such barriers raise domestic prices. Governments recognize that there is an external Phillips curve and that trade measures can export unemployment only at the cost of importing inflation. Thus inflation has had at least the one beneficial effect of helping to check protectionism.

Second, the parity changes of 1971-1973 and subsequent advent of flexible exchange rates have eliminated (or even reversed) most of the earlier balance-of-payments disequilibria, and defused that justification for protectionism. In the United States, there was less pressure for general import controls with unemployment above 8 percent in 1975 than with unemployment at 5 percent in 1971 because the dollar devaluations had sharply reduced the contribution of the foreign sector to the underutilization of capacity.

In addition, the commencement of the Multilateral Trade Negotiations (MTN) in early 1975 came just in time to provide the usual protection against protectionism that derives from a concerted international effort to liberalize trade. Successful completion of those negotiations is the principal item on the agenda of the world trading system at present.

Successful completion of the MTN, however, requires more than the traditional reduction of tariffs, although that should be an important ingredient. Progress is needed in reducing a number of nontariff barriers, most notably government procurement rules and the "voluntary" export restraints that are even more damaging than equivalent import quotas and represent a giant loophole in existing trade rules.[19] And as in the case of the international monetary system, reform of the rules themselves is sorely needed.[20]

The most important concept of this reform should be the extension of the rules to cover export controls and other issues surrounding the problem of access to supplies, modeled on the rules that throughout the postwar period have covered import controls and other issues surrounding access to markets.[21] As noted above, the advent of rapid inflation has triggered the widespread use of export controls as countries seek to check domestic prices by keeping goods at home. In addition, the new aggressiveness of primary producing countries in seeking to improve their terms of trade, both unilaterally and through the creation of "producers associations," often leads to the imposition of export controls or the domestic equivalents thereof.

Access to supplies is one of two important international economic issue-areas where no effective international rules and institutional arrangements exist. Yet it is potentially explosive, in both economic and political terms, as vividly demonstrated in the recent past by the Arab oil embargo and the several impositions of U.S. export controls on agricultural products. The creation of an international regime in this area is the most urgent task of international trade reform.

International Investment

Foreign direct investment and multinational enterprises are the second major area of international economic relations where new rules and institutional arrangements are required. The value of international production by foreign affiliates of multinational enterprises is roughly equal to the level of world trade. Yet there exist virtually no international rules of the game, in stark contrast to the highly elaborated rules that govern at least the import side of international trade.

National policies that seek to capture for individual countries the benefits of foreign direct investment have leaped into this vacuum. Indeed, the major trend in world investment matters today is the widespread success of countries that host the multinationals–industrialized and developing alike–to harness them to their own national objectives. The trend is clearest in the extractive sector and has gone further in some countries than in others, but it can be seen in all industries and in even the poorest nations. There are some issues on which the multinationals themselves raise important problems, because their global domains exceed the national jurisdictions of individual states, but sovereignty is clearly not at bay on the major aspects of foreign direct investment.[22]

Hence two basic sets of international rules and institutional arrangements are needed. One set should constrain both home and host governments from adopting national policies that seek to capture the benefits of foreign direct investment at the expense of other countries. On the part of host countries, such measures include both distorting incentives to attract investment, such as tax holidays, and performance requirements that force the firms to provide, such as a minimum level of domestic value added or exports if they are to be allowed to operate locally. Such measures are becoming so widespread, and the phenomenon of foreign direct investment so important, that an increasing share of world production–and thus jobs, balance-of-payments positions, and location of technology–is being negotiated between multinational enterprises and host-country governments. Home countries, whose national interests go unrepresented in the process, are already beginning to indicate that such a situation is untenable. Unless new international rules are put in place soon, major conflict between countries, through the firms, is a strong probability.

The second needed set of investment rules should cover those issues, such as transfer pricing and antitrust, where all governments have a common interest in checking the ability of the multinationals to evade the individual jurisdictions of any of them. These issues can also lead to conflict among nations, but simply because of inherent asymmetries between the multinational private sector and the national public sector rather than any conscious efforts by governments to tilt the net benefits in their favor. In addition to the substantive need for rules of this type, it is evident that few countries would accept the checks on their national policies toward multinationals as proposed above unless they were confident in the concomitant creation of alternative sources of countervailing power against the firms.

The creation of a new international regime to govern foreign direct investment and multinational enterprises will be extremely difficult, both because the issues are intellectually new and complex and because they are even more highly politicized than most other aspects of international economic relations. Indeed, the creation of such a regime will probably be the major task of the international economic order for the next generation, just as the creation of monetary and trade regimes was the major task of the past generation. But this largest of gaps in the Bretton Woods system must be filled if an effective new economic system is to replace the old.

Notes

1. This has been dubbed a "two-track" system by Richard N. Cooper, "Trade Policy is Foreign Policy," *Foreign Policy* 9 (Winter 1972-1973): 18-36.

2. Gabriel and Joyce Kolko, *The Limits of Power: The World and United States Foreign Policy, 1945-54* (New York: Harper and Row, 1972).

3. The importance of this issue is stressed in Charles P. Kindleberger, *World in Depression, 1931-1939* (Berkeley: University of California Press, 1974).

4. For an enumeration of the different economic and political goals that can be sought through alternative international economic arrangements, and an analysis of the tradeoffs among them, see C. Fred Bergsten, Robert O. Keohane, and Joseph S. Nye, "International Economics and International Politics: A Framework for Analysis," in C. Fred Bergsten and Lawrence B. Krause (eds.), *International Economics and World Politics* (Washington, D.C.: Brookings Institution, 1975).

5. See Stanley Hoffman, *Gulliver's Troubles, or the Setting of American Foreign Policy* (New York: McGraw-Hill, 1968).

6. See C. Fred Bergsten, "The Threat From the Third World," *Foreign Policy* 11 (Summer 1973), and "The Response to the Third World," *Foreign Policy* 17 (Winter 1974-1975). These and the other articles by the author cited in this chapter are reprinted in *Toward A New International Economic Order: Selected Papers of C. Fred Bergsten, 1972-1974* (Lexington, Mass.: Lexington Books, D.C. Heath and Company, 1975).

7. C. Fred Bergsten, "The New Economics and U.S. Foreign Policy," *Foreign Affairs* (January 1972): 199-222.

8. Jan Tinbergen, *On the Theory of Economic Policy*, 2nd ed. (Amsterdam: North Holland Publishing Company, 1963).

9. C. Fred Bergsten, "Coming Investment Wars?" *Foreign Affairs* (October 1974): 135-152.

10. See C. Fred Bergsten, "Crisis in U.S. Trade Policy," *Foreign Affairs* (July 1971): 619-635.

11. C. Fred Bergsten, "The New Era in World Commodity Markets," *Challenge* (September/October 1974): 32-41.

12. For a complete analysis of the issues raised by export controls, see C. Fred Bergsten, *Completing the GATT: Toward New International Rules to Govern Export Controls* (Washington, D.C.: British-North American Committee, October 1974).

13. C. Fred Bergsten, "Prospects for the Atlantic World: An American Perspective," *SAIS Review* (Summer 1974):21-31.

14. See "The United States and Germany: The Imperative of Economic Bigemony" in Bergsten, *Toward A New International Economic Order.*

15. For elaboration on this point and the following paragraphs, see Bergsten, *The Dilemmas of the Dollar.*

16. Richard N. Cooper, "The Future of the Dollar," *Foreign Policy* 9 (Summer 1973):3-23; and Marina von N. Whitman, "The Current and Future Role of the Dollar: How Much Symmetry?" *Brookings Papers on Economic Activity* 3 (1974):539-583.

17. E.g., Friedrich Lutz, "The Problem of International Liquidity and the Multiple-Currency Standard," *Princeton Essays in International Finance*, No. 41 (March 1963).

18. See C. Fred Bergsten, "New Urgency for Monetary Reform," *Foreign Policy* 19 (Summer 1975):79-93.

19. See C. Fred Bergsten, "On the Non-Equivalence of Import Quotas and 'Voluntary' Export Restraints," in Bergsten (ed.), *Toward A New World Trade Policy: The Maidenhead Papers* (Lexington, Mass.: Lexington Books, D.C. Heath and Company, 1975).

20. For one set of proposals see Eric Wyndham White, "The Prospect for Negotiation" in ibid.

21. Details can be found in Bergsten, *Completing the GATT.*

22. Data are provided in C. Fred Bergsten, Thomas Horst, and Theodore H. Moran, *American Multinationals and American Interests* (Washington, D.C.: Brookings Institution, 1976), as is elaboration of the points made in the following paragraphs. This particular aspect of foreign direct investment was highlighted in Bergsten, "Coming Investment Wars?"

2 The United States

Harald B. Malmgren

There has long been a kind of schizophrenia in United States foreign economic policy. On the one hand, there has been a strong attraction of policy towards economic isolationism because of the primacy of domestic concerns in U.S. politics. On the other hand, some U.S. goals in the world, particularly in the political-military area, could be achieved only with the aid of economic diplomacy, and so the U.S. found itself drawn outward during international political crises. Between these two poles, each magnetically attracting this or that sliver of policy, has been an uncertain pattern of pragmatism. Often this pragmatism combined elements of economic nationalism and unilateralism with international efforts to draw other nations together with the U.S. in multilateral diplomacy.

Between these opposing forces, policy sometimes shifts inward and sometimes outward. When a shift occurs, it is often associated with domestic political maneuvering. Coalition formation is often the means to a change in policy. However, political processes have a tendency to act like inert masses, the inert body being difficult to set in motion, but once moving it is difficult to stop abruptly. So U.S. economic policies that are externally oriented usually develop in waves, strengthening slowly, then receding slowly as they are drawn back by counterpressures or distractions. What has been remarkable about these shifts is that the United States has been able to afford the luxury of inattention to its economic relationships with the world whenever Washington was preoccupied with domestic matters. The U.S. could and usually did ignore the world in setting its own domestic economic policies. It could act unilaterally and get away with it, because its internal economy—its resources, its market size, its technological base—created a high degree of self-sufficiency.

Before the mid-1930s, the U.S. government was only barely involved in the international economy, and the famous Smoot-Hawley tariff of 1930 helped to demonstrate dramatically Washington's independent position and its lack of concern with other nations' trade interests. The U.S. was then, as it has continued to be until quite recently, insistent on the subordination of international to domestic policy.

In an absorbing account of the evolution of U.S. policy in the 1940s, R.N. Gardner cited four basic forces that drew the U.S. inward.[1] The first was the tradition of U.S. isolationism. This isolationism was part of the long-term process of withdrawal from involvement with, and the influence of, the Old World. A second force at work was economic self-sufficiency and market size. A third was the ideological devotion to the philosophy of laissez-faire. This entailed an effort tc minimize the role of government and keep it out of economic affairs if at all possible. And the fourth was the unusual constitutional and political structure of the United States:

> Any country with a widely dispersed and heterogeneous population would find it difficult to form an integrated and consistent foreign economic policy. In the United States this natural difficulty was further aggravated by a political system which tended to subordinate national to local interests and, as a corollary of this, international considerations of a domestic character. The bargaining among sectional groups, so essential a part of the American legislative process, often produced unfortunate results when it came to matters affecting the relations of the United States with the rest of the world.[2]

This ability to ignore the international consequences of national actions was linked to the very small role of trade and international investment in the U.S. economy in most of this century. Trade was perhaps more important about 1870, when the proportion of imports to GNP was 7 percent. But in following decades, trade fell in relative importance, averaging below 3 percent in recent decades. There was an exceptional rise during the Korean War period, but the average rose only slightly and only recently, during the 1964-1970 period. By 1970 the ratio was still less than 4 percent. It was not until the 1970s that the picture altered significantly. By 1974 imports had grown to 7 percent—back to the 1870 level.

U.S. investments abroad were also not very critical until recent years. In 1914 (an old date for data in this field), U.S. investment abroad, in terms of private long-term investment, stood at \$3.5 billion, of which \$2.6 billion was direct investment. In 1930 the figures were, respectively, \$15.2 billion and \$8.0 billion. But in the 1930s the figures dropped, and by 1946 the investment level was \$12.3 billion and \$7.2 billion respectively. The decade 1946-1955 saw a doubling for long-term investment and more than doubling for direct investment alone. Direct investment kept growing fast in recent years, so that the cumulative level of direct investment overseas in 1973 reached \$107.3 billion—nearly fifteen times as large as the 1930-1946 average level. But this history also reveals a decline in the proportionate impact on the U.S. economy, in relation to domestic income and other statistics, until recent years. And it was not until very recently, in the 1970s, that the income derived from U.S. investments abroad began to exceed the annual investment outflow by substantial amounts. (The income in 1974 was estimated by the Council on International Economic Policy to be \$18.0 billion, as compared with a \$4.5 billion outflow in 1974.)[3]

As far as the dollar itself was concerned, the world economy's dependence on U.S. aid, trade, and investment during and after World War II meant dependence on the dollar as the principal reserve currency. Since the dollar was a reserve currency, and the international monetary institutions were built around the dollar as the peg for other currencies, the U.S. could do what it wished for a long time without concern for the effects of domestic actions on the dollar in world markets. To the extent that the balance of payments was in deficit and dollars moved outwards, other nations could use those dollars to build up their own reserves and to strengthen their own capital markets. This also meant that there was minimal pressure on the U.S. to rectify domestic policy to reduce the balance-of-payments deficits.

Thus U.S. foreign economic policy came to be separated from domestic economic policy, with the foreign elements clearly subordinated to the domestic. The U.S. developed schizophrenia as more and more was demanded of it in relation to its political objectives in the world.

The "Economic Imperialism" Thesis

Politically, some analysts have viewed the period since the end of World War II as a period of U.S. hegemony in the West, and of U.S.-Soviet bipolarity in the global political-security context. From this point of perspective, it has been argued, particularly by D.P. Calleo, that this Western political hegemony fostered "economic imperialism" by the United States. In this interpretation, the U.S. consciously exploited world markets and raw materials and the economic system was kept in order by force.

> Modern imperialism seeks to gain control of key resources, markets, and strategic territories as cheaply as possible, that is, without having to assume the responsibility for government. Modern imperialism . . . thus tends to be more truly exploitive—precisely because it prefers to be indirect and irresponsible.
>
> If imperialism is seen in this way, then the vast American apparatus of military protectorates, bases, and alliances, along with great military power, the military and economic subsidies to foreign governments, the omnipresent diplomatic and intelligence network, the huge direct investments, and the preponderant position in the monetary system would seem to constitute a tolerable approximation of a modern empire.[4]

This line of argumentation is carried farther by reference to the hegemonic role of the U.S. in NATO, describing it as an alliance of dependence, not interdependence. Between East and West, the postwar period of cold war is viewed as a duopoly—the U.S. and the Soviet Union not only dominating the world, but in essence being the only major actors. Calleo views these elements of Western hegemony and cold war duopoly as unstable, with centrifugal forces constantly at work to pull apart the structure of the world political and economic order.[5]

This conception of the U.S. role suggests a self-awareness and consciousness of economic purpose that does not correspond with the way that policy actually evolved. It does not reflect the economic reality that the external elements of the economy were too small to have a major influence on the domestic decisions. And it does not reflect the fact that domestic policies were not designed to bring about external results. When trade policies were influenced by external considerations, the reaction usually was to seek to insulate domestic policy from foreign influences.

The size of the U.S. economy and the role of the dollar, in other words, allowed the U.S. to neglect or ignore the interconnections of domestic and foreign economic policies. Moreover, the nature of the political process in the country could not sustain a flexible and manipulative policy that could be continuously adapted to exploit targets of economic opportunity. The system simply was not geared to the management of foreign economic adventures—and where adverse developments took place, such as in the series of expropriations of American company interests by governments of developing nations, the U.S. government could not do much about them.

Another perspective sometimes taken is that U.S. policy regarding the world economy was coherent and clear in the late 1940s and early 1950s, but oriented toward an extension of American concepts of how economic systems ought to work: for the benefit of everyone globally. William Diebold argued in this vein that

> In the middle of the twentieth century the government of the United States had a clear view of the kind of world economy it would like to see created when the destruction and disorganization of war were overcome. For the next twenty-five years American foreign economic policy was largely shaped to achieve those aims. As the last quarter of the century approached, clarity was lost.[6]

An open world economy was a philosophic objective, in this view. It is doubtful that there was in fact such clarity of view throughout all parts of the U.S. government in the last twenty-five years. But in recent years, the picture has become even more unclear, and it will probably become even more so in the future. Growing economic interdependence of recent years, the conflicts between domestic and foreign objectives, and the changing structure of the world economy are combining to create confusion and uncertainty about the future. Moreover, a variety of other domestic and international objectives, some of conflicting natures, have operated to diffuse or distort the philosophic objective of more open, free world economic relations.

Foreign Economic Policy Themes

This does not mean that the U.S. had no policy; a number of strong themes did evolve. A major and continuing theme of policy, for example, has been economic ideology. Prominent among the ideological questions was the role of private enterprise and laissez-faire market policy—the invisible hand should be allowed to work unfettered by the bounds of government restrictions and distortions of world commerce and investment. As often happens to ideology in the real world, this principle was tampered with, by protectionist measures such as the Smoot-Hawley Tariff, by the tight restrictions on foreign products in relation to domestic agriculture, and by the use of export subsidies and tax incentives favoring international business activity.

Private investment was seen as beneficial, not so much for the U.S. as for the rest of the world. It was perceived as a better method of dealing with problems than were government programs. For example, many U.S. officials perceived private investment as the answer to the problems of recovery in war-ravaged Europe and the predicament of the developing countries. They argued that private investment would do the job if encouraged; but some officials also questioned whether private resources were large enough to do the job. The debate was clearly not a question of whether private investment *should* be relied on, but only whether it *could* be relied on.[7] As far as development assistance to poorer countries was concerned, the message was even clearer when the problems of Europe were set aside. The Commission on Conduct of Foreign Policy, jointly established by the president and Congress, recommended in 1975 that "The United States Government should make clear that primary reliance must be placed on private investment to undertake the job of assisting in economic development abroad."[8] This emphasis on private investment was tied in as a theme with laissez-faire concepts of how to set the world right.

Another basic theme was the principle of nondiscrimination. According to this principle, nations must not charge a higher duty on products from the U.S. than they do on products from other sources; the U.S. itself in turn avoids discriminating among the nations from which it imports. Even President Washington in his farewell address in 1796 stipulated that the U.S. should in its economic dealings with other nations proffer "an equal and impartial hand, neither seeking nor granting exclusive favors or preferences." Gardner points out that this doctrine had more than an economic basis, in terms of avoiding discrimination against U.S. products—it was also a political doctrine, aimed at preventing regional adventures and imperial relations that would work against U.S. objectives. As he notes, this type of consideration led to John Hay's Open Door Policy and the third of President Wilson's Fourteen Points on nondiscrimination. This policy proved to be a major, time-consuming source of policy dispute in Anglo-American relations during the World War II discussions on lend-lease and on planning for the postwar world economic system.[9] Even Roosevelt and Churchill managed to square off on this question repeatedly.

Nor did this issue die in later years as the Commonwealth withered to death. Instead, the battle was transferred to relations between the U.S. and the emerging European Community. The EC developed special preferential trade relations with formerly associated countries (and colonies), and it made special free trade arrangements with other European nations that did not choose to join the European Community. Eventually the EC broadened the scope of the special trade agreements to cover its relations with the Mediterranean nations, and with other selected countries.

In the early 1960s the fear of growing European discrimination gave birth to the Trade Expansion Act of 1962 and the Kennedy Round trade negotiations authorized by that act. By the late 1960s the U.S. was involved in an open political debate with the European Community about the perils of regional or bloc discrimination, and Congress was becoming gradually more bellicose, looking for means to retaliate.[10]

The U.S. itself nonetheless exercised discrimination, again compromising an ideological stance, in connection with the USSR, China, Cuba, and other "unfriendly" nations. The U.S. went further, and tried to coordinate (with some success) the trade policies of other Western nations toward these same countries, which were also potential adversaries for them. The intricate discussions about Western nations' export controls to Eastern Europe and the Soviet Union are but one example.

Fairness and equitable burden-sharing became another major theme. When the word "fair" is invoked in congressional debate, it often means "more for us." Thus "fair trade" could carry the meaning that unbalanced concessions should be made in favor of the U.S., as it did in the 1968-1974 period. Burden-sharing is undoubtedly one of the most complex areas of multilateral diplomacy and international negotiation ever confronted, because measurement of relative effort is so difficult.[11] For years the wastebaskets of the history of the OEEC and NATO were full of papers on relative burden-sharing among the NATO allies, not only in terms of military expenditures, but also defense "effort," foreign aid, and other theoretically common-objective activities.

Reciprocity has been another fundamental theme, closely associated with nondiscrimination and equitable burden-sharing. To an American trade negotiator, reciprocity often means that the effort of domestic adjustment involved in a trade concession will be as great in the other nation's economy as in your own, if a fair deal is to be struck. Reciprocity has been a fundamental part of the arsenal of American negotiators throughout the period of the Trade Agreements Program, from 1934 until the present. The Trade Act of 1974 includes a requirement that the president insure that major trading nations provide reciprocity. If that reciprocity is not provided, he is authorized to discriminate against such nations.

Reciprocity does not always have to be found in the same economic area, however. The chief executive, for example, chose to seek internationally agreed trade principles as reciprocity for lend-lease arrangements in the 1940s. In the early 1970s, reciprocity was openly interpreted to cover political and military tradeoffs with economic opportunities. And this interweaving became even more prominent in spring 1973, when Secretary of State Henry Kissinger called for a new Atlantic Charter to link economic, political, and security interests of the Atlantic nations (and Japan, if a way could be found to do so while remaining sensitive to the security issues in the Japanese case).

Alongside some of these basic policy concepts was the executive branch's interest in multilateralism, and the application of the "rule of law" to the world around us. International rules were believed to be needed to police nondiscrimination, reciprocity, and the "openness" of the world system. Rules were needed to provide order. International institutions were needed to provide a mechanism through which the rules could be implemented, arbitrated, or otherwise tailored to specific country problems through consultations.

The search for a new order during the early 1940s based on multilateral institutions was somewhat out of character for the U.S., given the experience of the League of Nations. It has to be emphasized, however, that this was a matter of executive branch policy. Its fruits were rejected, in the case of trade, by Congress, in the failure of the International Trade Organization to be given U.S. support. The GATT was instead set up as an interim arrangement, and Congress gave no recognition to it. Indeed, it was not until the Trade Act of 1974 that Congress finally gave the GATT its formal approval by explicitly authorizing GATT expenditures. In the case of the financial institutions, the history of U.S.-British—perhaps one should say Keynes-White—discussions during the early 1940s reflected a growing cynicism in Congress, and therefore a scaling back of the U.S. concepts for the postwar monetary system.

Still, any assessment today would have to acknowledge that in the long run, the push by the executive branch for multilateral diplomacy did work. The U.S. was drawn into a web of international rules and procedures that were of great benefit economically and politically, to the U.S. and to the other Western nations (including Japan). The IMF, the World Bank family, the GATT, and the OECD all came to perform important functions.

Assistance to other nations in economic trouble evolved in a more complex way. The Marshall plan combined anti-Soviet motivations and the doctrine of self-help and self-initiative. Development assistance policy also originated in a reaction to cold war fears and events, beginning with Greek-Turkish aid and the Point Four program Harry Truman proposed in his 1949 inaugural address. The humanitarian aspects also motivated some people in the United States throughout the years of foreign aid programs, but Congress and the executive branch in general perceived aid as a weapon to beat back the global octopus of Communism. This aid theme therefore faded with the apparent fading of the cold war and the growing desire of the Congress and the U.S. public to disentangle the United States from overseas involvements of a direct, face-to-face character.

There was some schizophrenia in aid policy, too, as the multilateral impulses worked in favor of using the World Bank and other multilateral lending institutions, while the cold war motivations worked in favor of bilateral aid programs where the U.S. could act directly, on the spot, in shaping the evolution of individual developing nations.

Alongside these themes one finds a strong defense of national sovereignty and the retention of the U.S.'s right to take actions to defend itself and its economy as it deemed necessary or desirable. Preservation of the right to take unilateral action—and in particular, the avoidance of binding Congress from taking unilateral actions—was prominent in instructions to negotiators over the years as executive branch lawyers were periodically called upon to advise in the drafting of agreements. The legal advisers were concerned, in economic matters, that international agreements provide "escape routes" for the U.S. to cover potential congressional decisions. When, for example, the U.S. took the lead in seeking a pledge from all the major trading nations that they would not take unilateral trade actions for balance-of-payments reasons during the 1973-1975 world economic disorders, the final drafting of the OECD and IMF pledges had to be watered down to keep freedom of action for Congress (even though no one in Congress had raised the question). The lawyers were in this case very worried about the U.S.'s sovereign rights and Congress's constitutional rights to act as it saw fit on trade, while the rest of the executive branch was concerned with preventing such action by other nations.

The unilateralism of U.S. policy cannot be ignored. Even in the areas where the U.S.-drafted rules for international institutions theoretically blocked unilateral action, the U.S. has acted unilaterally from time to time, particularly in trade policy, but also in the monetary area. The political appeal of machismo and the inherent belief that in the end we are right and can go it alone if we need to has kept alive the unilateral theme in government deliberations over the years. It is closely tied in with the widespread political belief that the domestic economy comes first anyway.

These themes will continue to influence policy, but in new ways in the last quarter of the century. The U.S.'s ability to ignore the world economy is rapidly diminishing with a rapidly increasing interdependence in the world economic structure. Changes set in motion years ago are now becoming visible. In the public eye and in Congress's eye, this new set of circumstances became apparent in the early 1970s. Food shortages appeared as a result of a combination of world developments: the Russians came into the market unexpectedly; Peruvian fish currents shifted, resulting in a worldwide shortage of fishmeal for feeding animals; drought came to Australia and Canada; and demand was rising worldwide, putting upward price pressure on the U.S. food prices. Mounting worldwide inflation interfered with domestic price controls and other anti-inflationary programs, as goods leaked out of the U.S. economy into exports destined for higher-priced markets abroad. The Arab-Israeli war of 1973 brought with it an oil embargo and an acceleration of oil price increases (which were already moving upward, and which would have moved up eventually regardless of the war), dramatizing to U.S. consumers how dependent and vulnerable they were becoming. These events came alongside growing unemployment. They were perceived in an increasingly unstable political context: Middle East instability, the shakiness of Portugal and Italy, the fall of Vietnam and Cambodia. Combined with this sense of shakiness abroad was the growing desire to withdraw from foreign entanglements, the growing fatigue of domestic political stress resulting from the foreign policy of earlier years. The mid-1970s brought, as Geoffrey Barraclough put it, "premonitions of ordinary people, in America and in Europe. Suddenly their whole future has become precarious."[12]

As far as the planning or devising of domestic economic policy is concerned, foreign developments have only rarely had much effect on, or been considered in, domestic economic decisions. The perception that foreign and domestic economic policy were separably persisted. Domestic policy-makers and foreign policy-makers continued to avoid each other for fear that communication between them might lead to adulteration of the purity of their respective purposes. But the era of clear separation of domestic and foreign preoccupations is drawing to a close. New forces are at work.

Money, The Balance of Payments, and Domestic Policy

The interaction of the U.S. monetary market with the world monetary situation did not appear to be a primary concern of U.S. economic policy-makers until recently. In the 1950s and 1960s there was growing concern over the U.S. balance of payments, in relation to national reserves and the ability to continue high levels of overseas official expenditures for defense and foreign assistance, but this did not impact heavily on domestic policy formulation.

The growth of official concern with the balance of payments and the role of the dollar probably began in the mid-1950s. The U.S. balance of payments was in deficit every year beginning in 1950. However, in the early 1950s it was believed desirable that there be a deficit, since this deficit or dollar outflow contributed to the rebuilding of international reserves in the hands of other nations. It was considered an essential element in the process of expanding world trade and enabling currency convertibility to take place. It was considered a natural concomitant to aid and military expenditures. According to Henry Wallich, a major policy-maker during that period, "The threshold of a real 'problem' was reached only with the dawning recognition that foreign aid and military expenditures both were likely to continue indefinitely."[13] A surplus in 1957 raised hopes, but 1958 brought an unusually large deficit of $3.2 billion. This latter deficit was financed with $2.3 billion of gold, creating worry that confidence in the dollar was fading. This led to substantial discussion of balance-of-payments problems and their relation to the FY1960 budget, although the effectiveness of such discussions in changing any policies remains in question.[14]

A balance-of-payments committee was formed under the National Advisory Council, and from then on through the 1960s the cabinet periodically deliberated on the country's balance-of-payments problems and what could be done about them. The first policy initiatives involved the tying of loans and a reduction in family residence arrangements for military personnel posted abroad. On February 6, 1961, only a few days after he took office, President Kennedy developed the balance-of-payments deficit reduction concept further, with proposals for additional tying and preferential purchasing of domestic products in federal purchases. Then in subsequent months the U.S. found itself entering into foreign exchange transactions for monetary purposes for the first time since the 1930s.[a] By 1963 the Federal Reserve was proudly announcing adjustments in interest rates and a change in Regulation Q (the board's regulations regarding interest rates and time deposits) "to aid in the U.S. efforts to combat its international balance-of-payments problem." At the same time, however, it was emphasized that these actions "do not constitute a change in the System's policy of maintaining monetary conditions conducive to fuller utilization of manpower and other resources in this country."[15] Domestic policy was still the preeminent consideration.

Since the deficit was the focus of so much attention, the question not unsurprisingly came up as to whether the way the deficit was measured was adequate or misleading. In 1963 President Kennedy commissioned a special report under the direction of Edward Bernstein. The Bernstein Report, published in 1965,[16] recommended a shift to the "official settlements" basis of accounting. Some experts disagreed. In any event, the old basis of measurement of the "liquidity" balance and the new official settlement basis gave different numbers, but which one was more favorable depended on the circumstances. The public became confused, and in the end the policy-makers in the executive branch benefited from the ambiguity thus created. In the meantime, the various cabinet balance-of-payments committees carried on, each year tightening further the perceived "leakages." By late 1967 a decision was reached to take drastic action. President Johnson ordered a program to be prepared. He arranged for his top economic and foreign policy advisers to fly in secret to his Texas ranch between Christmas and New Year's Day. On January 1, 1968, he announced measures that included direct controls on foreign investment outflows, and he hinted at restrictive trade measures if Europeans and others did not make some trade account adjustments to offset the border tax adjustments they applied to U.S. exports. (This latter issue, and the threat, were the precursors to the August 1971 import surcharge.) Even then, however, domestic policies remained

[a]"The Treasury began limited operations in March, 1961, acting through the Federal Reserve Bank of New York as its fiscal agent. In February of (1962) the Federal Reserve System announced its decision to enter the exchange market for its own account." Robert V. Roosa, Undersecretary of the Treasury of Monetary Affairs, in an address before the American Bankers Association meeting in Rome, May 17, 1962.

separate in everyone's minds, and the thrust of all this effort was still the reduction in the magic number of the balance-of-payments deficit. Overseas confidence in the dollar was still the major worry, but the link to domestic policies was not given significant consideration.

Then large volumes of dollars began shuttling across the Atlantic. First the so-called Eurodollars moved in an enormous adjustment toward the U.S. in 1969, and then back out in 1970 and 1971. This flow had very disruptive effects on the monetary policies of other nations. Some of this shuttling was related to interest rate differentials, some of it to the expectation of currency appreciation because of the general international uneasiness and obvious need for adjustment in exchange rates. It was beginning to be realized that the system of fixed parities, or at least the fixity of the U.S. dollar, had to be bent or it would break.

The apprehension in foreign capitals intensified as the Federal Reserve eased monetary policy and brought about a massive expansion in the U.S. money supply in the first half of 1971. While the U.S. was easing monetary and fiscal policy to promote domestic recovery, European nations were maintaining tight policies to limit an apparently accelerating cost-push inflation. Short-term interest rates were thus falling in the U.S. and rising in Europe, further stimulating an outflow of short-term funds from the U.S. In turn, speculation on appreciation of all or at least some European currencies intensified. The trade deficit simultaneously grew, and for the first time since 1893, U.S. imports exceeded exports. The official settlements deficit for 1971 was running at a level that would make the 1971 deficit about equal to the entire deficit of the 1961-1970 period taken together. The size of the deficit–and in particular the dramatic deterioration of the U.S.'s competitive position demonstrated by the rise in imports to exceed exports–"convinced the markets that the dollar's turn to be devalued had finally arrived."[17]

For the U.S., the international money crunch coincided with the need for dramatic action to stabilize the domestic economy. Domestic economic policy officials examined both international needs and domestic needs at Camp David in August 1971. Then, on August 15, the administration instituted an emergency program involving both domestic and international measures: an emergency freeze on prices, wages, and rents; a proposal for a preferential investment tax credit for purchase of U.S.-produced equipment; repeal of the automobile excise tax and adjustment of personal income tax exemptions; temporary surcharge of up to 10 percent on imports; and suspension of convertibility of dollars into gold for official settlements. The unilateral character of the international actions became known in some circles abroad as the "Connally shock."

Whatever the individual motivations of the policy officials involved, the international and domestic issues were viewed in a comprehensive, interrelated manner, and the package of actions was put forward as an integral package. The international forces had finally become recognized as relevant to domestic policies, and the U.S. entered a new phase of economic decision-making in which the world had to be taken into account in domestic planning.

However, it should also be noted that the Camp David meeting did not include representatives of the State Department or the agencies responsible for trade affairs. It was almost as if the domestic economic policy-makers, recognizing the linkage of international and domestic forces, were determined to avoid letting international policy considerations interfere with the decisions made.[18]

Anti-Inflationary Policy, Domestic Supplies, and Trade

Not until 1973 was there a full appreciation of the domestic consequences of the international exchange rate adjustments that had begun with the August 1971 measures and the restructuring brought about by the Smithsonian Agreement of December 1971. By 1973, U.S. exports of food and commodities were relatively cheap by world market standards, and this coincided with a run-up of demand throughout the world (partly a result of disappointments in crops in various parts of the world). The Cost of Living Council found that it could not keep an effective lid on prices domestically without some method of limiting the outflow of goods to higher price markets abroad. Building material prices soared as log exports appeared to accelerate; wheat and feedgrain sales abroad became far more attractive than home sales; even that end product of modern civilization, metal scrap, flowed outward at a rate that threatened price stability in domestic metals markets. Export controls were seen as a logical answer by the domestic price controllers. It was decided to put export controls on agricultural exports. This decision was made again without the participation of any of the administration's international trade experts. Only after the decision had been made in principle were the State Department and other officials responsible for international matters brought into the decision process—and then only to devise efficient controls and minimize the frictions with other governments. The governments of other nations considered this unilateral solution as both politically provocative and threatening to their own economic policies. While the U.S. had been preaching more open access to markets and foreign governments had gradually liberalized their trade policies, the foreign governments found that they had become more dependent on U.S. supplies. The export controls created a feeling, justified or not (the physical flow under the export control system was fairly high), that such a dependence was dangerous, for the supplies might not be there in a time of need. Some foreign officials likened the U.S. export limitations to the OPEC oil export limitations.

The European and Japanese concerns about this type of solution were made known to the White House, and another lesson was learned about the intertwining of domestic and international forces. From then on, arguments in favor of export controls were countered with arguments concerning the U.S.'s long-term competitive position in world markets and the paramount consideration of appearing to be a reliable supplier with predictable, steady export policies. In the spring of 1974, for example, domestic flour manufacturers and bakers called for export controls to dampen the price rises in wheat and flour ("We will have dollar-a-loaf bread by June."), but the executive branch was able to hold the line and to persuade Congress as well to keep cool and wait out the market adjustments. And later in 1974, when feedgrains were in very tight supply, the interagency process was able to devise a complex monitoring system as an alternative to export controls.

However, the new circumstances in which the U.S. found itself in the food area in 1974 could not be handled by U.S. actions alone. If export controls were to be avoided, and if domestic and international needs were to be met at the same time, there would have to be intensive, in-depth consultations with the U.S.'s trading partners about their own agricultural policies, external needs, and willingness to coordinate efforts with the U.S. An effort was mounted to open detailed discussions with several countries, involving much capital-to-capital travel by U.S. agricultural officials, with reasonable success. By the autumn of 1974 the world market for feedgrains and the U.S. position in it seemed to be under control.

Then late in 1974 the Russians unexpectedly entered the market for substantial purchases of corn as well as wheat. Once more the administration was thrown into shock over the external unpredictabilities and their effect on the U.S. economy. Not only were domestic corn prices at stake; but the price of meat was bound to reflect any disturbance of the feed market by the Russians, and the U.S. trading partners who had cooperated would lose interest in cooperation if the Russians were found to be having a "free ride." The White House was forced to make a tough decision concerning Russian relations at a time when many other U.S.-USSR issues were at stake. Should we have a confrontation with the Russians? Can we somehow bring about cancellation of contracts? Or were general export controls the easy way out, relative to a potential political confrontation with the Russians? The problem was ultimately settled through rapid and secret diplomacy, but another lesson was learned: that even the nonmarket economies were beginning to have a direct impact on domestic circumstances. This led to concern over other potential problems. Prominent among these were the problems that could be posed by the state-trading nations, or by operations of that character. Could not an oil-rich, state-trading government play a major role in destabilizing food markets if it so chose or if it decided to speculate without considering the delicate balance being maintained in the market through informal coordination of the major Western trading nations? The interim solution to the potential problems with the Russians and other state-traders was the establishment of an ad hoc approvals board to rule on all significant transactions, with a special eye on abnormally large transactions from unexpected quarters. The longer term impact of this kind of review on policy-making is only beginning to be felt.

The food and other commodity price problems stemmed from various factors, including simultaneous booms in many parts of the world economy, international exchange rate adjustments, and rising expectations. When the policy-makers considered those problems in combination with the monetary flow problems and their impact on domestic policies, they began to admit openly that there was a connection between internal and external developments. The Economic Report of the President, issued February 1, 1974, articulated the new awareness of the world as a major source of domestic inflationary pressure: "The price deflator for imports rose 26 percent during 1973. If these rising import prices were merely passed through dollar for dollar to final purchasers in the United States, they would have accounted for about one-fourth of the rise in prices paid by U.S. purchasers in 1973." Similarly, in explanation of the sharp increase in U.S. farm commodity prices that year, the report said that: "Two devaluations of the dollar in a 15-month period, followed by further depreciation in the dollar exchange rate after February, added to the export demand for U.S. food commodities, as did the widespread and strong economic expansion abroad."

Against the background of world market pressures on domestic interests and plans, even the president's own introductory statement to the annual report contained rhetoric acknowledging the interlinkage: "The events of 1973 brought our external economic relations sharply to our attention. Most simply put, it will be exceedingly hard for us to have a stable economy in an unstable world. We must contribute a stabilizing influence to the world economy of which we are a large part. We must promote concerted efforts to maintain the health of the world economy."[19] This official admission of external and internal interactions at the presidential level was of historic importance. It was not based on the cold war concept of the stability of the West versus the forces of Communism. It was a simple recognition that the world market order does affect the U.S. economy.

Other developments in the world economy during 1973 caught public attention as well as administration concern. The most prominent event was, of course, the Arab oil embargo and the organized rise in oil prices worldwide. While the public is unlikely to follow the complexities of international monetary manipulation or understand the impact of world monetary developments on individual circumstances, the effects of gasoline and home heating shortages and price rises were dramatically visible at that time. The dependence of Americans in their day-to-day living habits on foreign developments became vaguely understood. The dependence was resented. Congress began to churn out proposals for retaliatory actions. However, it was soon discovered that U.S. leverage would be minimal without coordinated action by all other consuming nations. Thus the U.S. depended not only on foreign suppliers but also on other consuming nations for effective influence on the suppliers.

Attention soon broadened to cover other potential commodity shortage problems. A major review was instituted within the executive branch on the raw material situation, including the degree of dependence of the U.S. economy on foreign supplies. A report, issued in December 1974,[20] acknowledged that price gouging and cartel action might occur in commodities other than oil. It assessed possibilities of supply interruptions and the impact on the U.S. economy and national security. The report concluded that U.S. supplies of chromium, bauxite, and platinum were vulnerable. Of the sixteen other materials examined, "market forces, with all their imperfections, appear adequate to deter price gouging or cartel-like action."

The degree of dependence of the U.S. economy on world resources is difficult to assess. It is a question of relationships. In relation to present circumstances and present world market prices in particular, the United States imports a high proportion of many of its raw material requirements. As a percent of domestic consumption in 1973, U.S. imports were at or close to 100 percent for chromium, bauxite, platinum, and tin; over 80 percent for mercury, manganese, cobalt, and nickel; and over 33 percent for tungsten, zinc, lead, and titanium. The relative percentages for other raw materials are less, but the impact of these imports on domestic markets is nonetheless significant. Oil in the mid-1970s provided a dramatic example of a relatively small import component in domestic energy consumption (about 15 percent), which had major implications for domestic supply availabilities and prices.

Other factors play a role too. First, there are substantial stocks of raw materials available in the U.S. Some of these stocks exist simply as a result of normal commercial behavior of trading companies and manufacturing companies, partly in the form of goods in transit, partly in the form of stocks withheld from sale as inventory protection against market uncertainties.

The government holds and owns some of the stocks in the U.S., as a consequence of national security policy or legislative developments in agricultural policy. In the federal stockpiles, for example, one can find enough tungsten for eight years, chromium and tin for about four years, and manganese and lead for a year or so.

In these circumstances the executive branch report was able to play down the prospects for further short-term supply disruptions on the U.S. economy. Moreover, it was suggested that the U.S. economy has within itself a wide range of alternatives to deal with potential pressures. The tradeoffs between coal and oil and the alternatives such as methanol and coal liquefaction are well known. There are also huge deposits of such base materials as alumina sands and shale.

The U.S.'s raw material role and position in world trade is special, even unique. The U.S. is both a major exporter and importer of raw materials. The two-way nonfood materials trade amounted to $72 billion in 1974. The only other industrialized countries that are major raw material exporters are Canada and Australia. The U.S. is a net exporter of food and feed, coal, phosphates, softwood logs, and ferrous scrap. Copper goes in both directions in almost equal amounts.

Consequently, even taking into account heavy reliance on certain imports noted earlier, the character of the U.S.'s problems of dependence seem different from those faced by Western Europe, which depends on imports for 75 percent of its raw materials, and Japan, which is 90-percent dependent. Interestingly, the U.S. does not rely heavily on developing countries. Canada, Australia, South Africa, and other developed countries supply over two-thirds of U.S. raw material imports, with Canada alone representing about one-half. This is why in recent decades the U.S. has felt able to take such a firm line in debates on commodity policy in international institutions where the developing countries may band together.

However, the argument that the U.S. need not worry as much as other nations because it depends on other developed nations for its limited external needs is subject to qualification. The raw materials policies of Australia and Canada are subject to political controversy in those countries and therefore are in transition. And if Europe and Japan run short, one can reasonably suppose that they will turn to the open U.S. market for additional supplies. This could put U.S. policy-makers again in the difficult position of choosing between export restrictions or feeling the effects of foreign shortages at home. Politically, could the U.S. turn its back on Western Europe or Japan, if they were under pressure?[21]

The Kissinger speech that Ambassador Daniel P. Moynihan delivered September 1, 1975, to the United Nations General Assembly (meeting in special session) opened the door to a new U.S. raw material and commodity policy posture. The results will unfold slowly, but this speech marked a new pragmatism concerning the changing economic and political realities.

Management of Foreign Economic Policy

The use of economic instruments in the pursuit of U.S. political objectives and the use of political leverage to obtain economic advantage have been sporadic. There has not been a consistent design of economic imperialism, nor a consistent policy of promoting the interests of private companies abroad. The principles of nondiscrimination, reciprocity, multilateralism, and fairness in burden-sharing were utilized to pursue U.S. cold war objectives, but many of the high policy-makers had little or no interest in the economic content of these policy instruments. To the extent that trade and monetary experts could take advantage of their political masters, they did so. Speeches for presidents and cabinet officers were drafted with high-flown rhetoric about open world economies, but the presidents and cabinet officers who actually spoke the words often had other things on their minds. Cordell Hull was an exception to this generalization. Hull probably believed what he often said, that "unhampered trade dovetailed with peace; high tariffs, trade barriers, and unfair economic competition, with war."[22] As Gardner described it, Hull accorded pride of place to economic factors, and particularly to trade policy, in his philosophy of world affairs.[23]

The making of foreign economic policy in Washington is an intricate process. Often it can best be described as Byzantine. The issues are technical and esoteric. The rhetoric has a Shakespearean richness and multiplicity of meaning—and deviousness—to it. What people say and what they do are often different. A particular problem abroad may be used as a pretext, or a political context, for a policy that a handful of people are committed to. Politically, one of the most attractive reasons to offer in defense of policy change is the need to react to something another nation has done that is widely perceived as unfair or discriminatory.

The history of trade policy under the Trade Agreements Program—with its primary reliance on the principles of nondiscrimination, reciprocity, and multilateral discipline—is an example of an attempt to block regional arrangements and bilateral ties elsewhere in the world.

The recent history of U.S. trade policy demonstrates the complexity of motivations, political maneuvers, and foreign policy considerations. A major motivation for the Kennedy Round was to react to the formation of the European Economic Community—and a major element of that reaction was the perceived need to offset the effects of growing discrimination in Western Europe. The rhetoric of President Kennedy was more bold and more comprehensive, it is true. At the time of the introduction of the Trade Expansion Act of 1962, he said:

> Our efforts to promote the strength and unity of the West are thus directly related to the strength and unity of Atlantic trade policies. An expanded export program is necessary to give this Nation both the balance of payments equilibrium and the economic growth we need to sustain our share of Western military security and economic advance. Equally important, a freer flow of trade across the Atlantic will enable the two giant markets on either side of the ocean to impart strength and vigor to each other, and to combine their resources and momentum to undertake the many enterprises which the security of free peoples demand. For the first time, as the world's greatest trading nation, we can welcome a single partner whose trade is even larger than our own—a partner no longer divided and dependent, but strong enough to share with us the responsibilities and initiatives of the free world.

The Kennedy rhetoric also contained more comprehensive elements, relating this initiative to the so-called Grand Design. For example, he went on to say:

> If we can take this step, Marxist predictions of "capitalist" empires warring over markets and stifling competition would be shattered for all time—Communist hopes for a trade war between these two great economic giants would be frustrated—and Communist efforts to split the West would be doomed to failure.

As members of the Atlantic Community we have concerted our military objectives through the North Atlantic Treaty Organization. We are concerting our monetary and economic policies through the Organization for Economic Cooperation and Development. It is time now to write a new chapter in the evolution of the Atlantic Community. The success of our foreign policy depends in large measure upon the success of our foreign trade, and our maintenance of Western political unity depends in equally large measure upon the degree of Western economic unity. An integrated Western Europe, joined in trading partnership with the United States, will further shift the world balance of power to the side of freedom.[24]

Thus there were elements of the residue of the cold war objectives of the Marshall Plan and the Mutual Security Program in the concept Kennedy put forward to Congress. The drafters of this message recognized that the political climate required more than trade policy or abstract economic efficiency reasons, and yet the cold war context was probably excessive, primarily aimed at firing up the congressional interest.

The effort succeeded, both with Congress and in subsequent years in the negotiations with other nations. Much log-rolling was required to put the Trade Expansion Act of 1962 through, however, including particular commitments to such special interest groups as the textile and cattle industries. The multilateral negotiations barely squeaked under the wire of the timetable set by law (the authorization terminated in June 1967 and the Geneva deals were agreed upon in May 1967). The results were clearly the most significant in trade negotiations history.

Then Congress reverted to protectionist pressure throughout the summer of 1967. The press did not carry much news of what was happening, but the various special interests were highly active in pressing for import restrictions, and only intensive, behind-the-scenes maneuvering by President Johnson and the White House staff succeeded in diffusing the pressures and preventing a rash of undesirable amendments. In 1968 the pressures were much worse, and the Senate added protectionist amendments to tax measures that were important to the president. Again these efforts were neutralized, but the pressure was clearly growing. The circumstances grew even more unfavorable as the Nixon administration took office in 1969.[25]

A complex countereffort was put together by U.S. people and groups who were interested in maintaining an open economy and an outward-looking trade policy. Within the administration, a new "housekeeping" piece of legislation—the Trade Act of 1970—was proposed as a means of providing some positive alternative. It failed to obtain serious consideration and died. In the meantime, the Burke-Hartke proposals for import quotas and drastic changes in tax laws affecting overseas activities of U.S. companies flourished in congressional debate, strongly supported by the AFL-CIO.

Outside the executive branch, a consensus was gradually forming in various circles. In the Senate, Abraham Ribicoff suggested creating a distinguished group of "wisemen" representing the major trading nations, to focus the attention of the international community on the trade issues. "Their deliberations on the outstanding problems of international trade could be the prelude to more formal negotia ons," he said.[26] This congressional initiative, at first resisted by the State Department, led to the creation of a high-level group in Paris at the OECD under the chairmanship of Jean Rey, former president of the European Communities. The group's report was instrumental in laying the foundation of a new international consensus.[27] Within the U.S., the National Planning Association, the U.S. Council of the International Chamber of Commerce, the Committee for Economic Development, and other groups generated thoughtful studies with recommendations for a new multilateral initiative.[28] And the presidential commission that President Nixon had established came forth with a positive call for a comprehensive new international negotiation to shape a new world economic order.[29] The idea caught on of using multilateral negotiations to solve some of the domestic complaints and to offer a positive alternative to protectionism.

Congress had to be asked for authority to negotiate, however. Under the U.S. Constitution, Congress regulates foreign commerce, not the president. Any powers to change tariffs or other trade measures have to be delegated from Congress to the president by law. If the U.S. were to negotiate under the president's residual foreign policy powers, Congress would still have to provide implementing legislation. Other nations said they would not work with the U.S. multilaterally unless the U.S. negotiators were given advance legislative authorization.

The process of maneuvering the Trade Act of 1974 through Congress may warrant a book; it cannot be adequately described in a paragraph or two.[30] A coalition of interests had to be mobilized to neutralize the maneuvers by organized labor to defeat the administration proposals. The legislative calendar had to be negotiated to make room for trade legislation in the Ways and Means Committee and the Senate Finance Committee, who were involved with other time-consuming domestic priorities such as tax legislation and health care legislation. The southern constitutionalists in the Senate had to be offered some kind of formula for transferring authority to the president that did not impinge on the congressional power to make law. The special problems of steel, textiles, and other industries had to be met by negotiated language for the so-called legislative history.

As some maneuvers succeeded, new issues were brought up. Among these were questions like cargo shipping legislation, with a procedural deal made to allow cargo preference legislation to come to a vote on the Senate floor in exchange for a commitment to get the trade act to the floor. The most troublesome question arose over the treatment of the Soviet Union in the bill. The bill provided power to grant most-favored-nation treatment to the Soviets under a bilateral trade agreement. Congress added conditions relating to the level of emigration of Soviet jewry, and when this did not appear to force the president to take action with the Russians, Congress added limitations on Export-Import Bank financing to the trade bill and also to the authorization of the Export-Import Bank itself. This brought in issues of détente policy, export financing questions, and the domestic politics associated with the emigration issue. Since organized labor opposed the entire trade bill, it liked the connection, because the trade bill was put in jeopardy and brakes were applied to détente policy. The Russians had great difficulty understanding the domestic U.S. politics, and only in the very last moment of the legislative process, during the House-Senate Conference, did they speak up against the trade act restrictions on the president's agreements with the Soviet Union.[b]

Interestingly, this legislative process did not become entangled in the politics of the presidency in 1973-1974 nor in the politics or other issues before Congress, except for procedural log-rolling. The reason was that the presidential trade office in the Executive Office of the President made every effort to handle the legislation itself, avoiding the use of presidential legislative staff, so that the bill was insulated against tradeoffs in relation to other presidential issues.

The politics of foreign economic policy involve special interests, stresses between domestic needs and foreign objectives, bureaucratic bargaining, presidential decision-making, a high level of congressional-executive interaction, and an apparent disinterest on the part of the general public. In recent decades, foreign economic policy in the executive branch was treated as technical subject to be left to technicians except when their recommendations ran counter to "high policy," in which case the technicians were simply overruled. In 1970, I wrote:

> In the U.S. . . . international economic issues rarely hold the high level of attention of foreign policy makers . . . The broad policy consequences of economic actions are hardly ever considered by Secretaries of State. Presidents never give international economics anything like the time and attention they devote to military and political problems.[31]

Special interests do have some influence on foreign economic policy occasionally, because they work through Congress (where local, constituent interests are vital) and rely on Congress to use leverage to get their special objectives accomplished. This points up a key element of the decision-making process: all foreign economic policy decisions are subject to appeal, whoever makes them. If a cabinet committee decides to go in a direction unfavorable to a powerful lobby, an appeal will be made to a White House staffer or to a key

[b]When the Soviet Embassy in Washington sent news to the Conference Committee that it would reject the U.S.-Soviet Agreement because of the trade act, the discussion in conference was simple: if the Russians were against it, said the conferees, it must be good. The title was approved without further debate.

congressman or senator. If the president digs in, more congressmen will be brought into battle, or the bureaucracy may begin undermining the presidential decision as a result of appeals to it. Foreign governments can make appeals through embassies or telephone calls between White House officials and foreign cabinet offices. The official who wants to make policy and make it stick must figure the certainty of numerous appeals into his battle plans.

Another key element of foreign economic policy management in the U.S. is its complexity. One might think of foreign policy issues as laid out in a spectrum of complexity. The relatively simple ones are associated with military problems, because the forces at work can be measured (how many missiles or men or tanks). Reaction times can be assessed. Domestic politics can be ignored for a time, because the domestic political forces do not follow the day-to-day technical or tactical developments internationally. Experts are few, and uncooperative outside experts can be kept uninformed by the clever use of security classifications. The relatively complex foreign policy issues are the economic issues. No two nations, no particular action, can be viewed in isolation. Every action has effects throughout the world economic system, leading to other, unanticipated developments. Special interests are directly affected, especially in connection with issues of international commerce. The special interest groups retain expert lawyers and expert economic advisers, who can second-guess the policy-maker. Congress has its own specialized experts. The press often gets interested in the tactics, and is able to watch more effectively than it can watch SALT negotiations or other security-protected areas of foreign policy. Other nations put foreign economic policy higher in their priorities and use other leverage to influence Washington where possible.

Vital to analyzing and understanding the complexity are the workings of the congressional role. Arms control or Middle East diplomacy can be explained to the Senate Foreign Relations Committee. This committee tends to be a debating forum, for airing public concerns as well as educating both the public and congress. The committee does not control the fate of other issues, especially domestic issues, so the executive branch sometimes assumes that it can be safely opposed. Economic issues in foreign policy are different, because there are a multiplicity of jurisdictions. The Finance Committee and Ways and Means Committee handle much of trade policy, but not all. Export controls and export financing have been handled by the banking committees. Foreign aid does go to the foreign affairs bodies. But shipping and certain other trade matters go to the commerce committees. The agriculture committees handle all the agricultural issues. The broad policy outlines are discussed by subcommittees of the Joint Economic Committee.

With the recent reforms of committees, this picture is even more complex, with numerous new subcommittees taking over, with increasingly overlapping jurisdictions. A secretary of state who concentrates consultation with the foreign relations bodies will find they are not jurisdictionally competent on most of these economic matters, and that consulting with them often offends the chairmen of the committees that do have legislative competence.

Since according to the Constitution Congress has major powers, a working relationship has to be developed with the members and their staffs. Consensus is necessary for support for economic proposals (especially in connection with votes, and the avoidance of appeals to the president), so that much time must be spent developing consensus. The executive official who works with Congress must know when to press and when to yield, because each time a firm stance is taken and a point is won it costs something somewhere else or sometime later, when the debt is called. Since these committees have vital domestic jurisdictions, the log-rolling potential for damaging the president is enormous, and the executive official must consequently approach with caution and humility, if he is to be successful.

Then there are the consensus-makers and industry experts and special interest groups. Usually some effort is made to form commissions or advisory committees so that their judgments can be interwoven with executive branch thinking—and if they are ignored or insufficiently appreciated, these parties to the decision process may end up testifying publicly before congressional committees against executive proposals. Under the new trade act, industry-government consultative processes are made more intimate and formal than ever before.

Within the executive branch, the number of agencies involved in particular economic policy issues varies—but in a typical trade policy question, there may be ten agencies with direct interests. Even in the monetary area, there has to be reconciliation of the views of the Federal Reserve, the Treasury, the Export-Import Bank, the Commerce Department, the State Department, the National Security Council staff, and other presidential aides. The number of interagency committees changes constantly, but it is always large. The level of reconciliation varies: some issues are handled primarily by office directors or deputy assistant secretaries, who then report directly to the White House; others are handled by the cabinet directly; and yet others are handled by the NSC in secret (as in the case of the USSR and China). The maze does have entrances and exits, but many newcomers to Washington never find the exits nor the paths through the mazes, and become lost in seemingly meaningless routines (cleverly devised by bureaucrats to keep them out of policy-making).[32]

Thus there are a number of possible channels for decisions, and their appeals, and the number is limited only by the ingenuity of the adversaries involved in or affected by the policy decision.

Transnational Policy Processes

Similar problems exist in other governments, though in different forms and degrees. What this means, however, is that there can be simultaneous but differing messages sent between capitals, as individual bureaucrats learn to avoid the normal bureaucratic channels and deal with sympathetic policy-makers in other capitals directly. The master of direct contact to end-run the system was Henry Kissinger, when serving as assistant to the president. In the White House, Kissinger and his personal staff were frequently in touch directly with high-level officials in other governments. Later, as secretary of state, he tried to limit the communications of other U.S. officials with foreign officials, but they had learned their lesson too well and could not be fully controlled.

Thus the economic policy-maker has to take into account transnational consensus formulation and underground warfare against his policies. He must become expert in the politics and procedures of other nations as well as his own—and this means the politics of economic policy in other nations. A casual acquaintance with a handful of interested writers and intellectuals around the world is not enough, as it may sometimes be when dealing with military-security affairs.

The decision-making complexity of domestic procedures is compounded by the complexities of multilateral diplomacy. The U.S. finds itself involved in a wide variety of international institutions and bilateral arrangements. Each institution is serviced from some particular bureaucratic base at home, in each capital. Foreign offices and the State Department dominate the U.N. institutions. The presidential trade office handles the GATT delegations. The Treasury handles the IMF and the World Bank. The Labor Department handles the ILO. The OECD is carved up, with different agencies backstopping different committees. Within the State Department, various offices backstop the various institutions, with minimal coordination and active competition.

The important roles of the IMF, the World Bank family, the GATT, and the OECD are clear enough. Some of the other bodies are looked on in Washington as political debating fora, to be utilized to extend debate and defer concrete actions. This is especially true of the U.N. bodies. Other nations make similar distinctions, using, for example, UNCTAD for strong attacks on the U.S. and other developed nations, and GATT for negotiating "real issues."

Which international bodies, if any, the U.S. utilizes in dealing with particular issues varies with the personal strength of the officials involved; the agency that has jurisdiction; the recent experience of frustration or success; and the responsiveness of the international secretariats to U.S. wishes. There is a great deal of "ad hocery." When the dominant Western financial powers that made up the G-Ten failed to move on U.S. monetary proposals, the C-20 was created, ostensibly to open the doors to developing nations but really to change the weight of political opinion against the European-dominated G-Ten. When issues came to dispute in these bodies, they were looked at in the OCED.

East-West issues have been dealt with bilaterally, tightly controlled by the State Department, in spite of the ceremonial role of the Commerce Department (except for the short reign of Peter Peterson as secretary of commerce), and an occasional outburst from the Agriculture Department. When political openings develop in connection with political maneuvers (for example, in relation to the Middle East recently), one sees the dominant personalities of the State Department and the Treasury Department developing personal relationships. These sometimes take the form of fiefdoms, through the creation of bilateral commissions (the U.S.-Saudi Arabia Commission, the U.S.-Egypt Commission). When big issues develop wherein personal glory and agency dominance can be exploited fully, the issues are split out for special multilateral activities. The follow-up to the 1974 World Food Conference is an example, where the world food reserve scheme has been split off to be negotiated by representatives of State and Agriculture in the London context of the International Wheat Council, even though most experts would argue that the issues ought to be connected with commercial questions in the Multilateral Trade Negotiations in Geneva. The proposal for a separate energy agency, in the OECD but essentially independent, is another example. The special oil producer-consumer dialogue, renamed the Conference on International Economic Cooperation in late 1975, is yet another case.

Interdependence and Policy Problems for the Future

This splitting off of important issues creates further confusion in Washington policy-making, and it makes it harder for foreign governments to assess U.S. objectives and whether the Americans will later be able to deliver congressional support for the ad hoc international adventures they propose.

While Washington speeches often refer to the interaction of all the foreign policy questions, the practice is to separate the issues in decision-making. While Washington speaks in cosmic themes, its negotiating stance tends to be narrowly defined and unrelated to the broader relations with other nations. While efforts to devise "grand designs" are periodically made, policy issues come up to the president in pieces, as do the political appeals and the bureaucratic differences. The amazing thing about the whole process is that it works at all—but the reason it could work in such a relaxed manner in the past is that the international pressures were never strongly felt. Washington could take its time; Washington felt it could even go it alone, if necessary.

In the new circumstances, of much greater global economic interdependence, the luxury of the policy process the U.S. has had in the past will become far more costly. Sudden developments of an unexpected character—such as the three state-trading purchased by the Russians in the early and mid-1970 period, or the unplanned rise in oil prices, or the absence of food stocks—are very hard for the system to handle. Consensus decision-making takes time; actions may be required quickly. But secrecy and concentration of power is not necessarily the answer. The issues are too complex to be handled by only a few people in one department—and even if that could be done, who would talk to Congress, or the White House, or the special interest groups?

Moreover, other nations' bureaucracies and political machineries cannot cope with the secrecy and concentration of power in Washington. Foreign officials need to be able to talk to their U.S. counterparts and discuss issues at a level where they feel expertise should be applied. The demise of the second Atlantic Charter in 1973 was primarily the result of the secrecy and closely held negotiating process on the U.S. side. Secretary Kissinger designated only two or three people to carry on the discussions and instructed them to operate in strictest secrecy. Nobody who understood the issues was involved, so the bureaucracy started its own guerrilla warfare against the concept and against specific drafts.

In addition to this critical dilemma of management, the U.S. must still face another fact: it is still the dominant power when economics, politics, and security matters are taken together. The rest of the Western world perceives the U.S. as the prime mover. The U.S. economy—and its meanderings on this or that path—is the benchmark for policies elsewhere. If the U.S. behaves in a steady, predictable manner, the policies of others will tend to adjust accordingly; but if the U.S. seems to move erratically, the others will act defensively to insulate themselves from the unknown side effects and the unknown objectives.

The frustrations of U.S. foreign policy-makers, when they work in the economic area, are often the product of the old-style diplomacy of private assurances, surprise initiatives, negotiations conducted in secret, and the inherent domestic differences.

The dilemma of economic policy in the coming decades will be to manage external affairs in a way that benefits national objectives, retaining a maximum degree of freedom for each nation to pursue its own interests, while at the same time keeping order in the world system so that economic disruptions and actions by one nation do not intrude on the well-being of other nations. A high degree of openness in economic policy, together with growing interdependence, tends to threaten national autonomy by allowing economic forces to flow over, under, and around national policies. This creates a need for government-to-government coordination or consultation, as Richard Cooper has so brilliantly explained,[33] in a variety of areas of economic policy.

Thus far, however, U.S. policy processes have only faintly reflected this need. There have been some recent efforts at close consultation, particularly in connection with interest rate policy and exchange rate management, in Working Party 3 and the Economic Policy Committee of the OECD, and in transnational contacts among central banks. However, the idea of highest-level cooperation and consultation was put forward first, somewhat surprisingly, by Chancellor Helmut Schmidt of West Germany and President Valéry Giscard d'Estaing of France, in their proposal for an "economic summit" at Rambouillet at the end of 1975. The U.S. was initially reluctant but eventually agreed to participate without any clear idea of what should be sought or how to explain it domestically. The circumstances of inflation, recession, budget crises, decline in world trade, and the special pains of oil price adjustments (causing structural adjustment problems in the energy field) in all the industrialized nations simultaneously clearly created serious difficulties for economic policy managers. Actions of one nation could and did affect other nations' economies. But while this high-level recognition of the new interdependence marks a new sophistication, it may or may not change the day-to-day practices of governments.

To summarize, U.S. foreign economic policy is characterized by a multiplicity of decision-makers and channels at home and abroad; a multiplicity of influences from political forces, bureaucrats, Congress, and opinion-makers; and conflicts between domestic and international objectives and political needs. Basic themes of policy are discernible, some of them in conflict with one another, and the basic themes are often overridden by domestic preoccupations.

The thesis of U.S. economic imperialism, noted at the outset of this chapter, does not correspond to the complex realities and conflicting policies. Nor can it be said that there has been one consistent, dominant theme.

The apparent confusion and kaleidoscopic images of policy are the result of the many processes at work. It is doubtful whether this way of coping with the world, and the U.S. relationship to it, can continue in the last quarter of the century. The economic forces require management more and more because of increasing economic interdependence and an increasing role of governments in other nations. The political forces, including those of détente and North-South relations, as well as those at home, will necessitate new approaches and therefore test the decision-making system. The easy part of economic multilateralism was developed in the mid-1940s and evolved further in the 1950s and 1960s. The hard tests for U.S. foreign economic policy, and the U.S. political machinery that lies behind it, lie ahead. Policy change can come only slowly, through new processes of consensus building, while economic challenges tend to come at an increasingly rapid rate. How the U.S. will react remains to be seen.

Notes

1. R.N. Gardner, *Sterling-Dollar Diplomacy* (London: Oxford University Press, 1956; rev. ed., New York: McGraw-Hill, 1969), Chapter 1.

2. Ibid., p. 3.

3. International Economic Report of the President (Washington, D.C.: U.S. Government Printing Office, 1975).

4. D.P. Calleo, *The Atlantic Fantasy: The U.S., NATO, and Europe* (Baltimore: Johns Hopkins Press, 1970), p. 13.

5. For further development of the Calleo thesis, see D.P. Calleo and B.M. Rowland, *America and the World Political Economy: Atlantic Dreams and National Realities* (Bloomington: Indiana University Press, 1973).

6. William Diebold, *United States and the Industrial World* (New York: Praeger, 1972), p. 1.

7. See T.C. Shelling, "International Investment," in *International Economics* (Boston: Allyn and Bacon, 1958), Chapter 25.

8. Commission on the Organization of the Government for the Conduct of Foreign Policy, June, 1975.

9. See, for example, Dean Acheson, *Present at the Creation* (New York: Norton, 1969), pp. 27-34; and Gardner, *Sterling-Dollar Diplomacy*, Chapters 1-4.

10. See H.B. Malmgren, "Europe, the United States, and the World Economy," in S.J. Warnecke, ed., *The European Community in the 1970's* (New York: Praeger, 1972), Chapter 7.

11. The best essay written on this problem is T.C. Schelling's "International Cost-Sharing Arrangements," *Essays in International Finance*, no. 24 (Princeton, N.J.: International Finance Section, Princeton University, September 1955).

12. "The World Crash," *The New York Review of Books*, January 23, 1975.

13. Henry C. Wallich, "Government Action," in Seymour E. Harris, ed., *The Dollar in Crisis* (New York: Harcourt, Brace and World, 1961).

14. Cf. Seymour Harris, "Introduction," in *The Dollar in Crisis*, p. 40.

15. Federal Reserve Press Release, July 16, 1963, reprinted in the statement of William McChesney Martin, in the Hearings before the Committee on Banking and Currency, House of Representatives, July 22, 1963 (88th Cong., 1st Sess.).

16. *The Balance of Payments Statistics of the United States: A Review and Appraisal* (Washington, D.C.: Government Printing Office, April 16, 1965).

17. Harold van Buren Cleveland, "How the Dollar Standard Died," *Foreign Policy*, no. 5 (Winter 1971-72):45.

18. For further discussion of this point, see Wilfrid Kohl's analysis in "The Nixon-Kissinger Foreign Policy System and U.S.-European Relations: Patterns of Policy-Making," *World Politics* (October 1975):19-20.

19. President Nixon, *The Economic Report of the President* (Washington, D.C.: U.S. Government Printing Office, 1974), p. 5.

20. Council on International Economic Policy, *Special Report: Critical Imported Materials*, Executive Office of the President, December, 1974.

21. For more on these complex issues, see H.B. Malmgren, *The Raw Material and Commodity Controversy*, Contemporary Issues no. 1 (a monograph) (Washington, D.C.: International Economic Studies Institute, October 1975).

22. Quoted in Gardner, *Sterling-Dollar Diplomacy*, p. 9, from Hull's memoirs.

23. Gardner, *Sterling-Dollar Diplomacy*, p. 9.

24. President John F. Kennedy, Special Message to the Congress on Foreign Trade Policy, January 25, 1962.

25. For a general discussion of the domestic and international developments, see H.B. Malmgren, *International Economic Peacekeeping in Phase II*, rev. ed. (New York: Quadrangle Books, 1973), Chapter 2.

26. Senator Abraham Ribicoff, *Trade Policies in the 1970's*, Report to the Committee on Finance, U.S. Senate, March 4, 1971, pp. 10-11.

27. *Policy Perspectives for International Trade and Economic Relations* (Paris: Organization for Economic Co-Operation and Development, 1972).

28. E.g., National Planning Association, *U.S. Foreign Economic Policy for the 1970's: A New Approach to New Realities* (Washington, D.C.: 1971); Committee for Economic Development, *The United States and the European Community* (New York, 1971).

29. Presidential Commission on International Trade and Investment Policy, *United States International Economic Policy in an Interdependent World* (Washington, D.C.: U.S. Government Printing Office, 1971).

30. For a discussion of the drafting concepts and the shaping of the various authorities, and the ultimate interpretations of the law, see M.J. Marks and H.B. Malmgren, "Negotiating Non-Tariff Distortions to Trade," *Law and Policy in International Business*, vol. 7, no. 2 (April 1975):327-411. For further discussion of the cumulative slow process of consensus formation in trade policy, see H.B. Malmgren, "Sources of Instability in the World Trading System," *Journal of International Affairs* (Spring 1976).

31. H.B. Malmgren, "Coming Trade Wars?" *Foreign Policy* 1 (Winter 1970-71):116.

32. I have examined the problems of Executive Branch management in much greater length elsewhere, in "Managing Foreign Economic Policy," *Foreign Policy* no. 6 (Spring 1972):42-63; and in my testimony before the Subcommittee on International Finance, Committee on Banking, Housing, and Urban Affairs, U.S. Senate, July 18, 1975, on the bill (S.1262) to authorize appropriations for the Council on International Economic Policy. See also Wilfrid Kohl's excellent analysis in "The Nixon-Kissinger Foreign Policy System."

33. R.N. Cooper, *The Economics of Interdependence* (New York: McGraw-Hill, 1968).

3 Great Britain

Benjamin J. Cohen

Britain's 1971 decision to join the Common Market was an event of the first magnitude in British economic history. Only twice before in the last century and a half had the country's foreign economic policy undergone a comparable transformation—once in 1846 when the repeal of the Corn Laws ushered in an era of free trade, and a second time in 1932 when free trade was abandoned in favor of the system known as Imperial Preference. At least until the early 1960s Britain still regarded itself as a major economic power—not the world's leading power certainly, but a force of some importance nonetheless, with widespread commercial and financial interests, particularly in the Commonwealth. But by the middle and late 1960s this conception had begun to fade. In place of the global and Commonwealth perspectives that had previously guided Britain's foreign economic policy, a new "European" orientation gradually emerged, culminating in Parliament's formal approval of British membership in the European Community in October 1971, and surviving even the Labor Party's pledge to renegotiate the terms of membership after Labor's return to power in 1974 and the referendum debate of 1975.

This chapter will discuss this dramatic transformation of British foreign economic policy, commenting on how it came about and suggesting some insights into the decision-making process that was involved. The first section develops in a rather cursory fashion—and with no particular claim to novelty—an abstract analytical framework that can be used generally to gain an understanding of the decision-making process in foreign economic policy. The second section gives content to the framework of analysis by applying it to the specific instance of Great Britain in the decade of the 1960s. The final section considers briefly some of the implications of the 1971 decision for the substance and direction of the decision-making process in British foreign economic policy in the future.

Analytical Framework

The analysis of the decision-making process in foreign economic policy generally may be approached in a variety of ways. For an economist, the most congenial approach views policy as a problem of "maximization under constraint."[1] Conventional economic analysis always begins with the assumption of scarcity: the things that people and societies value are limited in supply; the best things in life (Tin Pan Alley notwithstanding) are not all free. Choices therefore are necessary. The task for economic decision-makers (assuming they are rational) is to do the best they can to maximize some value or other—or several values simultaneously—under the constraint of scarcity. The task for the economic analyst seeking insight into such behavior is to focus on this problem of choice. As Walter Heller has written of the political economist: "Problems of choice are his meat and drink. His method is to factor out the costs, the benefits, and the net advantage or disadvantage of alternative courses of action."[2]

The traditional analytic mode of economics concentrates attention on three sets of interrelated variables: (1) independent variables, which are the instruments available to decision-makers; (2) dependent variables, which are the targets of decision-makers; and (3) parameters, which are the constraints on decision-makers. For analytical purposes these three sets of variables are combined, implicitly or explicitly, to form "models," in which the dependent variables are assumed to be functionally related to the independent variables, and the nature of each functional relationship (in mathematical terms, the magnitude and sign of each partial derivative) is assumed to be determined by the parametric constraints. For any given problem, specifying a model (implicit or explicit) enables the economist to analyze how he can use available instruments, subject to the constraints imposed by objective circumstances, to maximize a certain target. When the model incorporates multiple targets, the problem becomes one of joint maximization, with analysis focusing as well on the tradeoffs at the margin among the several targets.

This mode of analysis has always lent itself quite readily to explaining the behavior of private economic units. Economic theory speaks of the firm, for example, rationally maximizing the target of profit by making use of the instruments at its disposal—principally, its price and quantity of output—subject to such constraints as input costs, demand for output, and the prices of related goods. Or theory speaks of the consumer, rationally maximizing the target of personal utility by varying purchases subject to the constraints of income and tastes. Analysis of this sort has proved to be highly relevant and rich in practical insights. It is also relatively straightforward, because in dealing with private economic units discussion can usually proceed in terms of a single dependent variable, and also because the specified targets of private economic units normally, though not always, can be quantified.

On the other hand, when it comes to explaining the behavior of public (political) economic units, analysis of this sort becomes a bit more complex. In the first place, governmental decision-makers usually have multiple rather than single policy targets. Specifically, political variables enter alongside economic variables as separate and independent objectives of action, which means that realistically, public economic policy must be viewed as a problem of *joint* maximization with much of the focus of analysis thus being trained directly on the marginal tradeoffs among objectives. Furthermore, since political variables usually cannot be easily quantified, analysis also must necessarily be rather more qualitative than quantitative. For both these reasons, the economist's traditional analytic mode does not lend itself quite so readily to the study of public economic policy as it does to the study of private economic units. And the analysis becomes even more complex yet as we move from domestic economic policy-making to foreign economic policy, where foreign political targets must be added to the already crowded array of economic and domestic political variables. Nevertheless, I would maintain that the mode of analysis can be highly relevant and useful. Even though our actual knowledge of all the complex functional relationships involved may be quite limited, organizing thinking in these terms at least has the virtue of adding clarity to discussions. So long as policy-makers can be assumed to be rational, significant insights can be gained by approaching the problem of foreign economic policy in this way, as will become apparent later.

What specific variables should be included in a realistic model of rational decision-making in foreign economic policy? In my opinion, at least the following dozen variables should be considered for analytical purposes:

1. Independent variables
   a. trade policy
   b. investment policy
   c. aid policy
   d. financial policy
2. Dependent variables
   a. economic welfare
   b. distribution
   c. national security
   d. national prestige
3. Parameters
   a. geography
   b. demography
   c. development
   d. history

No explanation ought to be necessary of the four independent variables listed, for they are the familiar instruments of governmental action in international economics.[3] Trade policy is concerned with the international movement of goods and services; investment policy, with the movement of money, both short-term and long-term; aid policy, with the movement of either goods, services, or money on concessional terms; and financial policy, with the balance of payments and exchange rate of the country as well as with the international status (if any) of the national currency.

The four dependent variables listed constitute, I believe, the principal independent targets of governmental action in international economics. Economic welfare stands for real income—that is, the real volume of goods and services available for final use by the nation's consumers, businesses, and government sector. This is the traditional objective identified in economic analysis. It is not a simple concept; despite more than two centuries of development of modern economic theory, we still do not know precisely how to go about maximizing economic welfare. One reason is the existence of competing economic theories. Economists disagree among themselves, in large part because of the impossibility of testing competing theories against one another. In the physical sciences, more often than not, it is possible to test one theory against another by means of a controlled experiment in a laboratory. In the social sciences, controlled experiments are out of the question: the laboratory is the real world, and all the samples are samples of one. Accordingly, honest people can honestly disagree on such matters as how to maximize economic welfare.

A second reason for such disagreements is that economic welfare is decomposable. At the micro level, welfare may be identified with efficiency of resource allocation; at the macro level, with both full employment and relative price stability. These three dimensions may not always be mutually compatible. The famous Phillips curve, for instance, defines a tradeoff between employment and price stability. Likewise, situations may arise when policy-makers must choose between promoting either employment or efficiency (e.g., when a balance-of-payments deficit forces the government to choose between domestic deflation or import controls). Since such choices necessarily involve value judgments regarding the relative weights to be attached to each of the three dimensions of economic welfare, normative differences can also cause disagreements about how this objective may be maximized.

The second dependent variable, distribution, stands as a proxy for the set of relevant domestic political goals of policy. I take for granted that policy-makers do have political goals in mind. Being politicians and not disinterested statesmen or philosopher-kings, they may be assumed to concern themselves not only (if at all) with the general interests of the national society as a whole, but also with the specific interests of certain narrower constituencies within the national society, and to seek through policy to maximize the gains of such domestic groups or to minimize their losses. In other words, they may be assumed to aim at some particular distribution of the costs and benefits of policy. This of course is the traditional objective identified in political analysis, the meat and drink of the political scientist: whose ox is gored if one policy is chosen rather than another? It is also, like economic welfare, not at all a simple concept. As in the case of economic welfare, we still do not know precisely how to go about achieving some particular distribution of the costs and benefits of policy, again in part because of competing theories, but even more importantly because this objective too is decomposable. Distribution implies not only gains or losses of real income, but also of relative rank, prestige, privileges, and so forth, and since here too value judgments are necessarily involved in weighing the tradeoffs between the pecuniary and nonpecuniary costs and benefits of policy, honest disagreements among honest people are possible with respect to this objective also.

Analogous points may be made regarding the remaining two dependent variables, national security and national prestige, which embody the two most important foreign political targets that must be added when we move from domestic policy-making to foreign economic policy. These concepts are hardly simple either. National security is mainly concerned with issues of territorial integrity and political independence and can be logically translated into an imperative to maximize national power.[4] National prestige is listed separately because it appears to operate with considerable force as an independent influence on the foreign economic policies of many states. The problem here is to know just what constitutes power or prestige, and to understand precisely how in fact either may be enhanced.

Turning lastly to the parameters, geography stands for the whole variety of physical attributes of a country—its size, location (is it maritime or landlocked? is it near major transportation routes?), natural resources, topography, arability, and climate. Demography refers to both the size and the composition of a country's population. Development represents the variety of economic characteristics of a country—e.g., its degree of industrialization and urbanization, its overall and per capita levels of income, the depth and breadth of its financial markets, and so on. And history stands for the entire cultural, social, political, and economic background that is embodied in the structure of the contemporary national society. These four multivariate factors are, I believe, the most important of the many constraints operating on the decision-making process in foreign economic policy. All are influential in determining the nature of the functional relationships between independent and dependent variables.

For example, consider the functional relationship between trade policy and economic welfare. Some countries may be able to use protectionist commercial regulations (e.g., export quotas, import tariffs) to gain an improvement of their terms of trade if their geography gives them some degree of monopoly power in the sale of their principal export commodities, or if their population size, level of development, or historical commercial ties give them some degree of monopsony power in the purchase of their imports. Countries less favorably endowed geographically and historically and with lower populations and levels of development, on the other hand, are apt conversely to find that a protectionist trade policy produces only a negative impact on the nation's real income. Similar differences may be noted with respect to all the other functional relationships between instruments and targets as well. The point is that in every country foreign economic policy must be conducted under the constraint of objective circumstances, and these circumstances will vary greatly from country to country. The essential task for policy-makers is to take account of these constraints in deciding how to use the several instruments at their disposal to achieve their preferred objectives. The "maximization under constraint" approach can give a useful insight into how this decision-making process works.

In particular, the approach can give a useful insight into how *changes* in foreign economic policy come about. The fact that there is at least a quartet of independent targets of governmental action in international economics means that policy-makers are continually obliged to make decisions about tradeoffs among objectives at the margin. When a substantial shift of foreign economic policy does occur, it must be because of a decision to modify these marginal tradeoffs. The "maximization under constraint" approach suggests that such a decision could be attributed either to a change of objective circumstances that has altered the functional relationships between instruments and targets of policy; or to a change of the government's "utility function," reflecting altered preferences in policy-making circles. The usefulness of the approach lies in the framework of analysis that it provides. But the framework itself is nothing more than a set of "empty boxes." It is the individual analyst's responsibility to give the boxes some actual content, as is attempted for one specific case in the next section of this chapter.

The Transformation of British Foreign Economic Policy

What explains the dramatic transformation that occurred in British foreign economic policy in the 1960s? I have already suggested that this shift compares with only two others in the last century and a half. Britain's transition in the 1840s and 1850s from mercantilism to free trade was associated mainly with a redistribution of domestic political power from the Tory landed gentry and aristocracy to the rising Whig bourgeoisie (and hence it may be attributed largely to altered preferences in policy-making circles). The adoption of Imperial Preference in the 1930s may be interpreted primarily, though not exclusively, in terms of a concern for assuring national economic welfare in the midst of the Great Depression (and hence it may be attributed largely to changed objective circumstances). What factors account for the current European orientation of British foreign economic policy?

To begin with, Britain is a small, crowded island archipelago that has always been relatively poorly endowed with natural resources or arable land. As Table 3-1 indicates, mining and agriculture tend to account for very little of the country's gross domestic output or employment. Britain's structure of production is heavily skewed in favor of manufacturing and service activities, reflecting the fact that this is a country that has learned to trade to survive. Quite early in the Industrial Revolution, the British people seem to have realized that if they were to achieve anything significantly above an uncomfortable subsistence standard of living, they would have to obtain considerable amounts of food,

Table 3-1
Sectoral Structure of the British Economy
(In Percentages)

	Share of each sector in:	
	Gross Domestic Product[a]	*Employment*
Mining and quarrying	1.5	1.5
Agriculture, forestry, and fishing	3.0	1.5
Manufacturing	32.0	34.0
Services	63.5	63.0

Source: Central Statistical Office.
Note: Data are for 1971.
[a]Gross domestic product equals gross national product less net overseas investment earnings.

fuel, and raw materials from abroad; and in order to pay for the imports they required, they would have to promote a high level of exports. Britain therefore became a trading nation—for many years, the world's leading trading nation. The movement toward free trade in the middle of the nineteenth century was an entirely rational act from the British economy's point of view, and so was the effort in the uncertain atmosphere of the 1930s to secure the country's export markets and sources of supply by formalizing the Imperial Preference system.

The structure of Britain's domestic economy is reflected in the volume and composition of its foreign trade. Foreign trade accounts for approximately one-sixth of the country's gross domestic product; fully half of all exports are finished manufactures, as can be seen in Table 3-2. Imports, on the other hand, consist primarily of foods, fuels, raw materials, and semimanufactured industrial inputs. Britain trades to promote its own economic welfare. Of course, in principle the British could eschew foreign trade if they wanted to—but only if they were willing to trade off almost totally the goal of economic welfare for other policy objectives, and to tolerate not much more than a Stone Age standard of living. Such forbearance is hard to imagine, even given the long-suffering imperturbability for which the British people are justifiably noted. In practice, therefore, autarky (self-sufficiency) cannot be considered a feasible policy option for Britain. Objective circumstances constrain the country to accept a relatively high degree of involvement in the international economy.

But the international economy is not a homogeneous entity. It consists rather of a multitude of partially overlapping congeries of nations—some tightly organized into different types of economic blocs, others related more loosely through varying degrees and modes of economic intercourse—and in such a fragmented, differentiated world, states like Britain must make choices not just about the degree of their involvement in the international economy but also about the orientation of their commercial and financial relations. For the British

Table 3-2
Composition of British Foreign Trade
(In Percentages)

Imports		100.0
Foodstuffs		22.0
Fuels		12.5
Raw materials		13.0
Manufactured goods		51.0
Semimanufactures	26.5	
Finished manufactures	24.5	
Unclassified		1.5
Exports		100.0
Foodstuffs		6.5
Fuels		2.5
Raw materials		3.0
Manufactured goods		85.0
Semimanufactures	35.0	
Finished manufactures	50.0	
Unclassified		3.0

Source: Central Statistical Office.
Note: Data are for 1971.

from at least the 1930s onward, the preferred choice was an orientation toward the remnants of the old empire—that is, toward that disparate, widely scattered group of nations, dominions, and dependencies that has since come to be known simply as the Commonwealth. Until recently the fundamental *leitmotif* of Britain's foreign economic policy was this Commonwealth "connection." The twin pillars of the connection were Imperial Preference and the Sterling Area.

Imperial Preference, first instituted at the Ottawa Conference of Commonwealth nations in 1932, consisted simply of a set of mutual tariff preferences arranged between Britain and the other members of the Commonwealth. British duties on imports from the Commonwealth were reduced relative to the tariffs on goods originating elsewhere; and likewise Commonwealth members levied relatively lower duties on products originating in Britain. From the British point of view, the advantages of the system were twofold. First, an extra incentive was provided to Commonwealth countries to supply Britain with the foods, fuels, and raw materials it needed. And second, Britain obtained extra leverage in valuable export markets required to earn the wherewithal with which to pay for imports. Imperial Preference promised both a continuity of supply of imports and a "captive" demand for exports. (The advantages offered to overseas Commonwealth members were of course complementary.)

The Sterling Area consisted of a parallel set of financial relationships arranged between Britain and the other members of the Commonwealth (with the exception of Canada, which has always been more closely linked financially with the United States than with Britain). The system first emerged in 1931, following the suspension of sterling convertibility, when a number of countries that had customarily relied on the pound for private and official international monetary uses–including a variety of non-Commonwealth countries–elected informally to peg their currency rates to sterling and to hold the bulk of their official monetary reserves in the form of sterling balances in London. After 1939, the initiation of a common regime of exchange control regulations applying to the group as a whole gave formal definition to Sterling Area membership; subsequently, most non-Commonwealth countries chose to exclude themselves from this more formal arrangement. From the end of World War II, therefore, membership of the Sterling Area was practically conterminous with the borders of the Commonwealth. The principal features of the group were: (1) freedom of monetary transfers between members; and (2) continued reliance on sterling as the currency for both private transfers and official reserve holdings.

The advantages offered to overseas members by the Sterling Area derived mainly from the first of these two features. Freedom of monetary transfers between members meant above all freedom of access to the British capital market. In effect, it meant that British investment policy would be biased in favor of the Commonwealth. Sterling Area arrangements assured Commonwealth countries first claim on British capital resources. Likewise, these arrangements (to say nothing of historical ties) assured a Commonwealth bias in British aid policy as well.

Although the British of course also benefited (economically or otherwise) from these biases, the main advantages the Sterling Area offered Britain derived from the second of the group's two principal features–the continued use of sterling for private and official international monetary purposes. The major thrust of Britain's financial policy, at least until the late 1960s, was to sustain and promote the pound's status as an international currency, in the belief that such status was essential to a continued high level of so-called invisible earnings in the country's balance of payments. Historically, Britain's visible trade balance has always tended toward deficit: only rarely have the country's merchandise exports ever exceeded imports. Consequently, the British have always had to rely on a high level of income from services–"invisibles"–to make up the difference on trade balance and in addition to provide some surplus for capital export. Most such services, including banking, insurance, merchanting, and brokerage, have traditionally centered on the "City of London" (Britain's equivalent of Wall Street). And until recently it was a cardinal tenet of faith in the City of London that the foreign income from these services was highly dependent on the international use of sterling. The status of the City as an international financial center had grown from the middle of the nineteenth century onward *pari passu* with the status of sterling as an international currency: as foreign use of the pound for private and official monetary purposes had prospered, so too had the City's overseas earnings. It was only natural, therefore, to believe that without the support of a great international currency much of that business would be taken elsewhere, and the City's earnings would begin to crumble away. Accordingly, it was only natural that British financial policy would be directed toward preserving the pound's international roles to the extent possible through continuation and reinforcement of Sterling Area arrangements.

Thus all four instruments of British foreign economic policy were orchestrated in support of the Commonwealth connection—trade policy through the system of Imperial Preference; and investment, aid, and financial policy through the customary practices and formal regulations of the Sterling Area. This orientation reflected Britain's historic conception of itself as a major economic power, a conception that survived World War II and in a sense may even have been strengthened by that experience. In the 1940s and 1950s the British still viewed their role in the international economy largely in global rather than in regional terms. Britain was the leader of the Commonwealth and enjoyed a "special relationship" with the United States. Britain's commercial and financial interests were worldwide. Britain's industrial output put the country among the world's leaders. It was difficult for a majority of the British people at the time even to conceive of any alternative orientation for the nation's foreign economic policy.

Still, a few lonely voices could be heard raising the possibility of alternatives, and these voices grew progressively louder following the failure of negotiations for a European-wide free trade area in 1958. In 1955 the six original members of the European Community initiated planning for the Common Market; by the time the Rome Treaty was signed in 1957, the remaining countries of Europe, Britain included, were feeling seriously threatened by exclusion from such a rich export area. Negotiations were therefore begun to establish a broader free trade zone in Europe to include the Six, but these talks foundered in 1958, most crucially over the issue of Britain's Imperial Preference system. While the Six, led by France, insisted on a common external tariff for all European countries, the British were as yet unprepared to abandon their Commonwealth connection. As a result, Western Europe became divided into two economic camps—the Common Market (the "Inner Six") and the European Free Trade Association (the "Outer Seven"). In Britain, the failure of the talks with the Six led some people to raise basic questions about the underlying value of the Commonwealth connection, and to consider possible alternative options for British foreign economic policy. Two diametrically opposed reactions predominated.

One of these reactions was like that of a rejected lover: "If the Common

Market doesn't want us, then we don't want them." Some Britons thus advocated turning away from Europe completely, hoping instead to formalize the "special relationship" with the United States in a broad free trade area encompassing both sides of the Atlantic Ocean (but excluding the Six). By the middle of the 1960s the proposal for a North Atlantic Free Trade Area (NAFTA) was receiving serious consideration in several quarters.[5] Membership of NAFTA was projected to include not just the United States and Britain but also the other Outer Seven and Canada, and perhaps also even Japan, Australia, and New Zealand—effectively isolating the Six from the rest of the non-Communist industrial world. Parallel proposals were made for bringing sterling and the Sterling Area under the aegis of the U.S. dollar.[6] The opposite of the two reactions was more like that of a resigned loser: "If you can't lick them, join them." These Britons preferred to apply for formal membership in the Common Market more or less on the Community's own terms, with the Sterling Area eventually to be either dissolved or else absorbed into a European monetary system. This European alternative began to receive attention almost immediately after the breakdown of talks with the Six in 1958.[7]

By the beginning of the 1960s, therefore, three quite different conceptions of British foreign economic policy were competing for official acceptance—the traditional Commonwealth connection, an "American connection," and a "European connection." As we know, in the grand national debate that followed, the European connection ultimately prevailed. The framework of analysis outlined earlier can help in explaining why.

First of all, recalling the four dependent variables included in that analytical framework, it should immediately be evident why the option of an American connection never managed to gain widespread popular support. Essentially it was because the British people were manifestly unwilling to trade off the goal of national prestige for other policy objectives. Historical preferences could not be easily altered. To join with the United States in NAFTA would have meant giving up the country's cherished conception of itself as a major economic power. Compared to the United States, Britain was a decidedly second-ranking economy. At the start of the 1960s, British gross national output amounted to just 15 percent of the U.S.'s GNP. Britain had only a fraction of the U.S. population or natural resources, and its currency had long since yielded the place of honor to the dollar in international finance. In short, Britain would have had to resign itself to being a relatively small fish in a relatively big pond—in effect, the U.S.'s fifty-first state. This was an eventuality British policy-makers were clearly reluctant to accept, despite the apparent benefits of the course.

Britain certainly would have benefited from the course in the area of national security. Closer economic ties formalizing Britain's "special relationship" with the United States would undoubtedly have reinforced America's existing commitments to protect British territorial and political interests. Likewise, the objective of economic welfare would in all likelihood have been promoted by a free trade zone spanning the Atlantic, giving Britain access to what was by far the richest export market in the world. Any risk that the British economy might be depressed by superior U.S. competitiveness could easily have been forestalled by an adequate system of safeguards. In any event, with assurance of access to America's technologies and capital resources, Britain—as economic fifty-first state—quite probably would have turned out to be more of a California than a West Virginia inside NAFTA. Yet British policy-makers were unimpressed. They were simply unwilling to surrender their remaining global presence and their residual leadership role in world affairs to retreat under the American shadow. Historical attitudes proved too enduring.

On the other hand, historical attitudes could not rule out considering the alternative option of a European connection. The prospect of membership in the Common Market represented nothing like the same threat to Britain's great-power pretensions as the American connection. Compared to France or Germany, Britain was still an economy of the first rank: along with the French and Germans, the British stood to become part of a triumvirate managing the affairs of the new Europe. For many Britons this possibility carried with it at least as much national prestige as the country's traditional leadership role in the old Commonwealth. Indeed, it was clear that in either pond, Europe or Commonwealth, Britain would continue to be a relatively big fish.

The real contest, therefore, was between the Commonwealth connection and the alternative of a European connection. During the 1960s the relative merits of these two policy options were debated publicly at great length and in exhaustive—and exhausting—detail.[8] The focus of the debate was on the tradeoffs among the three objectives of economic welfare, distribution, and national prestige. (Interestingly, comparatively little attention was paid to the remaining objective of foreign economic policy, national security.) The key question for analysis is: Was the decision to choose the European connection dictated by altered preferences in policy-making circles or by changed objective circumstances?

The answer to this question, in my opinion, is clear: the choice was dictated by changed objective circumstances. Despite recurrent shifts of electoral sentiment in Britain during the 1960s, underlying preferences in policy-making circles remained remarkably stable (as we shall see below). What did change were the constraints on British policy-makers, the parameters of foreign economic policy. As the decade progressed, it became increasingly evident that Britain's economic world had altered—that the old Commonwealth connection no longer served to maximize important national objectives, and that the continued isolation from Europe was blocking effective use of economic policy instruments. Gradually, dominant elites in Britain became educated to the real gains and losses accruing from the Commonwealth connection; they learned what potential gains and losses were in fact likely to result from shifting instead to the alternative of a European orientation. Assumptions and perceptions underwent a significant modification, reflecting (albeit with a lag) the substantial changes that had actually occurred, and were continuing to occur, in the functional relationships between independent and dependent variables of policy.

British industrialists, for example, began to perceive that there were considerable costs entailed in continued reliance on Imperial Preference in trade policy. Through the 1950s and 1960s, Britain's trade grew at a far slower rate with the Commonwealth than with the European Community. Indeed, as Table 3-3 shows, by 1971 the Commonwealth was actually taking a smaller share of Britain's exports than was the Common Market—despite tariff discrimination by the Six—and was supplying virtually an equal share of Britain's imports. There were two main reasons for this marked change of trade patterns. In the first place, the economies of the Commonwealth (many of them less developed) were expanding much less rapidly than were the economies of the Six. "Captive" or not, demand in the Commonwealth was simply too weak to ensure a high level of exports for Britain; demand in the rich and dynamic European market, on the other hand, was strong enough to draw in goods even over the wall of the Community's common external tariff. And second, much of the Commonwealth for its part was deliberately diminishing its economic ties with Britain (an inevitable part of the process of decolonization). One of the first things most of Britain's former colonies sought following attainment of political independence was to reduce their remaining economic dependence on the British by diversifying export markets and sources of supply of imports. The result was a sharp drop during this period in Britain's share of both the Commonwealth's exports and imports, as can also be seen in Table 3-3.

The lesson of these developments was not lost on British industrialists. Gradually they came to recognize just how umpromising the Commonwealth

Table 3-3
Changing Shares in British and Commonwealth Trade, 1951-1971
(In Percentages)

	Exports					*Imports*				
	1951	*1956*	*1961*	*1966*	*1971*	*1951*	*1956*	*1961*	*1966*	*1971*
Share of British trade accounted for by:										
Commonwealth	50.5	46	35	25	18	40	44	37	27	22
European Economic Community	9	11.5	16.5	20	21	11.5	12.5	15	18.5	21.5
Share of Commonwealth trade accounted for by Britain	25	28	22	17	12	25	24	21	15	12

Sources: Central Statistical Office, Board of Trade, and Commonwealth Economic Committee.

really was as a long-term market for exports or source of import supply—even given Imperial Preference. The traditional trade policy simply was incapable of yielding the same economic gains as before, either for the national society as a whole or for many specific trading sectors. The truly fertile fields for commerce in the future, industrialists saw, lay rather in the European Community, particularly if mutual barriers to trade with the Six could be eliminated. During the 1960s, therefore, most of this influential constituency became solidly converted to the idea of a European connection.

So too did most of the British farming establishment, attracted principally by the prospect of high support prices embodied in the Community's common agricultural policy. Under Britain's traditional trade policy, the bulk of food imports entered the country duty-free; the only help British farmers received from the government to sustain their competitive position took the form of limited production subsidies ("deficiency payments"). Higher agricultural prices were universally expected to lead to expanded food production and farm incomes in Britain.

A third elite whose assumptions and perceptions changed during this period consisted of the leadership of the City of London—the officers and managers of the major banks, insurance companies, commodity exchanges, brokerage houses, and other financial institutions whose overseas earnings were such an important element in Britain's balance of payments. Throughout the 1950s and 1960s, Britain's external payments and currency were almost continually in trouble. There were sterling crises in 1951-1952, 1955, 1956-1957, 1959, 1961, and 1964-1967, culminating in the formal devaluation of the pound in November 1967. (Further crises in the early 1970s eventually resulted in a floating of the pound in June 1972.) Yet in spite of these recurrent difficulties the City's invisible earnings grew at a singularly healthy pace, topping £300 million annually in the middle and late 1960s.[9] This led at least some financial interests to question whether the pound really was so important to the City's fortunes after all.

Gradually it became clear that London could actually get along quite satisfactorily without the support of an international currency, and that in fact only a small fraction of the City's overseas income was directly or indirectly dependent on the international use of sterling—not more than one-fifth, according to one estimate.[10] By the early 1960s, London had already become the focal point of the vast and expanding Eurocurrency market: the City's banks no longer needed sterling and the Sterling Area to ensure a high level of earnings from foreign exchange operations or other services provided to foreigners. Likewise, most of London's other financial activities had grown independent of the pound. City interests began to realize therefore that they did not really have a need for sterling—indeed, that official efforts to preserve the international status of the pound could actually prove to be counterproductive as far as London was concerned. A financial policy directed toward preserving Sterling

Area arrangements, requiring ever-stricter exchange controls and other regulations, could result only in irreparable damage to the City's position as an international financial center. Continued isolation from Europe, where London stood the best chance of becoming the principal axis of the Community's money and capital markets, could only retard future growth of the City's invisible earnings. Thus by the end of the 1960s, most of this influential constituency too was solidly converted to the idea of a European connection.

One final elite to be considered in this connection was the government's own bureaucracy—the permanent civil servants in the ministries and in the Bank of England. It is impossible to overrate the influential role of these dimly known individuals in the framing of public policy in Britain. Governments and ministers may come and go, but the civil service remains throughout to provide unity and continuity to policy. Newly appointed ministers—in the British tradition, often nonexperts with little (if any) training or experience in their areas of ministerial responsibility—rely inordinately on their permanent secretaries and other nonpolitical subordinates for information, education, and guidance. This is perhaps the principal reason why underlying preferences in British policy-making circles tend to remain so remarkably stable, and why there have been so few major discontinuities in the last century and a half of British foreign economic policy. However much voter sentiment may fluctuate from one election to another, however frequently political power itself may change hands, the same bureaucrats sit in Whitehall and Threadneedle Street giving the same advice to their transient political "masters."

During the 1960s the bureaucracy too underwent a process of reeducation, not only with regard to the relative economic merits of the Commonwealth and European alternatives (as did the country's industrialists and other economic interests), but even more crucially with regard to the differing implications of these two options for Britain's national prestige. For the civil service, Britain's historic conception of itself as a major economic power was more than just a matter of patriotism or the "national interest" (as important as these concerns may have been); in addition, it was a matter of some purely personal self-interest. A global presence for Britain meant leadership roles for many Britons. Prestige for the nation also meant prestige for many individuals. And these individuals gradually became convinced that in these terms too, not just in terms of national economic welfare, a new connection with Europe would be far more rewarding than the old connection with the Commonwealth. Beset by centrifugal forces, the old Commonwealth was fast fading as an influence on the world stage. The new European Community, on the other hand, was clearly a bright and rising star. Many in the British government thus saw the prospect of membership in the Common Market as a unique opportunity. Here was a chance not only to reinvigorate the British economy. Here also was a chance to reestablish Britain's status as a great power—and incidentally to enhance the personal status of Britain's civil servants as well. Indeed, though their French and

German counterparts would likely have a say on certain issues, it was confidently expected within the British civil service that ultimately they themselves—qualified as they were by history, talent, and inherited skills—would become the natural leaders of the emergent Europe. Careers would certainly be made in London and in Brussels. Not surprisingly, therefore, much of the British governmental bureaucracy also eventually fell behind the idea of a European connection.

Of course, there were also constituencies that remained unreconciled to the idea. The labor union movement, in particular, persistently opposed Common Market membership throughout the 1960s—to some extent because of fears that Britain might lose control over its economic planning, but above all because of worries regarding the distributional implications of the Community's common agricultural policy. Higher prices for food, it was clear, would mean lower real purchasing power for workers; the gains to the British farming establishment would come largely, if not entirely, at the expense of the living standards of the laboring poor. The unions could not accept a foreign economic policy that threatened to gore mainly their own ox. The unions' opposition was reflected politically in the left wing of the Labor Party. Other groups hostile to the idea of a European connection included industrial and financial interests with business ties to the Commonwealth, who also stood to have their ox gored; and sentimental imperial types who were simply reluctant to see the sun finally set over the old British empire. The views of these groups were reflected politically, for the most part, in the right wing of the Conservative Party.

However, over the course of the 1960s the balance of opinion among dominant elites in Britain clearly swung in favor of a European connection.[11] Within the government, important elements of the permanent bureaucracy (particularly in the Foreign Office and the Board of Trade) began changing its advice to the politicians. Outside the government, pressures were applied by such influential lobbies as the Confederation of British Industries, the National Farmers Union (both of which, together with the Trades Union Congress, enjoy the right to consultation on a regular and continuing basis with the British government on matters of vital interest to their members), the British National Export Council, and the Committee on Invisible Exports. Inevitably members of both the Labor and Conservative Parties responded: the moderate wings of both parties, following the example of the Liberal Party (which had declared itself in favor of Community membership as early as 1958), gradually moved toward the idea of joining the Common Market on some terms or other. Organized opposition outside Parliament came mainly from the Trades Union Congress, but this proved insufficient to prevent the majority vote approving membership in October 1971.

The education of Britain's elites was hardly an instantaneous process. In 1961, when Harold Macmillan's cabinet made Britain's first application to join the Common Market, attitudes were still relatively uncompromising on such issues as Imperial Preference and the Sterling Area. Most Britons as yet did not really comprehend how much their economic world was changing and were still largely unprepared to abandon their traditional Commonwealth connection. In the negotiations of 1961-1962, the British delegation to Brussels, led by Edward Heath, adopted the hardest possible line, bargaining arrogantly and endlessly over a multitude of safeguards, modifications, and exceptions to the Rome Treaty. The government wanted membership for Britain—but its motivation was largely to avoid the potentially adverse economic consequences of nonmembership, rather than any genuine enthusiasm for participation in the European adventure. Consequently, it insisted on terms that would not interfere with any of the country's existing commercial or financial interests in the Commonwealth. Few concessions were offered. In effect, the government wanted to have its cake and eat it too. With the wisdom of hindsight, it is not difficult to see why Charles de Gaulle saw fit to veto Britain's application in January 1973.

By 1967, when Harold Wilson's cabinet made Britain's second application to the Common Market, attitudes had already begun to change significantly. The very fact that the approach was initiated by a Labor government, despite strong left-wing opposition in the party and in the unions, suggests the extent to which assumptions and perceptions were being modified during this period. Prime Minister Wilson apparently felt that he could cope satisfactorily with the problem of farm prices. He was most attracted by the prospective stimulus to economic growth that access to the European Community could provide. The hallmark of the moderate wing of the British Labor Party has always been a certain willingness to trade off the distribution objectives of policy for the goal of overall economic welfare—that is, to seek improvements for the laboring poor more through economic growth than through the redistribution of income shares. This seems to have been the strategy that the Wilson cabinet adopted in 1967, a strategy embodying preferences not noticeably different from those that the Macmillan cabinet evidently had in mind in 1961-1963. Despite Wilson's greater readiness to compromise, however, de Gaulle vetoed this application too.

Britain's third application in 1969, following de Gaulle's departure from the scene, marked the completion of the education process of the country's elites. No longer did the British try to set their own terms for membership in the Common Market. Throughout the lengthy negotiations in 1970-1971—which were begun by the Wilson cabinet and concluded, after the change of government, by the Heath cabinet—the British delegation's attitude in Brussels was refreshingly open and candid. Britain now wanted to join the Community even if it meant jettisoning the traditional Commonwealth connection. Neither Imperial Preference nor the Sterling Area would be allowed to stand in the way any longer. This was certainly a dramatic transformation in the orientation of British foreign economic policy. In this discussion I have argued that the explanation may be found in the sharply revised assessments of objective circumstances by nearly all the most influential groups in Britain.

Implications of Britain's Choice of Europe

What are the implications of this transformed orientation for the substance and direction of the decision-making process in British foreign economic policy in the future? Are there likely to be significant changes in either the machinery of government in Britain or in the country's prevailing attitudes toward major international economic organizations such as the GATT and the IMF?

In the short run, at least, changes are likely to be comparatively modest. The machinery of government in Britain is already well adapted to the decision-making requirements of membership in the European Community. The British have long belonged to a variety of multilateral intergovernmental organizations, and over the years London has effectively shaped its administrative apparatus to deal with the kinds of problems raised by participation in such organizations. Moreover, from 1961 onward, through their successive attempts to negotiate entry, the British acquired a considerable familiarity with the Community's administrative procedures as well. Consequently, the feeling in Whitehall is that no substantial changes in the established machinery of British government will be required, at least for the time being, particularly since very few governmental functions have as yet been transferred to the Community's institutions in Brussels. Wallace and Wallace say, "There appears to be general satisfaction with the efficient functioning of the machinery during the negotiations, which has bred confidence for the future. . . . The predominant mood is one of confidence in the capacity of existing structures and procedures."[12]

Likewise, for the time being, neither are existing attitudes toward major international economic organizations likely to be altered significantly because of the country's new European connection. Although Britain's high degree of involvement in the world economy has traditionally dictated a preference *in principle* for liberalism and multilateralism in global economic relations—as embodied in the rules and practices of the GATT and the IMF—*in practice* the country's policies were of course long qualified by the requirements of the Commonwealth connection. Imperial Preference constrained Britain's role in successive rounds of multilateral trade negotiations in the GATT; similarly, the Sterling Area moderated Britain's role in monetary reform negotiations in the IMF. British attitudes toward the GATT and the IMF are unlikely to change, in the short run at least, as a result of the shift from one regional orientation to another.

In the longer run, though, more substantial changes may be anticipated, as the European Community moves toward ever closer integration of its members' economies, and as more and more governmental functions are transferred directly to the Community's institutions in Brussels. The machinery of government in Britain will be challenged both by the blurring of distinctions between foreign and domestic economic policy and by the need for closer central coordination of the decision-making process in London. Traditionally, four departments monopolized responsibility for the management of British foreign economic policy–the Foreign Office, the Treasury, the Bank of England (nominally part of the Treasury, but in practice quite independent), and the Board of Trade (now the Department of Trade)–with the Foreign Office attempting to assure some semblance of central coordination.[13] However, as integration within the Community proceeds in future years, it will increasingly draw into international discussions questions that until now have been treated as matters solely of domestic concern, and as a result many of the "domestic" ministries will demand a louder voice in the decision-making process. This has already occurred in the case of the Ministry of Agriculture, owing to the supplanting of national farming policies by the Community's Common Agricultural Policy; other ministries (such as the Department of Industry) can be expected in time to follow the same pattern. Accordingly, machinery for more formal coordination among different policy areas will ultimately be required. Because of the growing sensitivity of Community questions for domestic policies, it is unlikely that the Foreign Office can continue to play this coordinating role. More probably, responsibility for the function will pass to the Cabinet Office, which is best suited for the purpose.[14]

In turn, these developments will inevitably influence as well Britain's attitudes toward the GATT and the IMF. Britain's regional orientation toward the Commonwealth was always limited in scope, the degree of integration remaining small. Accordingly, it was natural for Britain to continue to take a prominent (if not an unqualified) role in promoting liberal, global solutions to problems of international commerce or finance. However, as integration in the Common Market proceeds, the British will be called upon to "think European" on a growing range of issues, and increasingly to sacrifice external interests for the sake of the European connection.[15] Britain's foreign economic policy will necessarily become much more regional, in a fundamental sense, than it ever was in the days of Imperial Preference and the Sterling Area, and its prominent role in the GATT and the IMF will necessarily be compromised. British attitudes on international trade and monetary problems can be expected to become progressively less inclined toward multilateral solutions.

However, none of these changes are apt to come about very rapidly. Much will depend on the actual pace achieved in the integration process in Europe, which until now has been anything but rapid. On issues as disparate as exchange rates and energy, so far Britain's European connection has not prevented the pursuit of policies that can be described only as highly nationalistic. Also, the underlying stability of the British decision-making process cannot be overstressed. What is most probable is not radical discontinuity but rather a process of gradual adaptation and small marginal adjustments of policy. Many years will pass before the transformed orientation of British foreign economic policy is likely to find expression in terms of significant alterations of governmental machinery or of attitudes toward major international economic organizations.

Notes

1. See for example Benjamin J. Cohen, *American Foreign Economic Policy: Essays and Comments* (New York: Harper & Row, 1968), Part I.

2. Walter W. Heller, *New Dimensions of Political Economy* (New York: Norton, 1967), p. 5.

3. Cohen, *American Foreign Economic Policy*, pp. 20-29.

4. Cohen, *American Foreign Economic Policy*, pp. 1-10.

5. See for example, Maxwell Stamp Associates, *The Free Trade Area Option: Opportunity for Britain* (London: Atlantic Trade Study, 1967); Lionel Gelber, *World Politics and Foreign Trade: Britain, USA and the West* (London: Atlantic Trade Study, 1968); Hans Liesner, *Atlantic Harmonization: Making Free Trade Work* (London: Atlantic Trade Study, 1968).

6. See Sir Roy Harrod, *Dollar-Sterling Collaboration: Basis for Initiative* (London: Atlantic Trade Study, 1967).

7. See for example U.W. Kitzinger, *The Challenge of the Common Market* (Oxford: Basil Blackwell, 1961); R.W.G. Mackay, *Towards a United States of Europe* (London: Hutchinson, 1961); John Pinder, *Britain and the Common Market* (London: Cresset Press, 1961).

8. See for example Robert L. Pfaltzgraff, Jr., *Britain Faces Europe* (Philadelphia: University of Pennsylvania Press, 1969); William Pickles, *Britain and Europe–How Much Has Changed?* (Oxford: Basil Blackwell, 1967); Edgar Pisani et al., *Problems of British Entry into the EEC*, Reports to the Action Committee for the United States of Europe (London: Chatham House and PEP, 1969); Harry G. Johnson et al., *Economics: Britain and the EEC* (London: Longman, Green, 1969); James E. Meade, *UK, Commonwealth and Common Market: A Reappraisal*, 3rd ed. (London: Institute of Economic Affairs, 1970). (First edition was published in 1962.)

9. See Benjamin J. Cohen, *The Future of Sterling as an International Currency* (London: Macmillan, 1971), pp. 116-127.

10. Cohen, *The Future of Sterling*, pp. 128-141.

11. See for example Robert Pfaltzgraff, Jr., *Britain Faces Europe* and Robert Lieber, *British Politics and European Unity: Parties, Elites, and Pressure Groups* (Berkeley: University of California Press, 1970).

12. Helen Wallace and William Wallace, "The Impact of Community Membership on the British Machinery of Government," *Journal of Common Market Studies* (June 1973):254, 261.

13. William Wallace, "The Management of Foreign Economic Policy in Britain," *International Affairs* (London) (April 1974):251-267.

14. See Wallace and Wallace.

15. William Wallace, "British External Relations and the European Community: The Changing Context of Foreign Policy-Making," *Journal of Common Market Studies* (September 1973):28-52.

4 France

Edward L. Morse

There has been a striking evolution in French foreign economic policy since the beginning of the Fifth Republic in 1958. At the onset, economic policy was used largely as a set of instruments to support a rational and consistent approach to the government's external relationships. This was undoubtedly a result of the central role that foreign policy issues played in Charles de Gaulle's political thought. Increasingly, however, and especially since the end of the 1960s, foreign economic policy has been formulated in reaction to both external forces and domestic politics, which have intruded upon and severely constrained the government's ability to conduct a coherent foreign policy.

The explanation for this evolution in policy must take into account two fundamental sets of factors. First, changes in the structure of the international economy and of France's position in it have significantly altered the options available to the French government in conducting its foreign economic policy. As a result of the French economy's increased sensitivity and vulnerability to external phenomena, coupled with changes in international commercial and financial relationships and with structural changes within the French economy itself, foreign economic policy goals have been increasingly contradicted by a growing number of policy constraints. Second, changes in political leadership have also served to modify the scope and salience of foreign economic policy as well as the role it plays in the government's general approach to foreign affairs. At the same time, the importance of foreign policy after de Gaulle's resignation in spring 1969 as well as the nature of foreign policy goals themselves have been significantly modified; these changes have also had an important bearing on the conduct of economic policy.

I will first review the structure of the French economy and changes in it, as they affect the conduct of foreign economic policy. I will then turn to an examination of the major themes of foreign economic policy, which reflect the style and goals of France's political leadership. In the process I will also examine such issues as the relationship between the management of the French economy and other aspects of governance in France, the degree to which foreign economic policy has been integrated into the government's more global approach to external relationships, particular national preferences that affect foreign economic policy choices, and the balance between the government's focus on Europe and, alternatively, on other external targets of policy.

Economic Constraints on Foreign Policy

Foreign economic policy in France, as elsewhere, is built on a set of constraints that stem from the structure of the domestic economy and the role of that economy in a network of international relationships. While it is certainly the case that salient features of the domestic economy as well as linkages between it and other economies have resulted from past policy choices, it remains true that these fundamental factors narrow and limit the options available to the government.

The French economy can be generally described as relatively open and oriented primarily toward the other economies of Western Europe, in terms of the movement of factors of production and trade. During the quarter-century since the formation of the European Coal and Steel Community and other institutions in Western Europe, the French economy has become highly interdependent with the other economies of the European Communities. While the economic integration of France with these other societies was the principal foreign policy goal pursued by the French government after World War II, it has become the major factor constraining economic policy options—both domestically and in foreign affairs—for reasons that I will detail below.

Although the French economy has become increasingly open, and hence more vulnerable to foreign economic activities, it remains perhaps the most well-managed and flexible economy of Western Europe, and indeed perhaps of all the industrialized non-Communist societies. The government has a wide array of levers that it can use to achieve its economic policy goals, and by and large these policy instruments have proved to be relatively effective.

It has thus been able to meet a series of crises, including balance-of-payments adjustment crises in the late 1950s, inflationary problems in the mid-1960s, the economic consequences of the events of May 1968, and the recent energy crisis of 1973-1974, without at the same time jeopardizing the continued and rather high level of economic growth.

Many of the strands of foreign economic policy relate to the economy's size and its relative openness to the outside world. The French economy is middle-sized. In 1973, gross domestic product was $254.8 billion, which made it approximately one-fifth of the U.S. GDP, and the second largest economy in Europe, at two-thirds the size of the German economy. Its growth rate has been relatively high by European and world standards, averaging 6.0 percent since 1968. With a population of 52.1 million in 1973, France is the third most populous member of the European Communities, and with a gross domestic product per capita of $4900 in 1973, it ranks third among (European Community) members (see Table 4-1).[1]

Like most other economies of the industrialized world, the French economy has become increasingly open in recent years as international markets have become interpenetrated. This growth in interdependence has made it more

Table 4-1
Basic Statistics (1973) and International Comparisons (EEC, Japan, U.S.)

Country	*France*	*Belgium*	*Denmark*	*Germany*	*Ireland*	*Italy*	*Japan*	*Lux.*	*Neth.*	*U.K.*	*U.S.*
Population (thousands)	52,177	9,742	5,027	61,967	3,051	54,888	108,350	350	13,438	56,026	210,404
Employment:											
civilian (thousands)	20,953	3,818	2,385	26,202	1,042	18,310	52,330	154	4,564	24,553	84,409
agriculture (%)	12.2	3.9	9.5	7.5	25.1	17.4	13.4	9.0	6.8	3.0	4.1
industry (%)	39.3	43.3	33.8	49.5	30.7	44.0	37.2	48.6	36.2	42.3	31.7
other (%)	48.5	52.8	56.7	43.0	44.2	38.6	49.4	42.4	57.1	54.7	64.2
Production:											
GDP per head ($)	4,900	4,650	5,460	5,610	2,130	2,510	3,760	5,200	4,410	3,100	6,170
GDP by sector (%)											
agriculture	6.3	3.9	8.2	2.9	18.0	8.8	5.9	4.4	5.3	3.0	4.4
industry	93.7	40.1	39.9	52.1	33.8	41.2	48.3	57.5	44.9	42.4	33.9
other		56.1	51.9	45.0	48.2	50.0	45.9	38.1	49.8	54.6	61.7
GDP annual growth (5-year average)	6.0	5.5	4.7	5.1	4.6	4.3	11.0	5.2	5.3	2.8	3.6
Foreign trade											
Imports ($ millions)	32,070	14,570	6,080	51,150	2,240	23,600	24,910	1,050	20,100	33,620	74,830
(% GDP)	16.4	40.9	28.6	19.9	40.6	20.1	8.5	77.8	43.4	21.8	6.3
Exports ($ millions)	33,760	15,430	6,240	55,730	1,930	24,040	31,800	1,100	21,320	33,350	62,690
(% GDP)	17.2	43.4	29.4	21.6	35.0	20.4	10.8	81.5	46.1	21.6	5.3

Source: *France* (Paris: OECD, 1976), pp. 71-74.

difficult to manage the domestic economy, insofar as the growth in economic interdependence has both increased the sensitivity of the economy to foreign activities and also introduced a large number of uncontrollable factors, which affected national planning. Here, however, in spite of a clear trend toward increased openness, the French economy remains far more closed than other members of the European Communities, as can be seen from Table 4-2. A similar situation can be found in terms of the portion of world trade attributed to the French economy. As can be seen in Table 4-3, France's share of world trade, at 5.3 percent in 1968, is somewhat less than one-fifth of that of the United States, half that of Germany and more or less equivalent to Japan's.

Table 4-2
International Market Interpenetration

	Ratio of Average of Exports and Imports to GDP		
	1960-1962	*1968-1970*	*Change*
Netherlands	50.2	49.2	−1.0
Belgium	35.5	43.9	+8.4
Ireland	38.5	40.6	+2.1
Denmark	31.9	30.2	−1.7
U.K.	22.3	23.5	+1.2
Germany	18.8	21.9	+3.1
Italy	15.6	19.0	+3.4
France	12.8	15.6	+2.8
Japan	10.5	10.7	+0.2
U.S.	4.9	5.9	+1.0

Source: *L'Expansion*, January 1974, p. 53.

Table 4-3
Portion of World Exports of Selected Economies
($ Billion Current)

	1939	*1948*	*1958*	*1968*	*% (1968)*
U.S.	3.19	12.8	17.7	34.2	14.2%
Germany	2.26[a]	0.7	8.8	24.8	10.4
U.K.	2.19	6.8	8.9	14.8	6.4
Japan	1.13	0.2	2.9	12.9	5.3
France	0.8	2.0	5.1	12.6	5.3
Canada	0.9	3.1	5.0	12.5	5.2

Source: Jean Autin, *Vingt ans de politique financière* (Paris: Seuil, 1972), p. 135.
[a]Includes prewar borders.

The French economy has undergone extraordinary structural change throughout the post-World War II period, including the time since France joined with five other governments to create the European Economic Community in 1958. As is clear from Table 4-4, increases in industrial output have been second only to Japan among major industrialized societies in the years 1963-1971. During the same period, industrial growth and modernization have been reflected in continued growth in the industrial and service sectors and a shift in the labor force from agriculture to other activities (see Table 4-5). They have also been reflected in the rapid growth of French exports, in shifts in the structure of France's markets, and in the relative position of industrial and agricultural exports.

For most of the twentieth century, French exports had been oriented toward traditional markets in primary producing areas of the less developed world. This had been typical of the trade relations of other European economies, which had been early comers to the process of industrialization. Guaranteed markets for French industrial exports were found within the French empire and trade was characteristically an exchange of industrial products emanating from the metropole and primary products from the dependent areas. As recently as 1956, 32 percent of French exports went to franc-zone countries,[2] while only 51.6 percent were oriented to other countries who later became members of the OECD, and 24.9 percent went to the Six. By 1966 only 16 percent of French exports went to franc-zone countries and by 1972 that portion had fallen to 5.3 percent. Meanwhile, by 1966, 70.9 percent of exports went to OECD countries and 47.9 percent to the EEC, and by 1972 exports to the OECD area accounted for 76 percent of all exports, and 56 percent went to the original EC members.[3]

This rapid change in the external orientation of the French economy has paralleled structural changes both within the international economy and French society. The growth in trade among industrialized societies and the relative decline in trade between industrialized and nonindustrialized societies has been reflected in changes in the major orientation of French trade. Similarly, the growth in economic interdependence among industrialized societies and espe-

Table 4-4
Increases in Output per Man-Hour in Manufacturing, 1971 (1963 = 100)

Japan	240
France	168
Italy	155
Germany	153
U.K.	139
U.S.	130

Source: "Survey: France," *The Economist* (December 2, 1972), p. 36.

Table 4-5
Evolution of the Structure of the Labor Force, 1957-70, with International Comparisons
(% of Active Civilian Population by Sector)

		Agriculture	*Industry*	*Other*
France	1957	24.6	37.4	38.0
	1970	14.0	38.9	47.1
Germany	1957	16.3	47.9	35.8
	1970	9.0	50.3	40.7
Belgium	1957	9.6	48.4	42.0
	1970	4.8	44.7	50.5
Italy	1957	35.6	35.3	29.1
	1970	19.6	43.7	36.7
Netherlands	1957	12.8	42.1	45.1
	1970	7.2	41.0	51.8
U.K.	1957	4.4	49.2	46.4
	1970	2.9	46.5	50.6
Japan	1957	34.3	26.7	39.0
	1970	17.4	35.7	46.9
U.S.	1957	9.3	35.5	55.2
	1970	4.4	32.3	63.3

Source: *France* (Paris: OECD, February 1973), p. 40.

cially among the members of the EC have both oriented France's economic relations toward Europe and limited the number of policy options available to the government.[4] Within France, changes in the attitudes of elites in both governmental and business circles after World War II, the development of machinery for reconstruction and indicative planning after 1946, the impetus to growth provided by the implementation of the EC as well as by demographic shifts, also indicated major changes.[5] In turn, structural and social transformations have had an enormous impact on French politics, and hence on the conduct of foreign economic policy, especially after 1968, as I will attempt to demonstrate later.

Nowhere is this better demonstrated than in a brief review of the recent evolution of France's demographic structure. At the end of the eighteenth century France was among the most populous states in Europe, with a population of 28.2 million. But by the end of the Napoleonic Wars, the population began to stagnate and even underwent decline during several years. Although the French population had reached 35.8 million by 1850, it remained more or less constant at the level of 40 million for the next century. After World War II, for reasons that are still not well understood, the French population began to grow again, so that by 1961 it reached 46 million, and by 1971, 51 million, with an annual growth rate of 1.05 percent (as compared to 0.5 percent in the U.K., 0.87 percent in Germany, and 0.65 percent in Italy). As will be shown below, this shift from demographic stagnation to demographic growth was both a reflection of a new dynamism in French society and also a spur to industrial growth, since a growing population required both the development of new sources of employment and a higher level of consumer expenditure.

In summary, the French economy is middle-sized and moderately open by world standards. It is highly dynamic and interactive with the other industrialized societies of the non-Communist world and has been increasingly oriented toward the other economies of the EC. This situation has reflected general trends that transcend the French case and policy options that have been explicitly chosen by successive French governments. I will now turn to a specific examination of strands of foreign economic policy to see better how they have reflected conscious policy choice as well as constraints upon the French government.

The Economics of Grandeur

While the roots of contemporary foreign economic policy can be traced to conditions in the Fourth Republic (1946-1958), and in ideological terms even to the seventeenth century, the role of foreign policy in the political views of Charles de Gaulle was predominant in the conduct of foreign economic policy between 1958 and 1969. Gaullian foreign economic policy was therefore inspired far more by a general program of action than it was by prevailing economic conditions. To be sure, France's position and role in the international economic system and in the European arena influenced foreign economic policy, but this was the case more by way of providing issues of policy and limits on the achievement of goals than it was of the initial articulation of policy objectives and targets.

The most central characteristic of foreign economic policy under de Gaulle's presidency was the way economic policy was used to achieve more general political purposes in both the European and global settings. Gaullian diplomacy can be readily summarized, since the simplicity of de Gaulle's general strategy in the international arena had the virtues of elegance and coherence.[6] If one is to begin an analysis of foreign policy with the traditional tensions between the conduct of foreign and domestic affairs, it is critical to underscore that for de Gaulle there was little question but that foreign policy ought to predominate and that the management of the domestic economy and the mobilization of domestic support were to be oriented toward larger foreign policy objectives. This did not mean that de Gaulle abided by the traditional notion that foreign and domestic policies belonged to their separate realms or that the conduct of one could be divorced from the conduct of the other. Although the original constitution of the Fifth Republic was based on that more traditional notion,[7] changes in it that were implemented in 1962–especially the institutionalization of a plebiscitary presidency–recognized that public policy, both foreign and domestic, formed a seamless web.[8]

Foreign policy had to be primary for de Gaulle for several reasons. Dangers to the integrity of the state abounded as a result of the inherent condition of international anarchy in the international arena. De Gaulle's Republic had to recognize "the present state of the world," with its "opposed ideologies, behind which lurk the powerful states that surround us [and which] do not cease to inject in our own political struggle an element of passionate controversy."[9] The *telos* of France also required it, since de Gaulle believed that it was France's destiny to be in the front rank of states.

Primacy in the contemporary world depended on two minimal conditions. First, the executive had to have the ability to act autonomously, unconstrained by domestic political factions and interest groups. This was required both by foreign dangers to the state's integrity and by the need to achieve strategic consistency in foreign policy. Second, the politics of primacy required that the domestic economy be modernized and, in a highly technological age, that France develop all the leading economic sectors so that national unity and autonomy could be secured.

In constitutional terms, the Fifth Republic's framework stood alone among democratic constitutions drawn up over the course of the last two centuries in that rather than looking toward an enhancement of legislative participation in foreign affairs, it "vest[ed] the supreme authority to conduct foreign relations in the Head of State again."[10] The exclusive powers of the president and the advisory capacities of the prime minister and foreign minister in matters of external relations were defined in Articles 14, 15, 20, 21, and 49, and were enhanced further by the inclusion of Article 5, which defined the president as the "protector of the independence of the nation" and by Article 16, which gave the president virtually unrestrained "emergency powers" whenever he considered the independence of the state to be in danger.

These constitutional mechanisms, which were designed to assure the autonomy of the president in foreign policy matters and to perpetuate the primacy of foreign policy, were reinforced by political conditions that lay behind the movement toward a plebiscitary presidency in 1962.[11] At that time de Gaulle thought that his own legitimacy as president had to be enhanced through direct elections because of specific problems he encountered in negotiating a settlement to the last of France's colonial wars in Algeria. But the change also reflected his realization that the political system had to be mobilized in order for him to achieve his foreign policy objectives. The office of president was central to the conduct of foreign policy, which would be based on a series of great undertakings, both domestic and foreign, and which would serve as a basis of securing national unity (undermined by colonial wars and ideological disputes). National unity itself was required if a singularly defined national interest was to be satisfied. Both the population and material resources had to be mobilized to support great undertakings, which were themselves necessary for the achievement of national unity and the fulfillment of national destiny. Hence the modernization of the domestic economy, including the rapid technological development of France's industrial base, were essential ingredients in de Gaulle's grand designs.

The strategic content underlying Gaullian foreign policy was predicated on the securing of national autonomy and freedom and the discerning of long-term international trends that de Gaulle's diplomacy could support. As French political analyst Pierre Hassner has argued, de Gaulle's designs for France consisted of a series of diplomatic triads, each of which centered on France:

> In her anti-American undertakings, France was conceived to be in competition with the United States serving as the interlocutor of Germany and of Russia. In her conception of a desirable international balance, she wished to serve as intermediary and arbitrator between Russia and Germany in Europe and between Russia and the United States in the world.[12]

The unfolding of this strategic concept proceeded in three stages.[13] In a first phase, from 1958 to 1962, de Gaulle tried simultaneously to terminate the Algerian War and to set the basis for reversing the trend of French global decline. In a second phase, which began with the independence of Algeria and proceeded through mid-1968, the progressive implementation of a policy of autonomy was central to French foreign policy and seemed to encounter few constraints either from the domestic political and economic environment or from the international setting. In a third and final phase, which began with the events of May 1968 and lasted until de Gaulle's resignation nearly a year later, severe limitations on French independence and autonomy became increasingly visible, so that this final phase was one of retrenchment and dependence on others.

This overall strategic design could be observed in the parallel moves de Gaulle undertook in both nuclear diplomacy and in efforts to reform the international monetary system. Thus with respect to a defense strategy, de Gaulle began to reassert French presence in the first phase, 1958-1962, although he was hampered in this regard both by the need to bring the Algerian War to a close and to develop a nuclear striking force. His efforts were principally diplomatic and began with an attempt to reorganize the leadership of the Atlantic Alliance by securing a French voice in a NATO directorate, which would include France, Britain, and the United States. Although Eisenhower rebuffed this effort, it did fulfill French fears of a sellout of French interests through superpower diplomacy similar to the combined Soviet-American effort to rebuke France and Britain after the 1956 Suez invasion.[14]

In the second phase, de Gaulle changed his tactics. Rather than continue his efforts to gain control over NATO strategy, de Gaulle pursued a course of progressively implementing an independent French position. The independent nuclear striking force became the heart of a French strategy, which continually articulated a policy of foreign policy autonomy frequently smacking of neutralism. The strategic rationale of this policy hinted at the desirability of creating a third force that expressed a Franco-European humanitarian doctrine, different from both U.S. capitalism and Soviet socialism. This phase of Gaullian diplomacy involved two vetoes of British efforts to gain entrance into the European Communities (1963 and 1967); tactical maneuvers associated with the "empty chair" or efforts to boycott institutions where French autonomy was curtailed (especially in the European Communities in 1965); anti-American postures especially concerning the MLF and the withdrawal of France from the NATO military infrastructure (1966); and independent efforts to deal with members of the Soviet bloc, including the recognition of the People's Republic of China and a series of bilateral economic treaties both with Russia and with members of the Warsaw Pact. The apotheosis of this policy came in the form of a strategic rationale articulated by General Charles Ailleret in early 1968. It involved the projection of the eighteenth-century Vauban fortifications to the level of France by means of nuclear weapons that could strike any enemy in any direction and at all points.[15]

The third phase, which clearly depicted the limits to French independence, began in early 1968 and continued through the presidency of Georges Pompidou. This phase of retrenchment involved effective efforts to coordinate defense planning with the other members of the Atlantic Alliance and recognized the tremendous economic costs to France of developing an independent nuclear striking force. While the rhetoric of independence and autonomy continued to pervade French policy, in fact the policy seemed to recognize that fundamental domestic and international factors impeded its implementation.

In economic matters, the policy of autonomy and grandeur served to structure both foreign commercial and monetary policy, but especially the latter. In the early months of the Fifth Republic, the government devalued the franc by 15 percent to redress pressing balance-of-payments difficulties. The devaluation, which was orchestrated by de Gaulle's one-time financial adviser, Jacques Rueff, had three principal aims: (1) it was designed to eliminate some of the financial difficulties encountered as a result of the Algerian War; (2) it was a means of preparing the French economy for the freeing of exchange rates, the reconvertibility of European currencies (after post-World War II recovery), and the opening of the European Economic Community; and (3) it was designed to create a strong franc by restraining domestic demand for imports, making exports cheaper for foreign purchasers, and, in the process, reverse the trend of growing balance-of-payments difficulties.[16]

By the time the second phase of Gaullian policy began, the devaluation of 1958 had started to reap its benefits. The French economy had become surprisingly competitive in the context of the new EEC, deficits had been reversed, and France's foreign reserves had begun to mount. It was especially in the second phase of foreign policy that de Gaulle discovered the political implications of Rueff's reforms. At the same time, due to growing U.S. balance-of-payments deficits, efforts had begun to reform the international monetary system. It was in this context that Gaullian diplomacy found opportunities. Rueff had argued for the necessity of a return to a pure gold standard as a means of assuring international economic equilibrium, ending asymmetries in the operation of the monetary system that had given undue freedom to the United States, and providing an external means of "discipline" on domestic economic management. Not coincidentally, since in a pure gold stand the United States would no longer be able to enjoy an exceptional position, French efforts to reform the monetary system assumed the same anti-American posture as did other aspects of French policy. By attempting to guide the direction of reform, de Gaulle believed France could achieve both greater autonomy and reflected glory.

The years after 1962 were characterized, then, by efforts to diagnose what was wrong with the international monetary system—efforts that placed much of the blame on U.S. policy and on a system deemed to benefit the United States more than other societies—and by a series of actions designed to implement a new system in which French autonomy would be enhanced. French views were clearly summarized in de Gaulle's noted press conference of February 4, 1965, which is worth citing at length:

> The conditions which formerly were able to give rise to the "gold exchange standard" have changed. The currencies of the Western European States are today restored, to the extent that the total gold reserves of the Six today equal those of the Americans. They would exceed them if the Six decided to convert all their dollar holdings into gold. This means that the custom of ascribing a superior value to the dollar as an international currency no longer rests on its initial foundation—I mean America's possession of the largest share of the world's gold. But, in addition, the fact that many States in principle accept dollars on the same basis as gold so as to offset, if need be, the deficits in their favor in the American balance of payments, leads the United States to indebt itself abroad at no cost. Indeed, what it owed abroad, it pays for, at least partially, with dollars which it alone can issue, instead of paying entirely with gold, which has a real value, which must be earned to be possessed, and which cannot be transferred to others without risks and sacrifices. This unilateral facility which is granted to America is serving to cloud the idea that the dollar is an impartial and international medium of exchange, when it is a means of credit belonging to one State.[17]

The French position on international monetary reform involved three major economic issues and two political questions, all of which seemed to pose France in opposition to the United States. First, the economic matters related to the question of liquidity. While the U.S. and British authorities were interested in reform primarily as a means of creating new liquidity that would aid their deficitary positions, the French government argued that dollar—and to a lesser degree, sterling—deficits resulted in an overabundance of global liquidity, which was inflationary for Europe. A second economic issue concerned the means of creating liquidity in the future. Here the Anglo-Saxon countries concentrated their efforts on new facilities created in the International Monetary Fund while the French wished to eliminate both the dollar and sterling as official international media and at the same time also were reluctant to accept an "artificial" currency or unit of reserve. Rather, they preferred to reinstitute the "neutral" gold standard with its "eternal" values.

The third economic issue was the fear of inflation. France was almost unique in the 1960s insofar as official governmental policy placed emphasis on ending what was considered the danger of imported inflation as a result of U.S. deficits. The political questions raised by the French position reflected the French government's desire to reform economic relations so that they would better reflect the economic recovery of Europe and the secular economic decline of the United States. On the one hand, the French wanted to enhance their autonomy and freedom of action that they felt was hampered by a U.S.-dominated monetary system based on the dollar. On the other hand, they were highly suspicious of focusing any reform within international institutions, like the International Monetary Fund, where reform could either bolster the U.S. position, or, quite the opposite, result in an enhanced role for Third World countries who could outvote the industrialized world as a whole.[18]

During this second phase of Gaullian foreign policy, the French position was bolstered by France's strong balance-of-payments position and by the growth in French reserves (from less than $2 billion to more than $7 billion). While France seemed to be a singular voice in calling for reform, its position was bolstered by the government's efforts to exchange its dollar reserves for gold, which the United States government was trying to phase out of the system. Moreover, French isolation also served Gaullist interests by reinforcing the position of independence that de Gaulle wished to pursue. Thus the movement toward a strategic position of neutralism in defense matters was paralleled by the movement toward independence in the monetary field.

In the third and last phase of Gaullian diplomacy, a hardened French position quickly tested the limits of independence and autonomy and a series of domestic and international incidents forced the government to retrench its position severely. The French diplomatic position on monetary reform had been precarious since the mid-1960s, as the government realized that it was isolated from other industrialized societies on the issue of reform. The *coup de grâce* to the French position, however, came with a series of international and domestic events in France in the spring of 1968. In the international monetary system, foreign exchange crises began to build up with a momentum that eventually led to the demise of the Bretton Woods system. In the meantime, however, the crisis made a U.S.-backed scheme to create special drawing rights in the International Monetary Fund acceptable to all major governments, and undermined the French position.[19]

More important were the domestic events of May in France—the spontaneous uprisings of students and workers, which led to widespread strike and disorders, and which ended with large wage increases. The relatively stable economic foundation upon which the strong franc had been based was thus lost, and internal political weakness was paralleled by a run on the franc and the need of the French government to rely on aid from foreign central banks—principally those of the United States and Britain. The government thus found itself in a position that made tactical maneuvers against the United States impossible and reliance on a system of interdependent relations with other industrialized societies both necessary and urgent.

The politics of grandeur thus had a rather short but glorious life in the Fifth Republic. It was limited primarily to the last seven years of de Gaulle's presidency—from the end of the Algerian War through the events of May 1968 to de Gaulle's resignation when his proposal for regional reform was voted down in the referendum of April 1969. The policy had been made possible by a set of general as well as accidental circumstances. The most important of these was certainly de Gaulle's return to political leadership in 1958 and his successful handling of the final acts of French decolonization. Once obligations to colonies were terminated, freedom to maneuver on the international political stage was greatly enhanced, for decolonization terminated the financial costs of administration, the keeping of political order, and also the social and political costs of divisions within French society that had been exacerbated by colonial conflicts.

French freedom to implement a policy of autonomy through grandiose Gaullian designs was also enhanced significantly by general changes in the structure of the international system in the 1960s. European economic recovery was complete when the European Economic Community began to implement the plans for a customs union and Common Agricultural Policy (CAP) according to the Rome Treaty's outlines. European economic separation from the United States, based on the assumption of continued secular growth of the European economies and relative secular decline of the U.S. economy, provided a base for increased French assertiveness. Playing out the logic of the nuclear deterrence relationship between the United States and the Soviet Union served the same end. On the one hand, the development of a stable nuclear relationship between the two superpowers resulted in a perceived lowering of the Soviet threat in the eyes of French leadership. On the other hand, the growth in a commonality of interests between the two major nuclear powers reinforced differences in the security interests of the Americans and their European partners, for it made it less plausible for the Europeans to assume an automatic U.S. commitment to Europe's fate and a willingness of the Americans to sacrifice their European allies to preserve America's physical integrity in the eventuality of nuclear war.

Both aspects of the nuclear relationship reinforced de Gaulle's efforts to develop an independent nuclear striking force.[20] The increased separation of European and U.S. security interests could be overcome by a modest but credible French nuclear force, which could both serve as a trigger for the U.S. deterrent and also preserve France's national security. The diminished Soviet threat gave de Gaulle the freedom to reinforce bilateral relations between France and Russia in the hopes that a viable European détente could thereby be created as the basis of a new European security arrangement, especially concerning a non-nuclear Germany.

Similarly, changes in the international monetary system also appeared to reinforce the trend toward greater national autonomy. The Bretton Woods system, with the dollar at the heart of international monetary relations, was clearly in the process of breaking down. The dollar had come increasingly under attack in international markets as a result of continuous U.S. balance-of-payments deficits. De Gaulle's own attack on the dollar thus reinforced prevailing trends in the system. It differed from the policies of other governments in the kind of reform that de Gaulle sought. Whereas other governments generally preferred to reform the monetary system, de Gaulle took steps to try to change its underlying rules by ending what he felt to be the U.S.'s "exorbitant privilege" to live on the credit of others and while U.S. corporations were able to buy up European competitors.

A final general characteristic of both the international monetary system and nuclear diplomacy was that in each instance the configuration of international relationships was such as to enable French policy to pursue an independent policy at virtually no risk. An independent nuclear striking force could be implemented because in the last analysis de Gaulle knew that for a long time to come the United States automatically provided nuclear protection to France by maintaining its own nuclear protection. And an independent monetary policy could be pursued because the network of international financial relationships had become so interdependent that even if France found itself in financial difficulty, it knew that other industrialized societies, including the United States, would inevitably be forced to come to its aid. In the meantime, however, French foreign economic policy could be perfectly congruent with a consistent and general orientation to France's external relationships, which was irksome to France's European and Atlantic economic and security partners.

From Grandeur to Interdependence

When Georges Pompidou succeeded Charles de Gaulle as second president of the Fifth Republic in the spring of 1969, the bases of a policy of grandeur had already begun to disintegrate. Pompidou and his ministers were, however, the political and ideological heirs of Charles de Gaulle and they represented the various branches of Gaullist thought. They therefore had to emphasize a declaratory policy that stressed: (1) the desirability of maintaining French economic and political autonomy and independence; (2) the continued and rapid industrialization of France through investment in social and economic infrastructure and in areas of high technology; (3) suspicions of Soviet and U.S. predominance in Europe; and (4) the desirability of encouraging the emergence of an independent West European economic bloc with France as the leading foreign policy spokesman. But there was a great discrepancy between a declaratory policy of independence and autonomy and the circumscribed choices taken by the Pompidou government—and later by the government of Valéry Giscard d'Estaing. Increasingly, French foreign policy has focused on economic matters and has been formulated more as a function of domestic economic imperatives than as a result of a coherent foreign policy orientation.

The more circumscribed policies pursued by de Gaulle's successors are, in the first instance, the result of a diagnosis of de Gaulle's failure to achieve his goals of autonomy and independence. It is therefore proper that this discussion begin with an analysis of the factors that made the policy of independence decreasingly feasible for France and that turned French governmental attention to domestic economic needs and the construction of Europe.

No aspect of contemporary French policy can be understood without first reviewing the effects of the worker and student demonstrations of May 1968.[21] Fear of the repetition of those events came to haunt the French political leadership, and governmental policy has since largely focused on methods of bolstering the legitimacy of the government—principally by attempting to satisfy domestic demands, which has also served to decrease the salience of foreign policy over domestic policy.

It should be recalled that the initial measure taken by the French government in ending the series of strikes that erupted spontaneously in spring 1968 consisted of a series of inflationary wage settlements. Minimum statutory wages were increased by 35 percent. Fringe benefits, including new opportunities for worker advancement through education, were dramatically increased. After 1968, wage packages involved disproportionately large increases to blue-collar workers, modest increases to middle-ranking white-collar workers and civil servants, and relatively small increases to those in the administrative ranks.[22] These step-level increases were designed to meet grievances that had built up in France during the first decade of the Fifth Republic. A fiscal system that has traditionally relied on indirect taxation has done little to remove glaring social inequalities and a maldistribution of national income.[23] One of the traditional means of coping with maldistribution has been through the "trickle-down" effect of growth on national income. But the Gaullist primacy of foreign policy had placed a premium on wage stability rather than growth in income in order to bolster an international policy based on a strong franc (and hence on restricted levels of consumption). It was also based on a high rate of investment (further restricting personal consumption). As Henry Ehrmann has argued, the results fed into worker demands in the spring of 1968, when

> a feeling of having been denied a fair share in an expanding economy, the abnormally low rate of minimum wages, the longest working hours in Europe, unpopular reforms, especially those of the social security system [which increased worker contributions and decreased payments] and also a widely felt need for recognition of trade-union activities at places of work, motivated the workers' demands in private and public enterprises.[24]

No longer could the government risk a foreign economic policy that was domestically costly and increasingly resented.

The May events had direct effects, moreover, on the government's general policy of autonomy because they struck at the heart of that policy, the nuclear striking force. Constrained, especially in the fall of 1968, to limit governmental expenditures on defense to less than 5 percent of the GNP, the political leadership was forced to sacrifice and postpone full implementation of the nuclear striking force. The government found itself squeezed between rising costs of high technology in the field of weapons acquisitions, the need to meet pent-up domestic demands, high costs of personnel and manpower, and the need to bolster the *gendarmérie* for domestic security purposes. Thus the government was forced in fact to alter its defense priorities. In the aftermath of the events of 1968, the government thus in fact curtailed its military programs and progressively moved back toward cooperation with NATO allies, although it remained outside the alliance's military superstructure.[25]

These changes in the construction of the French nuclear striking force were reinforced by additional changes in French strategic thinking after 1968. Following the settlement of the May events almost immediately, the Soviet invasion of Czechoslovakia challenged the assumptions upon which the eastern policy aspects of de Gaulle's policy of autonomy had been built. That policy had been predicated on the belief that Soviet objectives in Eastern and Western Europe had mollified, that U.S. preponderance in Western Europe had become as much a danger as Soviet hegemony over Eastern Europe, and that the French government was in a better position to pursue a policy of relaxation of tensions in Europe than either the United States (as a result of preoccupation with Vietnam) or Germany (whose then-existing Grand Coalition government was pursuing a policy of détente through the East European governments rather than through Moscow).[26]

The Soviet invasion of Czechoslovakia demonstrated the unchanging nature of Soviet objectives in Europe and thus made the French government realize that continued deployment of U.S. troops in Europe, and hence continued reliance on NATO, was critical to West European security.[27] Moreover, the prevailing view that France held a favored position in Soviet diplomacy that gave it autonomy to pursue a policy of détente on its own initiative was no longer strongly held. The invasion made it clear that the Soviet government wished only to ratify the military status quo in Europe, and that by dealing directly with Germany and the United States it could gain more than through bilateral negotiations with France. Moreover, the German policy toward the East that had been pursued under Willy Brandt's government in Germany (after 1969) enabled the Soviet government to have its way and also raised French suspicions concerning ultimate German objectives.[28] Cooperative relations with the Soviet Union remained useful for France, even if they no longer were believed to hold the key to change in Eastern Europe. Rather, cooperation with Russia continued to have a role to play in French domestic politics by weakening the opposition of the French Communist Party to Gaullist or center-right governments.

De Gaulle's successors thus realized that little was to be gained for foreign or domestic policy in the older policy of autonomy and independence and that there were other reasons to concentrate on a European rather than a global policy—a policy that focused on economic rather than on political or security relations. This change can be seen in terms of the policy the French government pursued under President Georges Pompidou at the summit of heads of state of the European Economic Community in December 1969 at The Hague. Three major decisions were taken at that meeting. First, the Community members decided to open negotiations for enlargement to Britain and other members of EFTA (European Free Trade Association), whose earlier applications for membership de Gaulle had vetoed. Second, preliminary planning was set for the development of a monetary union in Europe. Third, efforts were made to coordinate the foreign policies of the EEC members under a new committee of foreign ministers under the Belgian Etienne Davignon. Each of these decisions was pursued as part of a French policy, which had been reappraised in the aftermath of the events of May.

The decision to open negotiations for the enlargement of the Communities was taken in light of a reevaluation that began while de Gaulle was still president. One of the lessons drawn from the May events was that over the medium term or even long term, the German economy was likely to predominate in the European Communities. This view, however ambivalently it was held (the French economy had a higher long-term growth rate than Germany's), was coupled with the belief that the French government had perhaps made a wrong bet in relying on an implicit Franco-German axis in Europe. Moreover, German foreign policy remained too closely tied to the United States and had potential conflicts of interest with French objectives in Europe. Britain was the logical alternative to Germany, since in most economic and military-security issues with regard to Western Europe's future, French and British views were highly compatible. De Gaulle had recognized this before his resignation in April 1969, as evidenced by his overtures to British Ambassador Christopher Soames to involve Britain in a free trade area in Europe as a replacement for the EEC.

The second decision taken at The Hague—the establishment of plans to implement a monetary union—was also tied closely to the May events. Loss of confidence in the French government and economy, coupled with high inflation that followed the Grenelle wage agreements that helped end the events of May, had deleterious consequences on the franc's stability. The renewed prospective of a perennially weak franc—which did not in fact eventuate—had detrimental effects on the French government's major foreign policy objectives.[29]

First, it severely constrained French efforts to influence the United States to accept a reform of the international monetary system that would severely curtail the dollar's role. The French now were forced to rely on U.S. aid and credit as well as on a stable monetary system in order to assure the viability of their program to strengthen the French reserve position. Second, and perhaps of greater importance, the weakened franc and the eventual change that was forced between the exchange rates of the franc and the Deutsche mark in the fall of 1969 were of major significance to the European policy of the French government. The Common Agricultural Policy (CAP) was viewed as the chief French benefit from membership in the EEC, and the CAP was predicated on fixed exchange rates among the members. The prospect of frequent currency adjustments was incompatible with that policy, because of the need for (and the difficulties with) obtaining annual agreements on the pricing of agricultural products in Europe. Moreover, large-scale currency realignments like that between the franc and the mark in 1969 appeared to have unsettling effects on trade between those two countries and on their competitive positions in the EEC as a whole. The lesson of the experience was the urgency of creating some form of monetary union in Europe, which would guarantee fixed exchange rates and thereby obviate the danger to the CAP that would occur through parity changes. Moreover, a monetary union would also serve the same purposes as a strong franc in bargaining with the United States over restructuring the world economic system: it would serve to decrease the dollar's role and the predominant influence of the United States. That such a union also contradicted the French foreign policy goal of autonomy was a dilemma whose solution was put off to future confrontation.

The efforts to coordinate foreign policy with the other members of the EEC in the context of the extra-institutional Davignon Committee was merely an additional factor representing the new European-based strategy of cooperation of the post-Gaullian French government. It was to lay the basis for a political union, whose constitutional makeup was yet undetermined and which was to be implemented together with the formation of a true economic union in Europe.

The policy of cooperation in the European context can thus be explained partially as a result of the lessons of the experience of the Gaullist years, when efforts to implement a strategy of autonomy had detrimental consequences for the French government. But the substance of foreign economic policy in France in the post-Gaullian period requires that one take a more detailed look at the structure of the domestic economy than at any overarching foreign policy strategy. In many ways an effort to look at the policy must start with the factor of demographic growth, which was discussed briefly above. The 1.06-percent annual growth of France's population has been a mixed blessing for the French government. It has resulted in a rejuvenated population; but with an increased number of young people entering the labor force, the French government has had to be concerned with creating sufficient employment. This is translated into a need to invest heavily in the domestic economy and to enhance the growth of export industries as a means of increasing production and employment. This concern is especially acute in France, where fears of unemployment exist because of the assumption that high levels of unemployment will lead to political protest and thus political instability.

The employment situation has been worsened by the prospect of far greater numbers entering the labor market than would be indicated by a simple analysis of past demographic growth. In the period from 1962 to 1965, the normal demographic growth was accelerated by the return of French inhabitants from Algeria to the metropolitan mainland. The active population then grew slowly for a few years, but the growth rate again began to accelerate after 1968 as a result of the entry into the labor force of an unprecedented number of women between the ages of twenty-five and fifty. Although the entry of youth into the working force was reduced somewhat by the extention of mandatory education to the age of sixteen and by a growth in the number of students seeking higher education, the working force available for industry and the service sector grew as a result of the continued movement of workers out of rural areas and agriculture into cities and the other sectors.[30]

Governmental policies to come to grips with continued growth in the labor force were both short-term and long-term. Short-term measures included the extension of obligatory education, as well as reductions in the work week. Long-term policy was more complex and was outlined in the Sixth Economic Plan (1971-1975).[31] The plan foresaw the need to double French economic capacity between 1970 and 1980 through an annual growth rate of about 6 percent, a high level of sustained investment, and the fostering of exports. If France was to meet its obligation to provide employment for its labor force and to complete the modernization of French society, the plan argued that the government would have to aim for nothing less than France's becoming the largest economy in Western Europe.

The enormity of the objectives that were undertaken for the economy posed a number of problems for the government.[32] Through what means was the government to achieve its objectives? What industries was it to foster? Where was it to obtain the capitalization necessary for the achievement of these objectives? The problem was all the more severe insofar as the French economy is relatively middle-sized and, unlike the German or British economies, does not have many industries on the scale of the world's giant multinationals. The need for capitalization required two types of measures. First, the government had to continue to manage an economy in which industrial production would grow at a faster rate than consumption so that large savings could be generated. The Sixth Plan thus called for annual increases in industrial productivity of 7.5 percent and increases in consumption of only 5.5 percent. (Both were scaled down in the Seventh Plan, whose estimates for the period 1975-1980 are 5.0 percent to 6.6 percent for GDP and 4.0 percent to 4.7 percent for consumption). Second, access to capital from the international finance markets was also required. Both options, however, had their own difficulties. Efforts to generate capital out of domestic savings ran into the problems that had brought about the events of May 1968. The restriction of domestic consumption for the purposes of investment could once again create pent-up demands that would explode in strikes or riots and thus weaken the government's legitimacy. Access to international financial markets created the possibility of the takeover of French companies by foreign multinational corporation, thus risking one of the major stakes of French national economic planning: the creation of large-scale indigenous industry. This series of dilemmas could be resolved only by a tightrope act on the part of the government, which seemed well within its ability given the way the French economy is run, as will be discussed below. As *The Economist* described the government's approach:

> The philosophy is simple. In the not too distant future European industry in the main bread and butter sectors is going to be run by a few multinational firms, or by the joint subsidiaries of national giants. But while West Germany and Britain have got most of their basic building blocks for this European game into shape, France is behind in all but a few industries, the notable exceptions being Pechiney in non-ferrous metals, Michelin in tyres and BSN and St. Gobain in glass. . . .
>
> So, where possible, the government has put together two groups, bringing in European participation when needed. Two examples are Rhône-Poulenc and Erap-CFP in chemicals, and Compagnie Générale Electrique and Thompson in electricals, with their various satellites in ancillary sectors.[33]

Paradoxically, the government's policy has required far more in the way of a labor force than the French population has been able to supply, in spite of the rapid growth in French workers. Before the economic slowdown caused by the oil shortages and energy crisis of 1973-1974, the number of foreign workers increased annually at 4 percent in order to make up this gap. Increasingly, these workers have come less from the former French empire, and more from the poorer regions of the EEC (notably Italy) and from other countries around the Mediterranean basin (Portugal, Spain, Morocco, Tunisia, Turkey, and Yugoslavia). They have assumed positions in industry—especially in housing and the mechanical industries—that French workers have been decreasingly willing to accept. Similarly, they have entered the service sector in menial positions—domestic work and street cleaning. By 1968 foreign workers comprised 6.2 percent of the labor force and an enormous share of new positions in blue collar work—70 percent of new positions in construction, mechanical and electrical manufacture, and fishing.[34] While this is not very different from the situation in other centers of industrial growth in the EEC, it does represent a new social problem with international implication.

As left-wing economists like to point out, importing foreign workers is a form of neomercantilism. It has allowed industrial France several luxuries. It permits industrial production to increase by taking advantage of low paid foreign workers and thus it also enables the economy to keep its export price levels relatively low in comparison to what they would be with higher-priced unionized labor. It not only serves, therefore, as a means of fostering exports, but also gives the economy a cushion to fall back on either in periods of recession or when the government wishes to curtail industrial expansion as a means of containing inflation and stabilizing prices. For with economic slowdowns, the first workers to lose their positions are foreign workers who then return home. Thus this form of neomercantilism results in the exporting of unemployment and the preservation of jobs for French citizens. This is more or less what occurred in 1974-1975 as a result of the international recession that followed the quadrupling of oil prices by OPEC.

As noted above, an additional aspect of French foreign economic policy has to do with fostering exports. In the period of relatively fixed exchange rates, which ended with the demise of the Bretton Woods system in 1971, one means of fostering exports and export-led domestic growth was through currency devaluation. The devaluations of 1958 and 1969 were major stimuli to the French economy and especially to the export sector, in spite of relatively high rates in inflation and the consumer boom that followed the events of May 1968.

France of course has benefited greatly from the boom in world trade that took place in the three decades since World War II. But the export boom in France has been exceptional, even by global standards. In the decade from 1962 to 1972, French exports increased from a level of $5.3 billion to more than $25.8 billion, which is all the more noteworthy because that period involved two devaluations whose combined effect was nearly 30 percent.[35] As discussed earlier, these exports are closely tied to the growth of the Common Market in Europe and to France's two major customers, Germany and Italy. In spite of the dramatic increase in French exports of machinery, manufactured goods, and chemicals, which now comprise two-thirds of all exports, France still depends on the exporting of sizable quantities of agricultural products (just under 15 percent of all exports). The government is thus acutely aware that the health of the French economy depends on the growth of exports markets within the European Communities and will remain for some time dependent on produce and livestock sales.

In summary, while French foreign economic policy has retained many elements of the Gaullian quest for autonomy and interdependence, it has become far more dependent on the achievement of goals associated with domestic economic growth. The policy still retains a general coherence, but consistency is provided less by reason of an explicit and highly articulated foreign policy strategy than by domestic economic needs. The transition from de Gaulle to Georges Pompidou to Valéry Giscard d'Estaing, president since May 1974, represents a trend away from a policy that attempted to mold a domestic economy in order to meet explicit foreign policy criteria to a policy that directs a foreign policy toward the achievement of domestic ends. This has not meant that foreign economic policy or the relations between it and domestic economic management are less coherent. Indeed, domestic and foreign economic policy still form a coherent whole. Commercial policy is predicated largely upon the European Communities, which provide the bulk of French imports and France's major external markets. It remains the forum out of which the French government hopes to create an economic and monetary union, even if plans for its consummation have been postponed as a result of the general global movement toward flexible exchange rates and by the dependence of France and the rest of Europe on imports of energy sources from the Middle East. But foreign policy is no longer defined by an effort to enhance France's prestige and autonomy. Nor does defense policy any longer play a central or even a major role. As commentators have frequently noted, President d'Estaing does not share the Gaullian taste for grandeur, and he has deemphasized defense policy to such a degree that the full reintegration of France into NATO is no longer out of the question.[36] If there are states whose foreign policy is now almost solely concerned with economic issues, France is one.

Inconsistencies do appear, however, in France's foreign economic policy, and they relate to the dilemmas posed by the European option. The French government seemingly has no choice but to base its foreign economic policy on the desirability of creating an economic union in Europe. At the same time, however, the implementation of such a union has become less and less feasible. This has been strikingly the case since the oil crisis of 1973-1974. French policy choices have no longer either fully coincided with or complemented those of the other major members of the Communities. The German government, for example, had been playing the role of loyal European before the oil crisis in part because such a policy was a requisite to the successful pursuit of its Ostopolitik (lest movement toward the East raise suspicions on the part of Germany's Western partners). By the winter of 1973-1974, that policy had been played out and Western support was no longer required. At the same time, domestic critics began to attack the German government for having ignored domestic issues while pursuing its Eastern policy. These issues ranged from inflation to reform of the German welfare system and the further implementation of the comanagement of businesses by workers and owners. Moreover, the German government politically could no longer foot what many members of the electorate thought were exorbitant bills for common market programs, including the CAP and the nascent regional policy. The domestic reactions against the Ostpolitik and

Common Market policies were reinforced by the German leadership's growing belief that new problems being encountered on the international level, including the oil crisis, required cooperation with the United States and Japan, and that the European option made decreasing sense as a means of confronting them.

The British position also changed directions. The Conservative government of Edward Heath, which came into office in mid-1970, had European ambitions that were based on the understanding that Britain's future economic and political options were extremely limited and had to be based on membership in the EEC. Such membership might spur British industrial growth and provide a solution to the lingering problems associated with outstanding sterling balances. Moreover, as an applicant for membership in the Communities, the British government could not be overly demanding of its future European partners and had to act the role of good European. Yet, by the winter of 1973-1974, British support for the Common Market also came under severe domestic attack. British hopes for support of its regional policy through membership in the Common Market had been stymied, and the European option—which was never popularly supported in Britain—lost even more domestic political credibility. Moreover, the British government was facing a series of extraordinarily difficult domestic economic problems by late 1973, including union restiveness leading to a prolonged coal miners' strike, and endemic high rates of inflation. Its attention was thus also focused on domestic issues when in early 1974 the Conservative government lost power in parliamentary elections.

The support of Britain and Germany, which had made France's European option feasible, thus began to break apart. Even if it had not, new international conditions made the implementation of the European option extremely difficult. The logic that led to the need to create a monetary union was part of this. One of the major French incentives for monetary union was the desirability of maintaining the CAP and its pricing system, which kept European products generally at a higher price level than that prevailing in world markets. This in turn guaranteed a secured market for French exports. Inflation in primary products in the early 1970s led to a new situation by 1973, where target prices in the Common Market were below world prices. This weakened the rationale of the price support system and thus also made fixed exchange rates in Europe a less urgent issue than in 1969.

The international monetary system, moreover, had been moving in a direction that contradicted the goal of fixed exchange rates and monetary union in Europe. After a series of foreign exchange crises in the period from 1968 to 1972, governments of most industrialized societies realized that moving toward a regime of flexible exchange rates was far more congruent with new international monetary conditions than was a regime of fixed exchange rates. Flexible exchange rates, determined more by market forces than by governmental policy, reduced the incentive for international speculation and therefore reduced the occasion for monetary crises. At the same time, a flexible exchange rate regime permitted governments greater autonomy to pursue domestic economic policies without regard for deflationary or expansionary policies that might have been required for maintaining fixed rates. Since most of these governments sought new instruments to deal with domestic economic problems, they also welcomed the new flexibility of exchange rates. European economic and monetary union, in short, no matter how desirable as a political goal, represented a movement contradictory to prevailing international economic trends. This was recognized in January 1974 when the French government joined with the other major monetary countries in Jamaica to "ratify" an interim agreement to maintain an international regime of flexible exchange rates.[a]

The breakdown of the European coalition and the demise of the rationale for monetary and economic union were coupled with another factor that made the European option less viable for the French government: the change in general economic conditions in the industrialized world. The European option unfolded in a climate of general economic expansion in Europe, Japan, and North America. So long as this expansion could be maintained, no government in Europe was forced to make a difficult choice between domestic and European goals. By late 1973, however, especially (but not only) because of governmental reactions to the energy crisis, all Western economies entered a period of recession, or at least lowered economic growth. In such circumstances, domestic policies designed to maintain full employment, such as in a drive to sustain exports and limit imports, tend to create international conflict. So long as governments are elected by their own citizens and have a natural inclination to place a priority on domestic conditions, internationalism will be more difficult to pursue under limited growth conditions than under full growth conditions. While the French were not alone in reverting to nationalistic economic policies by the end of 1973, their choice to do so certainly affected the viability of the European option.

Finally, and perhaps of greatest importance for the interim shift by the French government away from the European option and toward the policy of relative autonomy, were domestic political factors. The upshot of these domestic factors was the severe limitation on options that the government could select, because of loss of popular support as well as electoral support. One of the motivations of President Pompidou's European policy after 1969 had been the

[a]Technically, the Jamaica Agreement enables countries to opt for fixed rates. In practice, however, it has meant the beginning of an effort to work out rules for the collective management of a flexible rate system and to suspend efforts at constitutional reform of the Articles of Agreement of the International Monetary Fund. French policy in the development of the Jamaica Agreement was, however, instrumental in providing, through the agreement, for a resusitation of the role of gold in the international monetary system. Gold sales from the IMF will be used as an instrument of development finance, thus indicating a phasing out of gold. But, central banks will again be able to purchase gold, thus presenting the possibility that the IMF will regain its centerpiece role in the system. See Tom de Vries, "Jamaica, or the Non-reform of the International Monetary System," *Foreign Affairs* (April 1976): 577-605.

desire to mold support for an issue that had been generally popular in the French electorate and that would also serve to free him from constraints imposed by conservative Gaullists like Michel Debré. If Pompidou could demonstrate that the European option would bring success, he would be able to distance himself from Gaullist dogma. In 1972, in spite of his suspicions of referendums, he held a referendum on the expansion of the EC, in the hope that he could marshal an overwhelming "mandate" for his policy on a popular issue. That gambit was less than successful. His government was unable to assure the mandate, not because the issue was unpopular, but because electoral support for his government had dwindled.

There were several reasons for Pompidou's and the UDR's loss of electoral support. In the first place, the government was ridden with scandals by mid-1972. During 1971-1972 a series of scandals in the construction industry involving the letting of governmental contracts had filled the press, and just before the referendum, Prime Minister Chaban-Delmas had been exposed to a tax scandal involving a law passed under his leadership in Parliament. Having failed to receive his desired mandate, Pompidou was then attacked by conservative Gaullists who argued that Pompidou lost support because he meandered from traditional Gaullist foreign policy goals. Thus after the referendum, Pompidou replaced Chaban-Delmas with a conservative Gaullist, Pierre Messmer, as prime minister.

The legislative elections of 1973 were the next test of the government's policy. Before the election, the government was in fact running scared. Opinion polls had demonstrated the plausibility of a left-wing coalition majority in Parliament, after the PCF and socialists formed an electoral alliance. The government ran hard and continued to use its European foreign policy as a means of garnering electoral support, arguing that a left-wing majority would be tied to the PCF's antagonism to the Common Market. The Paris Summit of October 1972 was thus as much a part of electoral politics as it was a reflection of the government's foreign policy. While the government expected to lose its rather artificially gained and overwhelming majority in parliament—which had been gained in the aftermath of the events of May 1968—its loss of the majority and need to form a coalition came as a shock.

I argued earlier that domestic and foreign economic policy in France more often than not form a coherent whole. Part of that policy included curtailing consumption and massive investment for the modernization of French industry.[37] By 1973 the government's commitment to continued high growth and industrialization, for the purposes of assuring employment and international competitiveness, had affected much of French society, even at the grass roots. The conservative Gaullist government began to be viewed as disruptive of French social patterns—and in a society where individual group attachment to the status quo is well known, the Gaullist party, as a party of change, was rendered suspect. The left-wing electoral coalition, moreover, capitalized on this image of

Gaullism and, in the legislative elections, it presented an image of stability and attachment to the status quo that was far more congruent with traditional French patterns of political authority.[38]

Thus by 1973 the government was losing its bets on both domestic and foreign policy. The government's policy was based on the wager that the benefits of industrialization and of the European option would accrue soon enough and in a large enough sector of French society to reap electoral rewards. In the short run, however, electoral costs proved far greater than electoral payoffs. Worsening matters by the end of 1973 was Pompidou's failing health and the government's recognition of the likelihood of presidential elections before the expiration of Pompidou's term in 1976. A complex series of political maneuvers in preparation of new presidential elections finally signaled an end to the European option; by the winter of 1973-1974, in EC matters, in the handling of the energy crisis, and in policies toward the Soviet Union and the United States, the Gaullist dogma of independence and autonomy again assumed a prevailing policy position.[39]

The reemergence of Gaullist rhetoric in early 1974 was thus not difficult to trace. There were both fundamental underlying factors and immediate electoral reasons responsible for this. Confronting the likelihood of new presidential elections and the possibility of the left-wing alternative, there was every reason for the government to assume the older Gaullist policy. The policy of independence, after all, has an important dual purpose. On the one hand, it solidified Gaullist support for the government, which after 1962 hovered at 38 to 40 percent of the electorate. On the other hand, it served to split any left-wing coalition by offering the Communist voters the chance to retain a government whose foreign policy, involving a pro-Soviet and anti-American position, would be far more to their liking than would be the policy of the Western-oriented socialist party with which the PCF would have to rule.

The reversion to a policy of autonomy and independence was reinforced by the logic of the energy crisis. A world of scarce resources and of recession provided the base of a different form of foreign policy than did a world of abundant resources and economic growth. Now security of sources of supply of resources, especially energy resources, became priority issues for the government, simply to maintain the standard of living of its population. Since these resources lie outside Europe, great pressures existed for the government to make bilateral deals with its suppliers at the expense of international or European cooperation. The oil crisis of 1973-1974 thus reinforced the domestic political dilemmas of the failing Pompidou government. Unfortunately for the Gaullists, however, Pompidou's death resulted in new presidential elections that saw the victory of the first non-Gaullist candidate since the beginning of the Fifth Republic in 1958. However, the electoral victory of Valéry Giscard d'Estaing reinforced rather than solved the dilemma, for it indicated that in electoral terms as well as perhaps in terms of international constraints, the options of

(1) autonomy, (2) building up Europe, or (3) collaboration with the United States and other non-European industrialized societies were all difficult to maintain.

The government of M. Giscard d'Estaing was at first unable to pursue a decisive policy. At the outset it felt it had to oscillate between an effort to build domestic support–the president had won the election by less than 1 percent of the popular vote–and an attempt to secure the benefits of international interdependence. It recognized that while it would be judged largely by its performance in domestic economic life, it could never receive a wholly satisfactory judgment. There was thus a pervasive malaise in French foreign and domestic policy, arising from the feeling that the long-term objectives of Gaullian policy–national autonomy and European leadership–could never be attained and that domestic social change and intractable economic problems were neither well understood nor easily controlled.[40]

In spite of the domestic and foreign issues that fractionated French policy after 1974, the Giscard government had several strong suits that it was able to draw upon in playing out its foreign economic policy. Although Giscard had barely won the popular vote in May 1974, he was widely recognized for his expertise in economic diplomacy, since he had carried the economics and finance portfolio for most of the previous decade. This obviously served him well, given the preeminently economic issues that were now at stake–inflation, unemployment, scarcity of supply of raw materials, and so forth. Moreover, the belief that no European political system–and especially not the French–could long withstand high levels of unemployment proved to be wrong. Contemporary welfare states in the West as it is now clear, have a far greater tolerance both for unemployment and inflation than was once believed. As well, Giscard's eroding support among the traditional Gaullists was balanced by the inability of the left-wing parties (the Communists and Socialists) to maintain their unity. His freedom to choose unorthodox options was therefore not as constrained by domestic factors as was felt to be the case in mid-1974.

This freedom of choice was reflected in the balancing act that the French government displayed with respect to three major policy partners–the other members of the EC, Third World (including OPEC) trading partners, and the United States. In Europe, Giscard built on his long friendship with German Chancellor Helmut Schmidt to maintain the feasibility of a European option. While the fruits of this relationship made European Community affairs less acerbic and more "businesslike" than they had been since the founding of the EC. With respect to Third World and "New International Economic Order" issues, the French government gained prestige and, more importantly, avoided being stigmatized by Third World governments. This was accomplished only through France's role in convening the Conference on International Economic Cooperation in Paris, but also by proposals put before the U.N. Conference on Trade and Development (UNCTAD) and the Seventh Special Session of the U.N.

General Assembly.[41] With respect to the United States, the French government was instrumental in reducing tensions and fostering a spirit of pragmatic cooperation on selected issues. The summit meeting of leading Western economic powers, convened by France at Rambouillet in autumn 1975, and the Jamaica monetary agreement mentioned above are clear examples.

Nor are the reasons for greater cooperation across the Atlantic obscure. They include the emergence of a new generation of political leaders who, like Giscard, are less ideologically oriented than their predecessors, and who find it difficult to capitalize on "independent behavior" in their domestic political arenas. As well, there is the perception that in some functional areas–e.g., money, trade, the regulation of multinational enterprises–relations have become so interdependent that each one's actions in many areas (including domestic, economic management) is of interest to the others, and autonomous action is more often than not self-defeating. Related to these factors are the successive failures within Europe to achieve an economic union within a reasonable time horizon (i.e., one that reflects the requirements of different electoral cycles), or to strike a European policy independent of the U.S. The construction of Europe and Atlantic cooperation must proceed together, at least for the time being, and efforts to juxtopose them as options are likely to be self-defeating. Finally, there is a perceived community of interests (albeit schizophrenic) toward the "outside world" of OPEC and the less developed countries, and this too plays a role. However, it is important to emphasize that this new cooperation is filled with malaise rather than certainty. It seems to freeze out some desirable goals, including independence and autonomy, and it is not at all clear that it will succeed.

The Management of Economic Policy

In spite of this pervasive malaise in French policy, the government remains rather well equipped to handle problems of domestic economic management and foreign economic policy. This is the result of the long tradition of *dirigisme*, the large scale of government and its predominance in the economy, and a network of relations between governmental and business elite groups, each of which is worthy of some general discussion.

The governmental policy of fostering economic growth and expansion has been aided by a revolution that has taken place in the attitudes of France's administrative elite since World War II. For a century that elite was oriented far more toward economic stability than toward economic growth. But the expansionary attitudes that have infected the postwar world have firmly taken hold within the French bureaucracies.[42] This attitude is reinforced by the series of economic plans that have been formulated to direct domestic economic growth since World War II. Moreover, conflicts in attitudes take place less between the elite groups in charge of economic management and leaders of the industry than they do elsewhere. If there is one pervasive set of conflicts, it has to do with the quite natural inclination of the minister of finance to stress balanced budgets and the stability of the currency, which frequently runs against the expansionary desires of politicians and other ministers. This conflict is asymmetrical in that the ministry of finance holds most of the economic keys in France—a subject to which I will return in a moment.

The overall expansionary posture of the government has been based on the government's belief that its major economic and political objectives can be achieved only by means of a high level of sustained economic growth. This desire is fostered by the well-developed technocratic tradition in France and the reliance on direction from above and suspicion or even fear of permitting market mechanisms to operate. A well-trained administrative elite, which is specifically recruited from elite institutions, is now dominant within France's civil service. A recent study of domestic economic management in France has described them as follows:

The technocrats have replaced ideological references and commitments with their own brand of radical pragmatism. At the centre of their system of beliefs is the conviction that social problems are susceptible to technical solutions. They see social situations as sets of specific, solvable problems. Principles do not matter; only results count. Their economic policies often combine classical liberalism and extreme *dirigisme*. For example, direct price controls coupled with the abolition of tariffs is one of their favourite means for controlling prices in a given line of goods.[43]

The importance of technocrats in domestic economic policy stems largely from the public sector's role in orienting the French economy. Total governmental expenditures account for about 40 percent of the gross national product. Although this share of the public sector in the national economy has declined somewhat during the past few years, it represents an enormous and powerful voice in the management of the economy. Through the nationalization of industries, especially at the time of the Popular Front government during the depression (1936-1937) and in the period of liberation at the end of World War II (1944-1955), the government gained total control or predominance in a wide variety of sectors, summarized by Ehrmann as follows:

. . . railroading; almost all energy production (mining, electricity, etc.) and telecommunication (radio and television); most air and maritime transport; most of the aeronautic industry; 60 per cent of bank deposits; 40 per cent of insurance premiums; one-third of the automobile industry; one-third of the housing industry—in addition to the old state monopolies of post, telephone, telegraph, tobacco and match manufacture, and sundry less important activities. Public concerns account for more than 10 per cent of the gross national product; their investments represent more than one-third of the gross capital formation of all enterprises. Fifteen per cent of the total active population or 27 per cent of all salary and wage earners . . . are paid directly by the state either as civil servants or on a contractual basis. Their income comes close to one-third of the total sum of wages and salaries.[44]

Management of the economy cannot, of course, be as finely tuned as this summary would imply. The major problems that the government confronts are dual. On the one hand, control over the public sector is shared by a "giant cluster of ministries, agencies and firms, each of which has its own constituency to satisfy, a traditional area of competence to protect from encroachment . . . , a different order of investment priorities, and a different conception of its own role."[45] On the other hand, many nationalized industries operate with great autonomy and are large enough to have independence in planning their own rates of expansion, regardless of the government's overall economic plan. Nevertheless, the manifold controls of the government, and especially of the Ministry of Finance, are quite powerful in helping the government achieve its policy ends. In addition, of course, the government has lost a number of controls over domestic economic management as a result of the opening of French borders to trade and the movement of other factors of production. The reciprocal of the increased openness of the economy has been a loss of control over the implementation of domestic economic plans.

The strengths of economic management in France reside in a series of monetary controls centralized through the Ministry of Finance. Economic policy has relied traditionally far more on credit and monetary policy than it has on fiscal policy. The taxation system has been based on indirect taxes, which have benefited the largely conservative and privileged constituency of most French governments. Although several governmental studies have indicated the need for an overhaul of the fiscal system, no one had seriously undertaken to implement reform. Thus the burden of domestic economic management is placed on the same institutional mechanisms and policy instruments as is the conduct of foreign economic policy (especially monetary policy). These can be summarized as follows:[46] (1) quantitative controls, including modest use of rediscounting, openmarket operations (which have increased in scale since certain reforms instituted in the late 1960s), and the required reserve system for banks which was instituted only in 1967); and (2) qualitative controls, which have been based on credit policy, including selective credit to different sectors. The predilection for credit controls is reinforced by the use of price controls, which are both direct and indirect. The indirect form of controls consist of *contrats de programme* upon which the government has increasingly relied. These include permissions to corporations to limit the overall increase in their prices but within these general limitations to selectively increase some prices to a greater or to a lesser extent as management prefers.

Obviously, control over credit and prices permits the government to strongly influence both the exchange rate of the franc and the level of domestic economic growth. But the lack of sophisticated fiscal tools, coupled with severe limitations placed on open market operations, has also created dilemmas. These dilemmas are typical of societies that have become economically interdependent with others and stem from a lack in the number of political instruments available to the government to achieve the whole spectrum of its economic objectives simultaneously. For example, stabilization measures, like those taken in December 1963 to bolster the strength of the franc in international financial markets, also served to limit the growth in investments that was required for the government to meet the goals of its economic plans. This experience led the government to institute a set of reforms that would enhance its ability to achieve financial stability and domestic growth at the same time. Another dilemma between the two spheres stems from the relatively rudimentary form taken by open market operations in France to neutralize the impact on the domestic money supply of foreign exchange operations. Thus, as Hodgman has argued:

> For France a major capital inflow may pose problems not only because it expands the money supply and thus may add to domestic inflation, but also because it may bypass the carefully designed system of credit controls. Thus money obtained from a capital inflow may be spent for investment purposes other than those of high national priority since it is not subject to initial credit review.[47]

To cope with this dilemma, the French government has expanded its open market operations and also instituted a two-tier system for foreign exchange operations in 1971 (one for commercial and the other for financial operations). The system was dropped after the French implicitly accepted a flexible exchange rate regime rather than a fixed rate system in early 1974. Yet new dilemmas have been created in their place. For example, one effort of the French to increase control over the monetary base led to a reform of the banking system, whose end result was the creation of institutions that were sufficiently powerful to escape governmental influence. Moreover, as *The Economist* has pointed out, "the government is less and less able, as the economy grows larger, more complex and increasingly enmeshed with those of its European neighbors, to wield direct control over it. Power is seeping away from the government both to different levels of decision, international and regional, and towards pressure groups, which are becoming better and better organized."[48]

These difficulties must, however, be placed in their proper context. The French economy, after all, has been extraordinarily well managed since World War II. Levels of inflation have rarely gotten out of hand, and if they have been persistently higher than elsewhere over time, that has been the result of the government's conscious decision to foster inflation at the expense of either a lower level of economic growth or a higher level of unemployment than would otherwise be the case. Given the degree to which the economy had to be modernized and industrialized to catch up to France's European partners and to provide employment opportunities for future generations of Frenchmen, perhaps all but one problem in the political economy of France have been relatively well met. The poorest record is associated with the continued maldistribution of income within the society and the political inability of any government to date to confront this problem directly for fear it would lose domestic support. In other areas, especially domestic investment and sustained growth, the government has performed rather well.

Notes

1. OECD Economic Surveys, *France* (Paris, 1976), Appendix.

2. See Institut National de la Statistique et des Études Economiques, *Annuaire statistique de la France, 1967* (Paris, 1968), p. 608d.

3. OECD Economic Surveys, *France* (Paris, 1974), p. 82.

4. See especially Richard N. Cooper, *The Economics of Interdependence* (New York: McGraw-Hill, 1968) for an analysis of these trends.

5. See Charles P. Kindleberger, "The Postwar Resurgence of the French Economy," in Stanley Hoffman et al., eds., *In Search of France* (Cambridge, Mass.: Harvard University Press, 1963), pp. 118-58.

6. The standard English language works on the subject include Guy de Carmoy, *The Foreign Policies of France: 1944-1968*, trans. Elaine P. Halperin (Chicago: University of Chicago Press, 1970); Alfred Grosser, *French Foreign Policy Under De Gaulle*, trans. Lois Ames Pattison (Boston: Little, Brown, 1965); Stanley Hoffman, *Decline and Renewal? France Since the 1930's* (New York: Viking Press, 1974); W.W. Kulski, *De Gaulle and the World* (Syracuse, N.Y.: Syracuse University Press, 1966); and Edward A. Kolodziej, *French International Policy Under De Gaulle and Pompidou: The Politics of Grandeur* (Ithaca, N.Y.: Cornell University Press, 1974).

7. See Nicholas Wahl, "The French Constitution of 1958: The Initial Draft and its Origins," *American Political Science Review* 52 (1959): 358-382; and also Jean Chatelain, *La Nouvelle Constitution et la régime politique de la France* (Paris: Berger-Levrauet, 1959).

8. See William G. Andrews and Stanley Hoffman, "France: The Search for Presidentialism," in William G. Andrews, ed., *European Politics I* (Princeton, N.J.: Van Nostrand, 1966), pp. 77-138; and, François Goguel, "Refléxions sur le régime presidentiel," *Revue Française de Science Politique* 12 (1962): 289-311.

9. Quoted in Roy C. Macridis, ed., *De Gaulle: Implacable Ally* (New York: Harper & Row, 1966), p. 41.

10. Frans A.M. Alting von Gesau, *European Organizations and Foreign Relations of States: A Comparative Analysis of Decision-Making* (Leiden: A.W. Sythoff, 1964), p. 52.

11. This argument is further developed in Edward L. Morse, *Foreign Policy*

and Interdependence in Gaullist France (Princeton, N.J.: Princeton University Press, 1973, pp. 105-115.

12. Pierre Hassner, "La France aux Mains Libres!" *Prevues*, 204 (February 1968): 55. The translation is mine.

13. This argument is drawn on the framework developed in Wilfrid L. Kohl, *French Nuclear Diplomacy* (Princeton, N.J.: Princeton University Press, 1971), and summarized in Wilfrid L. Kohl, "The French Nuclear Deterrent," *Proceedings of the Academy of Political Science* 29 (1968): 80-94.

14. See William G. Andrews, "De Gaulle and NATO," in Roy C. Macridis, *Modern European Governments: Cases in Comparative Policy Making* ed., (Englewood Cliffs, N.J.: Prentice-Hall, 1968), pp. 92-115.

15. Charles Ailleret, "Défense 'dirigée' ou défense 'tous azimuts,' " *Revue de défense nationale* 23 (1967): 1923-1932.

16. See Jacques Rueff, *Combats pour l'ordre finançier* (Paris: Plon, 1972), chaps. 6, 7 and 8.

17. *Major Addresses, Statements and Press Conferences of General Charles de Gaulle, March 17, 1964-May 16, 1967* (New York: Ambassade de France, Service de Presse et d'Information, 1967), p. 80.

18. See the French position on these questions as defined in greater detail in Jacques Wolff, "La Diplomatie du franc (1962-1968), (1)," *Revue de Science Financière* 60 (1968): 782-804.

19. See Fritz Machlup, *Remaking the International Monetary System: The Rio Agreement and Beyond* (Baltimore: The Johns Hopkins Press, 1968).

20. In addition to Kohl, *French Nuclear Diplomacy*, see Raymond Aron, *The Great Debate*, trans. Ernst Parvel (Garden City, N.Y.: Doubleday, 1965), pp. 100-144; and Wolf Mendl, *Deterrence and Persuasion: French Nuclear Armament in the Context of National Policy, 1945-1969* (London: Faber and Faber, 1970); Edward A. Kolodziej, *Patterns of French Foreign Policy, 1958-1967* (McLean, Va.: Research Analysis Corporation, 1968).

21. See the excellent bibliography of works written on the events of May 1968 in Laurence Wylie, Franklin I. Chu, and Mary Terrall, *France: The Events of May-June 1968, A Critical Bibliography* (Pittsburgh: Council for European Studies, 1973).

22. See *Le Monde*, March 30, 1971, pp. 19-20.

23. See Roger Prioûet, *Les Français Mystifiés* (Paris: Grasset, 1973).

24. Henry Ehrmann, *Politics in France*, rev. ed. (Boston: Little, Brown, 1971), p. 189.

25. The detailed effects of the May events on the military program are spelled out in Edward L. Morse, *Defense Autonomy in Gaullist France: Welfare Versus Warfare and the Dilemma of Insufficient Resources*, (Morristown, N.J.: General Learning Press, 1972).

26. For an examination of the policies then being pursued by the Western governments concerning détente, see Josef Korbel, *Détente in Europe: Real or Imaginary?* (Princeton, N.J.: Princeton University Press, 1972).

27. See Livingston Merchant et al., *NATO after Czechoslavakia* (Washington, D.C.: Georgetown University, Center for Strategic and International Studies, 1969).

28. The effects of the invasion on French policy are clearly spelled out in Michel Tatu, *Le Triangle: Washington-Moscow-Pékin et Les Deux Europes* (Paris: Casterman, 1972), esp. pp. 94-133.

29. A review of the political factors lying behind efforts to create a European monetary union can be found in Joseph S. Nye, "The Political Context," in Lawrence B. Krause and Walter S. Salant, eds., *European Monetary Unification and Its Meaning for the United States* (Washington, D.C.: The Brookings Institution, 1973), pp. 37-55.

30. These trends are discussed and graphically presented in OECD Economic Surveys, *France* (Paris, 1973), pp. 38-69.

31. The major aspects of the Sixth Plan are presented in Commissariat Général au Plan, *VIe Plan de développement économique et sociâl, 1971-75: Report Général* (Paris, 15 July 1971).

32. See the discussion in Lionel Stoleru, *L'Impératif industriel* (Paris: Seuil, 1969).

33. Jonathan Radice, "Survey: France," *The Economist* (December 2, 1972), p. 13.

34. OECD Economic Surveys, *France* (Paris, 1973), pp. 47-53.

35. OECD Economic Surveys, *France* (Paris, 1973), p. 102, and OECD Economic Surveys, *France* (Paris, 1974), p. 83.

36. See Alan Ned Sabrosky, "French Foreign Policy Alternatives," *Orbis* 19, no. 4 (Winter 1976): 1429-1447. Also see Michel Tatu, "La Peur de Bouton Rouge," *Le Monde* (Hebdomadaire), June 10-16, 1976, p. 1, and Jacques Isnard, "Une Nouvelle Conception Strategegue," ibid., p. 7.

37. See arguments concerning this dilemma in Jack Hayward, *The One and Indivisible French Republic* (New York: Norton, 1973), pp. 269-274.

38. See the arguments on the loss of French social cohesion in "Survey: France, A Divided Nation," *The Economist* (February 23, 1974), supplement.

39. Robert Mauthier, "French Foreign Policy: Almost Like the Old Days," *The Financial Times* (February 26, 1974), p. 3.

40. See Alfred Grosser, "Europe: Community of Malaise," *Foreign Policy* 15 (Summer 1974): 169-182.

41. The intellectual roots of these proposals are clarified in Thierry de Montbrial, "For a New World Economic Order," *Foreign Affairs* (October 1975): 61-78.

42. The most complete study of attitudes of the governing elite in France and the network of relations that characterizes it can be found in Ezra N. Suleiman, *Politics, Power and Bureaucracy in France: The Administrative Elite* (Princeton, N.J.: Princeton University Press, 1974). For a good overview of the management of France's foreign economic policy in comparison to U.S. policy, see Peter J. Katzenstein, "International Relations and Domestic Structures: Foreign Economic Policies of Advanced Industrial States," *International Organization* 30, no. 1 (Winter 1976): 1-46.

43. Stephen S. Cohen, *Modern Capitalist Planning: The French Model* (Cambridge, Mass.: Harvard University Press, 1969), p. 46.

44. Ehrmann, *Politics in France*, p. 30.

45. Cohen, *Modern Capitalist Planning*, p. 27.

46. For more details, see Pierre Dieterlen and Huguette Durand, "Monetary Policy in France," in Karel Holbik, ed., *Monetary Policy in Twelve Industrial Countries* (Boston: Federal Reserve Bank, 1973), pp. 117-160; and Donald R. Hodgman, *National Monetary Policies and International Monetary Cooperation* (Boston: Little, Brown, 1974), pp. 27-52. The role of the budget and the process of budgetary decision-making is summarized in Guy Lord, *The French Budgetary Process* (Berkeley: University of California Press, 1973).

47. Hodgman, *National Monetary Policies*, p. 46.

48. See note 33.

5 West Germany

Wilhelm Hankel

West Germany's three "economic miracles" consisted of its reconstruction (1948-1952), the reversal from balance of payments deficits into chronic surpluses (since 1952), and its ascent to the richest among the Western nations in currency reserves (1975). Both in Germany and abroad, these economic phenomena were more admired than analyzed. Admiration seldom leads to critical analysis. Almost all analyses of West Germany's postwar economic development read like the market reports of a successful business firm: they report success, but any investigation of the background, problems, or conceivable alternatives is virtually nonexistent.[1]

In this chapter I would like to develop and comment on the following five theses:

1. West Germany's rapid reconstruction as well as its position abroad, obviously stronger from the beginning of the fifties on, represents the economic consequences of Germany's division. West Germany had lost large parts of its traditional domestic market and had to seek new ones beyond its national frontiers—on the world market.
2. The two new political doctrines, neoliberalism and the preference for stability in currency values (a preference propagated more extensively in Germany than in all other Western countries), were reactions to the excesses of the Hitler era. They strengthened German dependence on foreign markets, ostensibly made structural by the division of the country. The decade-long renunciation of a domestically active financial policy and the permanently restrictive character of the currency policy (which was strengthened at the beginning of the seventies by a period of permanent revaluations) put a brake on the natural tendency of domestic market expansion. The policy of stability directed German industries "away from themselves" to the freer foreign markets. Ideological liberalism functioned as an extremely subtle mercantilism.
3. There was never a centrally planned German foreign economic policy. There could be no central plan because the new executors of economic policy—the *Länder*, the federal reserve system (*Zentralbank*), and the Federation—did not allow any such planning because of their competing interests. Nor was such a policy needed, because the development of German foreign economic policy was so successful that it needed neither political stimulation nor direction.

Translated from the German by Miriam J. Levy.

4. The experiment of the politically motivated policy of European integration (1958-1973) foundered at the outset. The Treaty of Rome excluded currency policy as an instrument of integration. A customs union and common agricultural policy developed into a weak European counterweight to the worldwide might of monetary convertibility.
5. The German case of a long-lasting "export-led growth," which is overwhelmingly interpreted as a smart and clever macroeconomic management of protecting the economy against tensions coming from the outside world (oil crash, balance-of-payments crisis), has weakened the country's long-term position. Given this high degree of dependence on sufficient growth rates in exports and export surpluses, the Germany of today and tomorrow is more vulnerable than it is aware of. The performance of its national policies is relying on good, not bad, weather in world markets and in the international monetary system. So in reality, Germany is more dependent on integration and more unable to pursue an economic policy of "splendid isolation" that consciously as well as successfully ignores the links to the world economy.

The Postwar Rebirth of the German Economy

Economic Consequences of Germany's Division

The new West German state, pieced together in 1948-1949 from the Western occupation zones, began under entirely artificial premises. Neither the Allied nor the German authorities considered it "viable" (*lebensfähig*) because of its enormous reconstruction and import needs. Thus at the end of 1947 and beginning of 1948 the head of the renowned Institute for World Economy at the University of Kiel, Fritz Baade, "proved" that for years if not for decades the West German economy could be maintained only through "reverse reparations," massive subventions of capital by the victors.[2] Baade preached on entirely correct formula of West Germany as a "second, but poorer England."[a] (See

[a]Baade took the formula of the "second, but poorer England" from *The New York Times*, which wrote in its editorial of 21 February 1948:

> Western Germany has become another Britain, with approximately the same population living in an approximately similar area, with coal as the only important raw material, and with an ability to produce only about half the food needed. Yet Britain, with an unimpaired production apparatus and complete freedom to produce and trade, with vast resources in her Empire which more than offset her Empire obligations, and vast American aid already given, is able to live only under the severest kind of austerity on a diet, which, while still twice the total calories the Germans usually receive, is nevertheless considered to be close to the danger point. How, without any of these advantages, Western Germany is not only to live but also to contribute to European recovery, under a program which would leave her only 75% of the per capita production capacity of 1936 (when she produced more than 80% of her own food) is an unexplained mystery for which we can see only one solution, and that is continued American subsidies to Germany and to Europe.

Table 5-1.) Like Baade, however, almost all analysts of the situation at that time perceived that after an economic regeneration, the division of the German economy into an "industry-rich" region (West Germany) and a vast "industry-poor" region (the German Democratic Republic and the Soviet- or Polish-occupied area) inevitably had to make West Germany into an export-intensive country of surplus. The former (but now lost) internal markets for West German industry had to be replaced by foreign markets. The world market took the place of West Germany's now lost central and eastern German markets.

Table 5-2 shows what weight this structural factor had. Before World War II (1936) West Germany disposed of almost 60 percent of its "exports" in the other parts of Germany. Conversely, the other German state had to replace over 85 percent of its "imports" from West Germany either by new production or by opening other sources of imports. While the Federal Republic had to seek and find its compensation on the world markets, from the very beginning the GDR was burdened with the problem of creating its own entirely new investment industries and of intensifying—cost what it might—the economic interweaving of imports and exports with Eastern Europe.

Federalistic Taming of Executive Powers

The birth of West German political institutions was accomplished in several stages. First, the Länder were formed; they were made *fully* competent for the economic policy of their regions. As a common federal organ of monetary

Table 5-1
The United Kingdom and West Germany in 1949

	United Kingdom	*West Germany (including West Berlin)*
Population (midyear 1949)	50.3 million	50.0 million
Grain production (1947/1949 ave.)	6.9 million tons	7.7 million tons
Cropland	31.5 acres	35.25 acres
Arable land	18.75 million acres	20 million acres
1949 exports	$6.6 billion	$1.1 billion
Manufactures	$5.8 billion	$0.6 billion
Coal	$0.16 billion	$0.2 billion
Other raw materials	$0.1 billion	$0.13 billion

[Adapted from Institut für Weltwirtschaft and der Universität Kiel, Lebensfaehigkeit und Vollbeschäftigung: Ein Beitrag zur Frage des wirtschaftlichen Wiederaufbaus in Westdeutschland (Bonn, 1959), p. 4.]

Table 5-2
Interweaving of the Economies of East and West Germany Before and After World War II

	1936		*1957*	
	billion RM	*%*	*billion VE*	*%*
Soviet Zone				
Total exports:	5.3	100.0	4.0	100.0
to the present-day Federal Republic	2.7	50.9	0.4	11.3
to the other German territories	1.5	28.3	–	–
to foreign countries	1.1	20.8	3.6	
Total imports:	4.8	100.0	3.6	88.7
from the present-day Federal Republic	2.7	56.2	0.4	11.4
from the other German territories	1.4	29.2	–	–
from foreign countries	0.7	14.6	3.2	88.6
Federal Republic				
Total exports:	7.4	100.0	36.8	100.0
to the present-day Soviet zone	2.7	36.5	0.8	2.3
to the other German territories	1.5	20.3	–	–
to foreign countries	3.2	43.2	36.0	97.7
Total imports:				
from the present-day Soviet zone	2.7	39.7	0.8	2.5
from the other German territories	1.4	20.6	–	–
from foreign countries	2.7	39.7	31.7	97.5

Source: Wilhelm Hankel, *Die Zweite Kapital Verteilung, ein marktwirtschaftlicher Weg langfristiger Finanzierung*, Frankfurt/M 1961, p. 24. Data originally from the following sources, according to the Berliner Bank: Bruno Gleitze, *Ostdeutsche Wirtschaft, industrielle Standorte und volkswirtschaftliche Kapazitäten des ungeteilten Deutschland* (Berlin 1956); *Statistisches Jahrbuch für die Bundesrepublik Deutschland 1958, Statisches Jahrbuch der Deutschen Demokratischen Republik 1957.*

Abbreviations: RM–Reichsmark; VE–Verechnungseinheit, i.e., a special exchange unit used in inter-German trade to indicate Mark equivalents.

policy, they created the German Federal Reserve system: at the Länder level there were the so-called *Landeszentralbanken*, headed by the Bank Deutscher Länder in Frankfurt. In 1957 this Frankfurt bank became the Deutsche Bundesbank–completely free from the federal government's direction. The Bank Deutscher Länder was competent for all questions of domestic and foreign monetary policy. On the other hand, the federal government in Bonn came into being only in the summer of 1949, after the Parliamentary Council (the constitutional assembly) had completed the Fundamental Law (the new West German constitution) early in 1949.

As a result, the new federal government was confronted with extensively distributed competences for economic, financial, and monetary policy. Thus monetary policy too was the concern of the Bank Deutscher Länder, which was influenced only by the Länder through their Landeszentralbanken, but not by the federal government. The federal government received only what had not yet been allotted, thus inter alia the representation of West Germany in the various international economic, monetary, and trade councils such as the Marshall Plan, OEEC, GATT, and the European Payment Union (EPU).

Liberalism or Mercantilism? The Self-Defeating Stabilization Policy

From the very beginning, two economic ideologies put their stamp on the new state, ideologies that had arisen from an understandable reaction to the horrors of the Hitler regime, which had been characterized by inflation and control. These ideologies were neoliberalism and a strong preference for a stable currency—symbolized by a reserve bank "autonomous" from all governmental direction.

These ideologies are to be found in the concept of Social Market Economy, whose political father was Ludwig Erhard, the first West German minister of economics. Erhard had already made a name for himself before the founding of the federal government, when in the summer of 1948 he—then director of the Allied-formed economic administration of the so-called Bi-Zone—brought about a currency reform and an end to food rationing. The concept of Social Market Economy was originated by the Freiburg professor, Walter Eucken, and was shaped into a political program by Professor Mueller-Armack, Erhard's advisor in economic questions. This concept distinguished sharply between economic *order* and economic *process.*[3] The state and its economic policy were competent solely and only for the shaping of the economic order, not for the economic process. Economic process would be left to the market forces, which would provide the society with the required investments, jobs, and daily goods—as unencumbered as possible by state interference. The sole condition that was to be created for this purpose was a price structure reflecting the natural scarcity of goods, as free as possible from influences of monopoly or inflation. An antitrust office (*Kartellamt*), provided with rigorous legal authority, and the federal reserve system, established for the struggle against inflation and therefore kept as free as possible from state influence, were established—as it were—as "fourth powers," neutral to the government, as the true guardians of Social Market Economy.

In accordance with this concept, Erhard renounced any formulation of economic-political goals, such as full employment, economic growth, balance of trade, and so forth—as this occurred in 1967 in the so-called Law for the Furthering of Stability and of Economic Growth. Erhard also forbade the management by any ex-ante macrostatistics, of a so-called national budget, because of the risks that a "planned economy" might influence the economic process. Such statistics might be used only internally (in the Finance Ministry for estimating taxes) and externally in international councils for reasons of international comparison, but it must not be published.

Examples of the application of Social Market Economy are the numerous state-owned utilities (*Staatsbetriebe*) and public banks. Appropriate to the difference between the "order" and the "process" part of the market, they had to comport themselves as "market-regulated" to cover costs and to manage earnings. The liberal state refused to install them as instruments of state economic policy. (The single exception to the rule was the state management of railways and postal service, which for reasons of regional and social policy might be—or had to be—eliminated under costs of production and whose deficits would be taken over by the government.)

In the foreign economic area Erhard was able to develop his economic liberalism most successfully. As early as the beginning of the 1950s he favored a liberalization of trade and a convertibility of the Deutsche mark, against the stubborn opposition inter alia of the Bank Deutscher Länder, which feared further increases in the West German balance-of-payments deficit.

This situation greatly explains what happened next: (1) the dependence on foreign trade caused by the division of Germany made foreign trade and foreign demand a decisive factor in the growth of the new economy; and (2) in a less liberal and above all inflationary environment, economic liberalism and the preference for currency stability that was closely connected with liberalism strengthened this trend.

From West Germany's liberalism came an extremely successful though very subtle mercantilism. This was not mercantilism in the primitive sense that the federal government promoted exports and restricted imports, which it neither wanted to do for ideological reasons nor was able to do for lack of administrative means. This mercantilism was developed quite simply in a "process-immanent" manner, because an increasingly larger part of West German production was absorbed abroad rather than at home, a process facilitated by West Germany's price and cost advantage. The country had no need to develop concepts of full employment, growth, or other economic-political goals. It received all that it needed through its markets, which were increasingly found abroad, without having to fear dependency or pressure for integration.

Reconstruction and Export-Led Growth

Reconstruction (1948-1952)

The German reconstruction miracle lasted from 1948 to 1952. In these four years the country succeeded in clearing up the greatest part of the war damage, reducing to a normal number the socially explosive surplus work force that was the result of an influx of over 12 million refugees into West Germany. Thus the maintenance level (*Versorgungsniveau*) of the population was raised so that a modest standard of living was again possible. The gross national product, which in 1950 had already reached 100 billion Deutsche marks, increased a good 10 percent yearly in this four-year period; the gross domestic investment increased about 17 percent, and exports increased by 25 percent. On the other hand, imports were increased "only" in proportion to volume of investments (17 percent), while because of the backlogged needs of a starved population, private savings fell off "moderately" to about one-tenth of the domestic investment of that time. Appreciably more was invested than saved and significantly more exported than imported, and thus a considerable Keynesian inflation gap opened up (no less than 75 billion Deutsche marks in the three-year period from 1950 to 1952). The cost and price levels, however, remained extremely stable, with the exception of the 1951 price increases connected with the Korea boom. (See Table 5-3.)

The explanation for this relative price stability during the reconstruction boom is the real-cost constellation. Enterprises that invested rapidly made significant gains in productivity because of a favorable conjuncture, which was based on an increasingly better utilization of their capacity. Because of the surplus labor force that continued to exist, the trade unions were more concerned with creating jobs than with increasing salaries. They accepted the fact that salary as a share of income had fallen from its 1950 high point of 65.5

Table 5-3
Factors in West German Economic Expansion
(In Billions of Deutschemarks)

	1	2	3	4	5	6	7
	Gross Investments	*Exports*	*Expansive Factors (1 + 2)*	*Private Savings*	*Imports*	*Contractive Factors (4 + 5)*	*Expansion "Gaps" (3 – 6)*
1950	21.9	11.9	33.8	2.0	13.1	15.1	18.7
1951	26.4	19.4	45.8	2.3	17.1	19.4	26.4
1952	31.5	23.1	54.6	4.3	19.7	24.0	30.6
1953	31.4	26.4	57.8	5.4	20.9	26.3	31.5
1954	36.3	31.8	68.1	6.6	26.0	33.1	35.0
1955	47.0	37.4	84.4	6.8	33.2	40.0	44.4
1956	49.3	44.7	94.0	6.9	38.1	45.0	49.0
1957	52.0	53.1	105.1	10.8	44.4	55.2	49.9
1958	53.1	55.6	108.7	12.5	46.8	59.3	49.4
1959	58.7	62.1	120.8	13.3	53.0	66.3	54.5

Source: Statistisches Bundesamt, Deutsche Bundesbank.

percent; this falling proportion of salaries in turn explains why imports of that time increased only to the degree technically needed (for the level of domestic investment) and no more—a "relative underconsumption" prevailed.

This was a constellation similar to what Keynes had described in his glorified retrospect on the nineteenth century and his ideal conditions for an upswing: the newly enriched enterprises expended their profits not to "dissipate" them but to reinvest them, and thus could get by without private savings. And private individuals were so pleased with what had been achieved that they did not long for still higher incomes. They could not save more, nor did they want to.[b]

Henry Wallich was certainly right when in the mid-1950s he wrote retrospectively that Erhard's Social Market Economy made possible "the restoration of life and viability to a country that seemed too 'kaputt' to rise again for many years."[4] But he forgot to raise this question: What would have happened if there had been an equilibrium between Germany's domestic and foreign activities as well as between financing of investments by the Germans themselves and by foreign borrowing? The process would certainly have been significantly less "mercantilist"—it would have proceeded with an orientation toward foreign trade—if from the outset the Bundesbank and federal government had pursued an expansive financial and monetary policy.

The "balance-of-payments miracle," the sudden change of a passive into an active balance of payments, certainly would have occurred much later. But West Germany would have planned the structure of its industry more for the satisfaction of domestic needs, like infrastructure or public investment, than for foreign economies. Furthermore, the overly high proportion of self-financing by German enterprises and the correspondingly low savings capacity of private individuals of those years likewise would have been rectified, since they are to be understood as the long-range effects of a socially unjust monetary reform like that of 1948. To attain the new Deutsche mark margin, all savings and money titles existing in old reichsmarks had to be devalued as much as 93.5 percent. On the other hand, the owners of real assets (investors and stockholders) were exempted, while in the so-called Deutsche mark Opening Balance Law (*DM-Eröffnungsbilanzgesetz*) they were given the option of which new Deutsche mark value they would apply to their old assets. The result of this overly

[b]Compare John Maynard Keynes, *The Economic Consequences of the Peace* (New York, 1920), pp. 18 ff.:

> The new rich of the nineteenth century were not brought up to large expenditures, and preferred the power which investment gave them to the pleasures of indiscriminate consumption. In fact, it was precisely the inequality of the distribution of wealth which made possible those fast accumulations of fixed wealth and of capital improvements which distinguished that age from all others. Herein lay, in fact, the main justification of the capitalistic system. If the rich had spent their new wealth on their own enjoyment, the world would long ago have found such a regime intolerable. But like the bees they saved and accumulated not less to the advantage of the whole community because they themselves held narrower ends in prospect.

rigorous cut in currency value, which burdened the savers but not the investors, was that all required currency was created as "debtor's" currency. It could just as well have been made available as "creditor's" currency by *pari passu* release of old, blocked savings.

This analysis has shown that the German reconstruction miracle was largely made possible by a "social dumping." It limited the absorption capacity of the domestic market and at the same time provided expanding German industries with a relative cost advantage on the world market, thereby placing these industries in a position to build up their exports. This development could have been prevented only by politico-economic countermeasures, but these were not enacted.[5]

The Balance-of-Payments Shift (Since 1952)

The German balance-of-payments miracle began in 1952. For seventy years, since 1890, the German balance of trade and balance of payments had been passive. Only twice was there an exception to this rule: in 1926 when the British miners struck, and in 1931 when controls were placed on imports. It was therefore difficult for anyone to believe in the stability of the miracle, although the old hypotheses of "nonviability" had been replaced as early as 1950. At that time the Kiel Institute for World Economy and four other West German research institutes stated that Germany would be "viable" if by the mid-1950s it had succeeded in bringing imports and exports (in 1950 prices) to \$3.5 billion to \$4 billion and industrial production to the level of 150 (1938-1939 equals 100). These "conditions" had already been fulfilled by the end of 1952 or beginning of 1953.[c] Despite this, in 1953 Otmar Emminger of the German Bundesbank still spoke of the "take-off help of the Korea boom," whereby he meant to say that the new surpluses produced by fortunate circumstances could not be permanent.[6]

[c]Compare *Lebensfähigkeit und Vollbeschäftigung* (see note 2 at the end of the chapter). Although the four research institutes (the Kiel Institute for World Economy, the German Institute for Economic Research in Berlin, the Rhine-Westphalian Institute in Essen, and the Bremer Committee for Economic Research) basically revised Baade's original concept, three years later they came only to the relatively optimistic conclusion concerning West Germany's ability to reattain full employment. Whatever the ability for foreign economic viability derived from, it still was portrayed in relatively black terms in 1950. The exports that it at that time considered necessary as a minimum standard on the scale of \$3.5-\$4 billion (thus one-tenth of that attained in the meantime) were only somewhat secure if one allowed the Germans to reconstruct heavy industry still under allied control. Although the export goals established by these institutes were practically reached a few months after publication, they nevertheless did not believe in its durability because: "Germany's export chances probably mainly lie in machine tools, power plant equipment and heavy machines. After a development period of several years, German exports can be increased in the degree envisaged only if they include heavy and light machines. . . . The assumption of the US/UK military governments that the export of steel products can be decreased from 32% before the war to 14% in the future, also is incompatible with the export volume of \$3.5 to \$4 billion" (p. 39 of the English edition).

Actually, however, from 1953 on exports and currency reserves grew constantly. West Germany realized the greatest part of its export and currency surpluses in Europe, in its trade with the countries of the European Payment Union (EPU). This was no accident. Indeed, for regional reasons German foreign trade had always had its European center of gravity, but the new factor was the European position of *surplus.* In 1957 West Germany, which in 1950-1951 had still been the chief debtor of the EPU, became its main creditor. Why? The EPU, which in 1950 had included and had institutionally consolidated the loose multilateral compensations-agreements of internal European transactions existing at that time, not only facilitated German exports to Europe. Above all it established a premium: The surplus countries of the EPU got back at first 50 percent (later up to 75 percent) of their surplus in convertible currencies (gold and the U.S. dollar).[7] The Bundesbank, as is customary in Europe, immediately and without any waiting period had purchased the claims (payable in EPU currencies) of "their" exporters; thereby it secured in conformity with the system a payment advantage for those exporters. An exporter would then receive money without any time lag, that is, without interim indebtedness and without loss of interest. This was completely in the "national" interest because the central bank used the convertible currency that the exporter had thus received.

The German credit and currency policy, strict at first only for balance of payments reasons, soon had a second motive. With the advance toward full employment, not only the forces of social dumping weakened; with time the excess of investment over savings had an inflationary effect on cost and prices. On the other hand, the Bundesbank increasingly opposed this despite the balance-of-payments surplus that had become clearer in the meantime. From the "social" there came "monetary dumping"; from the attitude of subtle mercantilism there came a recognizable mercantilism. Because of the policy of tight money and high interest rates—pursued in West Germany more forcefully than in the other EPU countries—more and more currency reserves flowed into the country, although they were no longer needed as urgently as before.

The mercantilist attitude also appeared in a new philosophy of capital export. From 1952 on, the German export economy increasingly felt the lack of a means for long-term export financing. Then a multitiered system of long-term export financing was established. At first the Bundesbank declared itself ready to guarantee to the banks of the German exporters a supplementary and cheaper line of refinancing for up to five years to be used for the purchase of export claims, if the banks agreed on a common quota for the ceiling. Thereupon these banks merged into the German Export-Credit Society (ECS), a permanent banking consortium for export financing.

The federal government permitted the Kreditanstalt für Wiederaufbau (KW)—previously active only in financing reconstruction and founded by means of the Marshall Plan—to finance long-term export business, partly parallel to and partly complementary to the ECS. If the ECS primarily financed the German exporters, the KW increasingly financed the foreign buyers of German goods. Finally, the system of the so-called Export Credit Insurance concentrated at HERMES, a private insurance society, began to operate under the mandate of the federal government, and was shaped to fit the needs of the banking industry. A framework of state guaranties was created and continuously expanded. The state guaranties relieved the export economy and banks from political as well as from economic risks.[8]

The new capital export philosophy was established with a formal antimercantilist argument: by guaranty of long-term financing, the balance-of-payments burden of those partners with deficits would be eased and the stream of foreign currencies into West Germany would be decreased, at least temporarily. In fact, the German export surplus was financed and consolidated. The firms could now grant long-term credit, which the banks refinanced through their two main institutions (ECS and KW), and the risk lay with the state and its HERMES.

This system of an almost one-sided export of capital determined by export requirements indirectly hindered direct investment abroad (which did not enjoy state encouragement). Only at the beginning of the sixties was there a breakthrough here—ultimately not from the effects of discussions about international aid for development, which saw in direct investment one of the most important motive forces for the proper development of these countries. German direct investment, in a manner analogous to its export requirements was likewise given guaranteed state protection out of special funds in the federal budget, which—not at the very beginning, but only later—was aimed especially at investments in developing countries.[d]

Nevertheless, in contrast to the HERMES ceiling that required export, this ceiling was not fully utilized for a long time. Until the end of the sixties, German export industry remained oriented toward export rather than domestic investment. Only the increasing uncertainty after the first SPD government took office (1969), with its program allegedly "inimical to the economy," brought about a change: investments were increasingly made abroad, in shares and local factoring, and, indeed, from the need for security against undesired reforms (codetermination, redistribution of capital).

The market-securing character of this growing German export of capital remains unanalyzed to the present day.

National Strength and Regional Integration

The year 1958 marked a new era in West Germany's foreign economic policy. Erhard put through the absolute and undivided worldwide convertibility of the

[d]The Budget Law of 1960 (Bundesdrucksache 1400) contains for the first time in its Paragraph 22 the authority to incorporate capital expenditures abroad, which had not arisen on the basis of exporters' demands.

Deutsche mark, against the long-standing opposition of the Bundesbank, which preferred a step-by-step approach. But he also focused again on the economic integration of Europe. Konrad Adenauer's integration model, which was wary of political union as "a streetcar named desire," had to be run without the motive force of monetary integration. The European Monetary Agreement (EMA), planned in 1955, replaced the EPU on 1 January 1958. It in no way guarded against European currency preferences (neither automatic stand-by credit, nor the connecting of European currencies through their own currency unit and consequently no European monetary standard).[9] The Treaty of Rome came into force together with the EMA and was supposed to bring about political union by means of a common market. In general, it had no provisions for monetary integration. Currency and currency policies were again, as in the era of the old gold standard, within the exclusive jurisdiction of national governments. Everything that had previously existed in the EPU for de jure or de facto currency integration ceased; Europe had to be integrated through a common tariff and agricultural policy, not via its currencies.

The victory of the "economic universalist" Erhard over the political "regionalist" Adenauer has left a lasting imprint on German foreign economic policy. Europe, which had formed the basis for the German surplus and reserve position, became through the liberal customs union a free-trade zone for West Germany's industrial surpluses. France had not only supported this policy in a remarkable misunderstanding of its own economic interests, but at base had first made it possible. De Gaulle followed Erhard's banner of convertibility, since in 1958 he strove wherever possible for a still stronger convertibility of the franc—in gold instead of "merely" in dollars. But he also promoted the project for a liberal customs union, since he had decided to request in exchange for this support "only" the price of a common agricultural policy favorable to French farmers. Despite the marathon of debates over European import liberalization, European customs, and European agricultural prices that occupied the foreground, the German-French Accord led to a "fair" compromise of the interests of both partners in the Common Market: Germany could market its industrial surplus, France its agricultural surpluses.

There was an important difference, however: for West Germany the European export surplus was a progressive subsidy because it drove German export industries into newer and newer technologies and economies of scale; for France the accumulation of an agricultural surplus was a retrogressive subsidy because it slowed the conversion from agricultural to industrial techniques and, moreover, preserved the country's anachronistic economic and productive structure. The foreground compromise of export interests in Europe between Germany and France increasingly allowed the contour of the political union desired by Adenauer to dissolve. The longer one waited, the less the desired spillover effect appeared.[10]

West Germany's indirect (and never officially intended) policy of export promotion experienced a kind of vindication in the political conjuncture of the recession years 1966-1967. The overly rigorous monetary restrictions of 1966 produced a temporary standstill in the forces of domestic expansion, above all in investments. The result was that exports grew stronger than before. The first mild postwar recession of the FRG, which because of its political shock effect drove Erhard's government from office and prepared the way for the Social Democrats under Willy Brandt, was in truth cured by means of a wide-open export valve and not by the pump-priming program condoned by Karl Schiller (one of Erhard's successors in the Ministry of Economics). While this created a surge of orders (*Auftragsstoss*) to the extent of about 12 billion Deutsche marks, far more than double that amount came in through the swelling export surpluses of 1967 alone. For the financing of the export surpluses, which were proportionately exorbitant for Germany, up to 40 percent of domestic savings were temporarily employed. As a side effect of the recession, the German capital market was opened outward and by means of its Euro-Deutsche mark loans it became the leading financial center in Europe, for which the World Bank temporarily financed up to 60 percent of its year's program.

The 1966-1967 recession glaringly revealed how successfully the FRG had already integrated itself worldwide. From then on, its ascent to the largest nation in world trade was only logical—a question of when, no longer whether.

The idea of European monetary integration and political union experienced a short-lived euphoria through the Commission's attempt (in 1969 and 1970) to push forward a plan for a European monetary union. The German attitude toward the Werner Plan was divided from the outset. The old struggle between the political regionalists and the economic universalists was also repeated among the leading figures of the new federal government, now headed by the SPD and no longer by the CDU. Brandt, like Adenauer, favored the regional political solution and at the Hague summit conference of December 1969 subscribed to the idea of a "European monetary personality." Erhard's successor, Schiller, and the Deutsche Bundesbank had endeavored from the very beginning to preserve the political sovereignty of national jurisdiction over currency as much as possible and as long as possible. The Werner Report, with its step-by-step plans and its fixed "success clauses" revealed the laborious compromise between political and economic reason.[11]

Actually, however, the project ultimately foundered not on the dispute over the "political" or "economic" position, but on the partners' diverging interests with regard to the common currency policy *toward the outside.* Indeed, all agreed that they would have to defend themselves against the 1969-1972 influx of "unwanted" dollars, but there was still much dispute over the question of *how* to do so. West Germany and the Benelux countries, with their preponderantly worldwide interests, favored minimization of the effects of isolation; they wanted neither discriminatory measures nor controls, but—as a less harmful method—the float. France and Italy, with their predominantly European interests and only qualified worldwide interests, favored stronger protection and opposed every pressure for upward revaluation of their currencies vis-à-vis the dollar; they argued for controls and against a European float.

The idea of following the tradition of the EPU with a European Currency Union and a common defense of the dollar and of establishing a political union via the currency union ultimately foundered on this opposition of foreign economic interests.

Bloc Leader or Prisoner?

Even before the outbreak of the oil crisis in the fall of 1973, the foundering of the European Currency Union led to a complete turnaround of the European front. In 1973 France and Italy, both of which had rejected the European float, went over to a policy of worldwide but isolated floats of their currencies, and thus slipped into the earlier role of Germany and the Netherlands. West Germany, which likewise would have floated most happily alone, unwillingly took over the leadership of an expanded Deutsche mark bloc consisting of the Benelux countries, Scandanavia, Austria, and Switzerland. This European Deutsche mark bloc ultimately represented a compromise of the West Germans with their worldwide export interests and the important and stability interests of their most important European partners, to whose interests West Germany could not again be completely indifferent. The German policy of stability, which from the beginning of the seventies could endure only in combination with political measures concerning rates of exchange (revaluation or floating), increasingly threatened to become a beggar-thy-neighbor policy of the most important trading partners in Europe. Each new German revaluation raised the cost of the trading partners' imports and domestic markets and set in motion an inflationary spiral that could no longer be arrested by national means. Consequently, it seemed obvious to enter a currency exchange union with the most important import partner, West Germany—with a strong Deutsche mark connection and variable dollar exchange rates. The European bend in the tunnel consequently represented less of a European rump currency union and more the true image of a "friendly" currency and trade compromise. Currency aspects are dominant for the weaker partners, trade aspects for the stronger German partner. Germany can evolve its "internal trade" in this currency zone at firm exchange rates but its worldwide foreign trade—as earlier—at fluctuating exchange rates. Instead, however, it clearly has more stable costs and prices than its most important competitors.

Most recently, the subtle mercantilist content is more visible here. As long as the rate of Deutsche mark revaluation remained clearly *under* the rate of world inflation, it maintained a relative stability advantage for the Germans. The policy of constant Deutsche mark revaluation in truth consolidated the German export position and in no way weakened it. German policy toward credit and money not only could, but *had to* be just as firm as that of the other Western industrial countries, so it would not endanger the German price and cost advantage. Thus there was concern that, through adept management of the Deutsche mark exchange rate, the adjustment inflation in Germany would be only slowed down, not eliminated. The rate of revaluation was so balanced that its inflationary effects abroad were compensated for by deflationary effects in German costs and prices. The numbers in Table 5-4 show that up to now these figures have risen: thus between the end of 1970 and the first quarter of 1975 the cost of the Deutsche mark vis-à-vis the dollar rose only about 33 percent; in the same period the world market price increased about 175 to 178 percent. The revaluation effect was sufficient to arrest German domestic inflation (cost of living) at around 23 percent; in the same period the German export price was raised almost 30 percent. Thus at a time when the world market price rose to about 175 to 178 percent, the foreign importer of German wares had to pay for his purchases in Deutsche marks only a 33-percent revaluation increase and 30 percent for inflation—about a third of the international price and cost increase!

Thus only a Deutsche mark revaluation of around 100 percent of its parity at the end of 1970 would have fully compensated for the world inflation factor and completely protected German price and cost development, but in return it would certainly have plunged a country dependent on its rate of exports into a serious structural crisis with definite, more or less temporary, 5-percent unemployment (as in 1975).

Conclusion: From Legitimate Export-Led Growth to Neomercantilism

In the rise of Germany to one of the strongest world trade and world currency nations, three different phases or concepts can be clearly distinguished in retrospect.

1. Between 1948 and 1955 the fear of "nonviability" dominated. It was a must for the young state and economy to survive. Export-led growth was the only chance to safeguard simultaneously internal full employment and to overcome once and for all the nightmare of the tremendous balance-of-payments deficits that were the unavoidable consequence of the import and investment needs of the first hard recovery years.

2. From the mid-1950s on when the German economy had reached external and internal equilibrium, the continuation of this policy took on another aspect. The strength of German balance of payments and German currency, which was manifested in export surpluses and an increasing rise in currency reserves, supported the demand for a *worldwide* and not merely European convertibility of the Deutsche mark. One consciously worked toward replacing the regional

Table 5-4
Deutschmark Revaluation, World and German Domestic Inflation Since 1971

	DM-Dollar Parity 1971 = 100	*World Market Price 1971 = 100*	*German Export Price 1971 = 100*	*German Cost of Living 1971 = 100*
1971	95.1	101.7	100.0	101.4
1972	92.1	117.3	103.3	107.7
1973	73.3	201.8	111.7	115.6
1974	72.5	295.2	130.7	123.0
1975 (first quarter)	67.2	275.1	131.3	125.1

Sources: Hamburgisches Weltwirtschaftsarchiv, Deutsche Budnesbank, Deutsches Institut für Wirtschaftsforschung Berlin.

Note: Measured at the end of the year, sometimes at the end of the quarter.

currency preference and currency integration of the EPU through a worldwide one: the EPU would become the EMA, which in fact would "de-Europeanize" the Deutsche mark by binding it more strongly to the dollar zone than to Europe.

The Treaty of Rome confirmed this trend with its lack of monetary provisions, excluding any monetary policy for Europe. Germany got the double advantage of a liberal customs union, which held open the European market for industrial exports and at the same time permitted Germany to pursue worldwide interests. Instead of a political union, the imperfect European customs union became for Germany a kind of takeoff ramp for its further high flying into the world economy.

3. The real price for this policy of foreign strength was the sacrifice to fulfill the internal infrastructural needs of the expanding German economy. Instead of building in the right proportion with the productive capacities, new roads, hospitals, schools and so on internally Germany exported real and financial resources with the result of alimentation of all these needs outside the country. Germany paid for its strong surplus position with a growing deficit of internal infrastructure, living below its real possibility.

4. This concept of an export growth heavily forced and accelerated by a vigorously strengthened anti-inflation policy that increased the competitiveness of the German export industry was creating a twin conflict: Internally the permanent export surpluses threatened the stability of the Deutsche mark; externally the Deutsche mark's attractiveness was destroying the framework of European integration as well as international monetary order, based on stable exchange rates and undisturbed balance-of-payments equilibria.

The European scale had been for a long time too small, so the renaissance of Europe through the European currency union was a failure. The partners' divergent interests appeared behind the dispute about the common outside policy of the union (controls or float). West Germany had grown beyond Europe and therefore could no longer cast a biased vote for Europe as did France, Italy, and (notwithstanding its domestic political difficulties) Great Britain.

Since in the early seventies Germany was becoming the biggest creditor nation among the Western nations, it was playing a dominant role among the members of the Club of Ten. In spring 1971 German authorities decided to stop the permanent influx of the then unwanted U.S. dollar; they changed the old policy of dollar reserve accumulation and financed a substantial part of the U.S. balance-of-payments deficit. They adopted a more monetaristic explanation of the alarming increase of the inflation rate. Not the "real" export surplus (creating an overdemand) but the "nominal" overhang of imported liquidity was the decisive factor to let the Deutsche mark float.

The German neomercantilism was stranded at two shores: internally by the rising conflict between growth and stability and externally by the nonacceptance of the rules of game for an international community.

5. Germany's strong position in foreign trade, balance of payments, and accumulation of reserves seems to stress this policy of completely pursuing aims and goals of national welfare: full employment by more exports than imports—i.e., at the expense of the balance-of-payments equilibria of other nations—and monetary stability by breaking established rules—i.e., at the expense of the functioning of the European and worldwide monetary system.

The German attitude of opting out of European integration and the Bretton Woods system in May 1971 induced a chain reaction: the United States deconvertibilized the dollar in August 1971, and the emergency repairing of the international monetary machinery (the Smithsonian Agreement in December 1971) lasted only fourteen months. In spring 1973 the whole system blew up, definitely for the time being.

6. What role was played by the most recent regrouping of balance-of-payments problems as a consequence of the 1973 oil shock? The arrival of a new major creditor (OPEC) on the world economic scene caused Europe's surplus position to be wiped out, while it brought definite improvements to the U.S. deficit position. That the financing of European deficits via the so-called Euromarkets has surprisingly functioned smoothly this far has less to do with floating than with the new creditors' investment habits and preferences. The creditors invested their current surpluses and previously held reserves in readily marketable securities, doing so preferably in a "stateless" international money and capital market. As long as this goes on, these markets will continue growing, and thus will be able to finance the deficit-induced requirements of the European partners. The perverse part of the situation is that OPEC and the poor developing countries that lack raw material resources equalize the balance-of-payments deficits of the wealthy industrial nations. This situation will come to an abrupt halt when the creditor status of the OPEC countries vis-à-vis the world

economy is liquidated, which is only a question of time and of the speed of their internal development process. When the petrodollars are called home, we can expect no automatic equilibrium between money withdrawals (deficits on the capital account of the principal investment countries) and the newly surplus-generating balances on the current account (of the major supplier countries to the OPEC states). What is more likely is that a recall of OPEC loans would cause the present creditors in the Euromarkets to call the loans they had made to their Eurodebtors, resulting in a cumulative contraction process of credit. The Euromarkets would stop growing, in fact shrink, and the equalizing of payments balances via free markets would grind to a stop, just as after 1929.

The inherent weakness of Euromarkets that are once again shrinking is thus a major argument for getting ready in proper time a system of intercountry balance-of-payments equalization, a new currency system of state-managed balance-of-payments equalization.[12]

7. Beyond this fragility of the Eurodollar market and the floating system, Germany's long-term position is weaker than it appears in the short term. Although it can reach back on reserves and so avoid harsh restrictions for balance-of-payments reasons, it must be aware of its foreign markets. To secure these markets, more real capital has to be made available, especially in the long term. Thus Germany cannot further reduce production for export because it would risk increasing crashes on its internal markets, which is why Germany's foreign strength is at the same time indicating its internal weakness. Whether Germany likes it or not, it is economically more integrated in the Western system than before—as an unavoidable consequence of a quarter of a century of export-led growth and a consequent neomercantilism. Therefore it has to be interested, more than other nations, in reestablishing a new system in Europe and worldwide.

Notes

1. Examples of this kind of analysis are: Henry Wallich, *Main Springs of the German Revival*, Yale: Yale Studies in Economics no. 5 (New Haven, Conn.: Yale University, 1955); Hans Besters, "Deutschland-Analyse," in *Economic Policy in Our Time* (Amsterdam: 1961), pp. 398 ff.; Hans R. Krämer, "Untersuchung über die deutsche Aussenwirtschaftspolitik, Aussenpolitische Perspektiven des westdeutschen Staates," in *Schriften des Forschungsinstituts der Deutschen Gesellschaft für Auswärtige Politik e. V.*, vol. 34 (Munich and Vienna: Oldenbourg Verlag, 1972), pp. 152 ff.

2. Fritz Baade's first, but unpublished, opinion on West Germany's viability was reworked and published three years later by the Arbeitsgemeinschaft Deutscher Wirtschaftswissenschaftlicher Forschungsinstitute [*Lebensfähigkeit und Vollbeschäftigung, ein Beitrag zur Frage des wirtschaftlichen Wiederaufbaus in Westdeutschland* (Bonn: 1950), foreword, p. i.

3. The two main works in which Eucken developed his programmatic concept were: *Die Grundlagen der Nationaloekonomie*, the first edition of which had already appeared in 1939, and the fifth edition (Bad Godesberg, 1947), which contains all essential elements. In addition, there appeared posthumously, after Eucken's death in 1952, his *Grundsätze der Wirtschaftspolitik* (the most recent edition, Tubingen and Zurich, 1968) in which the consequences of separation were exemplified by order and course of concrete examples of economic policy.

4. Henry Wallich, *Mainsprings of the German Revival*, p. 147.

5. The sociopolitical, most undesirable long-term effects of the Deutsche mark currency reform and of the advantages of valuing and of writing off all assets in the new DM currency to the investors (through the so-called Deutsche mark Opening Balance Law and the Paragraph 7 group of the German income tax laws) was first of all analyzed by Herbert Ehrenberg. Compare Herbert Ehrenberg, *Die ErhardSaga, Analyse einer Wirtschaftspolitik, die keine war* (Stuttgart, 1965) and *Zwischen Marx und Markt, Konturer einer infrastrüktur orientierten verteilungswirksamen Wirtschaftspolitik* (Frankfurt, 1973).

6. Compare Otmar Emminger, "Deutschlands Stellung in der Weltwirtschaft," *Kieler Vorträge*, N.F., Heft 4, 1953, pp. 1 and 7.

7. Compare Hans Karl von Mangoldt, "Die Europäische Zahlungsunion und ihre Aufgaben bei der Neuordnung des internationalen Zahlungsverkehrs," *Kieler Vorträge*, N.F., Heft 3, 1953, pp. 15 ff.

8. Compare Wilhelm Hankel, *Die Zweite Kapitalverteilung, Ein marktwirtschaftlicher Weg langfristiger Finanzierungspolitik* (Frankfurt am Main, 1961), pp. 110 ff; further, Alfred Lukac, "Die eingleisige Exportfinanzierung," in *Der Volkswirt*, no. 26, 1957, pp. 1307 ff., which above all very instructively has worked out the historical connections for the origin of the West German system of export finance.

9. Compare Günther Schleiminger, "Das Europäische Währungsabkommen von 1955 und einige neuere währungspolitische Entwicklungen," *Kieler Vorträge*, N.F., Heft 9, 1953, pp. 10 ff.

10. Compare Wilhelm Hankel, "European Monetary Union–Dead or Still Alive?" (lecture held in the Center for European Studies of Harvard University, Cambridge, Mass., April 1975, mimeographed), where these connections are drawn from in particular.

11. Compare Rudolf Morawitz, "Perspektiven der Verflectung im Rahmen der Wirtschafts- und Währungsunion," in *Regionale Verflechtung der Bundesrepublik Deutschland, Schriften des Forschungsinstituts der Deutschen Gesellschaft für Auswärtige Politik e. V.*, vol. 33, Munich and Vienna, 1973, pp. 94 ff.

12. For more details, see Wilhelm Hankel, "The Taming of the Petro-Dollars," expert report prepared for the German Marshall Plan Fund of the United States, Washington, D.C., 1975.

6 Italy

Marcello de Cecco

Among the countries that now compose the EEC, Italy is without doubt the one that has experienced the most profound economic transformation in the course of the postwar decades. On the eve of the Second World War, Italy had completed an important stage in its industrialization process, with the establishment of large-scale basic industry in the north. Industrialization, however, had not been extended to the center and south of the country, except for sporadic, isolated instances. The industrial matrix, moreover, was by no means complete enough to be comparable to that of the other industrial countries of Europe, and the largest part of the Italian population had not been exposed to the industrialization process. Agriculture still provided the largest source of employment, and urbanization had begun but remained an altogether unimportant phenomenon. The world crisis and Fascist enmity toward urban workers had favored the persistence of the agrarian structure. In 1951 44 percent of total employment was in agriculture, and only 23 percent in manufacturing industry. In actual figures, this meant 8.5 million workers in agriculture and 4.5 million in manufacturing, while 1 million workers were employed in the construction industry. By 1961 the figures had changed considerably. Agriculture now provided only 30 percent of total jobs; the manufacturing industry provided 27 percent; and construction, 9 percent. By 1971 agriculture had fallen to providing only 19 percent of jobs, while the manufacturing industry had 31 percent of the workers and construction had 10 percent.

Today Italy has, both in actual figures and percentagewise, more industrial workers than France, and percentagewise almost as many as Germany and the U.K. It still has many more people in agriculture than any of its EEC partners, both in actual figures and percentagewise. And both in agriculture and in industry the product per capita of Italian workers is much lower than that of French or German workers, although some improvement has been achieved over the situation of the immediate postwar period, especially in the two decades ending in 1970. (See Table 6-1.) Urban population has also increased very rapidly over the same period, although this rapid urbanization has created a host of problems more typical of nineteenth-century Europe or of Third World urbanization processes than of the contemporary industrial metropolis. The last three decades have, overall, seen a profound improvement in the dietary, sanitary, and general welfare condition of the Italian population. In 1951, 61 people per 100,000 inhabitants died of infectious diseases. In 1974 this number had fallen to 11 per 100,000. Reported cases of typhoid and typhus fell, over

Table 6-1
Major Indicators of Italian Economic Growth, 1951-1971
(milliard lire, constant prices)

	1951	*1971*	*1971 Index (1951 = 100)*
Gross national product (market prices)	15,816	45,094	285.1
Gross national product per head (thousands of lire)	336.5	836.6	250.9
Exports (market prices)	1012	11,455	1131.5
Gross investment (market prices)	2649	8721	329.2
Value added at factor cost:			
agriculture	2892	4581	158.4
industry (including construction)	4146	16,168	390.0
manufacturing	2952	12,145	411.4
Value added per labor unit (thousands of lire)			
agriculture	433.2	1461.4	337.4
industry (including construction)	942.7	2077.0	220.3
manufacturing	709.2	2098.6	295.9

Source: Adapted from K.J. Allen and A.A. Stevenson, *An Introduction to the Italian Economy* (London: Martin Robertson, 1975). Data originally from ISTAT *Annuario di Contabilità Nazionale 1971* (Rome, 1972); ISTAT *Occupati Presenti in Italia 1951-1970* (Rome, 1971); ISTAT *Annuario Statistico Italiano 1972* (Rome, 1973).

the same period, from 69 per 100,000 inhabitants to 13 per 100,000. Malaria, diphtheria, and peurperal fever, which still occurred frequently in 1951, had virtually disappeared by 1974. Beef consumption per head rose, in the same period, from 5.3 kilograms per annum to 24 kilograms per annum; pork consumption rose from 3.4 kilograms to 14.6 kilograms; and consumption of other meats from 5 to 23 kilograms per annum. Beef consumption per head is now higher in Italy than in any other Common Market country. The Italian citizen now consumes the equivalent of 3110 calories and 98 grams of protein per day, compared to 3121 and 90 for the U.K., 3232 and 88 for Germany, and 3315 and 104 for the U.S.[1]

It is, however, extremely important to note one feature of the Italian economy that looms larger than any other in characterizing it and in differentiating it from other Western European economies. This is the difference that exists between the north and the south of the country, a difference that has existed for several centuries and that rapid postwar economic growth has, if anything, accentuated rather than reduced. The difference between the northern and the southern economic structures is so deep-seated that one could easily imagine that the two parts of the country constitute two separate economies (as they once did, until 1860). By and large, the north—and to a certain extent, the center—of Italy, can be assimilated to French or German regions, as far as economic structure is concerned. Industry prevails over other activities, agriculture is modern, high-yielding, mechanized, and export-oriented. Incomes are near the European average.

As one proceeds south, and certainly below Rome and Ancona, things change more and more markedly. Agriculture remains the most important source of employment, and it is still in many cases subsistence agriculture. Industry provides very few jobs, and the number of women in industry is almost insignificant. Incomes are much lower than in the upper part of the country. All the socioeconomic indicators one may choose, from sanitary conditions to infant mortality, car ownership, housing standards, meat consumption, and book and newspaper readership, drop dramatically as one goes south. Industry and agriculture are much less export-oriented than in northern Italy.

The gulf that divides Italy into two so different halves has remained as deep as ever, in spite of an avalanche of public money that has flowed into the south since the war, as a result of special government programs aimed at fostering the growth of the southern economy.

Without exaggeration, it can be said that the negative results that this powerful and protracted effort has had so far can be explained in much the same way the theoreticians of "dependencia" explain the permanence of underdevelopment in Latin America. The money that has poured into the south has contributed mainly to feeding a corrupt political class or to subsidizing, one way or another, the capital needs of Italian heavy industry, and of northern industry in general. Industrial plants that have been established in the south are almost invariably capital intensive, and they make very scant use of local labor, and of labor in general. They produce steel or basic chemicals, or refine crude oil. The only sizable attempt to introduce large-scale, relatively labor-intensive industry in the south remains is the Alfa Romeo automobile factory, located near Naples—a factory fraught with mismanagement, poor labor relations, and political corruption. Efforts to foster the emergence of small-scale enterprise in the south have failed miserably. In addition, the opening of the southern market to northern competition in light industry, especially because of radically improved transport and communications, has meant the virtual destruction of what local small-scale industry did exist in the south.

Paradoxically, as the postwar period has witnessed the influx of very large investment funds into the south, there has been an outflow of almost 10 million people from the same area, toward northern and central Italy and to other countries of Western Europe. Also paradoxically, the inflow of funds was nothing but the return home, after government intermediation, of southern bank savings. It has always been normal, in fact, for banks all over Europe to take rural area deposits and lend them in industrialized areas.

The pattern of economic relations that exists between southern and northern Italy is therefore quite similar to the one that links Germany and France to the countries of the Mediterranean. Like Greece, Portugal, or Turkey, southern Italy exports to northern Italy labor, Mediterranean agricultural products and bank deposits; it imports from northern Italy all sorts of manufactures. There is, however, a difference, which is represented by the fact that now southern Italy also exports to northern Italy basic industrial products, like steel and chemicals. This, however, also seems to be the future trend in relations between Western Europe and the Mediterranean if peace is preserved in the area and the logic of the international division of labor continues to prevail. Basic industrial production, which is land- and energy-intensive and ecologically unacceptable in crowded Western Europe, seems destined to emigrate to the Mediterranean countries and to the Middle East. In southern Italy we see a preview of the Mediterranean's future.

There is one more difference. The migrants from southern Italy are Italian citizens, with equal rights vis-à-vis the citizens of the Italian regions where they migrate. The continuous inflow of southern immigrants has therefore resulted in the short-term disruption of social services in the center-north, and a long-term profound transformation of the northern Italian population. The lack of local employment in the south has traditionally meant that government jobs from the most important to the most menial predominantly went to southerners; this trend was dramatically reinforced in the last decades, as southern agriculture expelled more and more people who tried to find jobs in the tertiary sector and in manufacturing. As birth rates remain higher in the south compared to the central or northern areas, the phenomenon seems bound to persist in the future.

We have dealt at some length with the problems accruing to the Italian economy from its dualistic nature for one important reason: it must be appreciated that since the war, the Italian economy has experienced two concomitant integrative processes, one internal and the other international. The international one is by far the best known and the most discussed, but the internal one is just as important. The unification of the Italian market has really happened only since the war, especially after the drastic improvement of the roads network and the establishment of a national television network that did much to standardize consumption and expectation patterns.

This has been immensely important especially for Italian light industry, which historically has been even more concentrated in the north than heavy industry. If one realizes that most of the south is as far from the Po Valley (where most industry is located even now) as most German, Belgian, Dutch, Swiss, and French cities, it is much easier to understand the revolutionary impact of the improvement in communications. The booms in domestic demand and in export demand resulting from these integrative processes coincided from 1958 to 1963. Previously Italian industry had relied on domestic demand. Historically it had grown behind high tariffs and had developed following a marked oligopolistic pattern, an almost textbook case of *finanz-Kapital* and state subsidization.

The novelty of postwar growth between 1955 and 1965 was the emergence of myriad small enterprises that manufactured light industrial products, which have previously lacked a sufficient internal market, and which came to utilize the cheap home-made steel produced by the integrated steel industry established by state-owned enterprises after the war and the cheap energy that came from the Po Valley gas fields exploited after the war by the government-owned oil industry.

This was a revolutionary phase for Italian industry. The old balance was broken and the oligopolistic equilibrium was deeply shaken. Small-scale enterprises were very labor-intensive, unlike the traditional oligopolies. They began to compete for labor, and they soon pushed up the wage rate and induced the reinforcement of trade unions. It must be noted that Italian industry had never experienced rapid and considerable wage increases, so the effect of the wage increase was shattering. They also relied almost exclusively on internal financing. Moreover, Italian financial institutions had been used to finance only large-scale industry, which almost always runs little or no risk of failure. When labor gradually became less cheap and foreign competition began to bite as a result of trade liberalization so that external financing would have been required, Italian financial institutions were unable and unwilling to step in. As a result, the investment rate, which in the boom years between 1958 and 1963 had been perhaps the highest in Europe, slumped dramatically, never to regain its previous heights. Subsequently, investment has been the business, again as in the old pattern, of large-scale industry and the government. The investment rate has been much lower than the Western European average for the whole decade from 1965 to 1975. Small-scale industry, however, has managed to survive mainly by economizing on labor, by adopting foreign patents and licenses rather than developing its own products, by cheating on taxes and social security contributions, and by resorting to a larger and larger extent to forms of co-ownership, which involves the workers directly in the risk of production, as they themselves own the machines they use and thus are their own masters. Of course, survival has meant retrenchment to the production sectors that require little investment, i.e., the sectors that produce labor-intensive light industrial goods, where technology levels are quite low.

These developments occurred at the same time when all sorts of social security legislation was passed that put Italy on the forefront of social protection. It is quite difficult to explain this schizophrenic behavior. What is certain is that it has produced a new form of dualism. On one side there are large-scale firms, where working conditions are among the best in Europe. Unfortunately, they do not employ more than one-third of the total industrial workers. On the other side are small-scale enterprises, which flout social legislation almost completely, so that the working conditions they offer to their workers resemble more those of the industrializing Third World than those of Western Europe. Between one-half and two-thirds of Italian workers belong to the second category.

One more feature of postwar industrial development in Italy is the polarization of firm and plant sizes. Medium-sized plants and firms are very few and far between, and their number has diminished since 1963. The Italian industrial landscape is now composed of a few giants and myriad midgets.

A further element that must be noted is the increasing importance of state-owned industry, particularly since 1963.[2] This is the consequence of two factors, the rising importance of government investment in industry since 1963 and the growing need to salvage an ever-increasing number of private enterprises that were going bankrupt and would have left tens of thousands of workers unemployed, in a context where industry's demand for labor has been eminently static. The recourse to takeover by government-sponsored financial holdings has become more and more fashionable as an instrument of short-term social stabilization. It is, of course, a very expensive system, but it has the advantage of involving little direct political choice. The political class prefers it exactly for this reason, and it must be added that the businessmen involved have fared at least as well as their workers in the system, at the taxpayers' expense.

Even the taxpayer, however, has been superficially little bothered. This is especially because the very large percentage of self-employed workers (40 percent, much higher than in the rest of Europe) makes tax evasion relatively easy.

Relative fiscal leniency has thus meant that the gap between revenue and expenditure has begun to yawn wider and wider. The percentage of government expenditure over GNP is no higher than in the rest of Europe, while the percentage of government revenue over GNP is much lower than in the rest of Europe. The ever-increasing gap has been filled by recourse to public debt, in all its forms, from long-term issues to treasury bills to straight money creation for the treasury's account. This has been another form of social stabilization. Personal savings in Italy are the highest in the world, and a very large proportion of them are kept as bank deposits or straight currency hoards. The only financial intermediaries that exist are banks, which pay very high interest rates on current account deposits. The government, confronted with ever-growing financial needs, has decided to compel banks to keep a fixed percentage of their assets in the form of public debt. In this fashion, the Italian political class has managed to reexpropriate the money it has given the Italian wage and salary earners. However, a complete neutralization of money created was not possible. The result was therefore a very high inflation rate, and the long-term disruption of economic life.

The Politics of Economic Policy-Making

It must be noted, however, that no Italian governments have, since 1963, been able to rely on a popular consensus strong and unqualified enough to permit a policy of stern restructuring of state finances, an industrial policy based on a strategy of gradual uplifting of the technological level of Italian industry, and a policy of increasing the efficiency of the service sector. In fact, the logic of political alliances that has presided over the succession of center-left governments since 1963 has demanded that objectives quite opposite to those just stated be pursued. As neither left- nor right-wing alternatives were feasible because of the untouchability of frank conservatism (a result of the disastrous end of Fascism) and the permanent exclusion of the Communist party imposed by the international situation, a number of center-left parties have enjoyed an oligopoly of power, forever assembling and dissembling coalitions where the distribution of power was effected on the strength of electoral results. This has induced a luring of electors by straight patronage and by successive concessions of privileges to various social categories and pressure groups with the aim of gaining (or not losing) very small percentages of the electorate.

Until 1974 electoral swings among the coalition parties were measured in fractions of percentage points. A resounding electoral victory or defeat involved two to three percentage points. In this static electoral context, such minuscule swings involved very large effects in terms of relative power and the number of cabinet posts each coalition party could demand. Hence the absolute unfeasibility of electoral platforms involving reforms, sacrifices, sweeping change: big gains, or losses, were not the stakes. Hence the absolute sectoralization of economic and social policy, the absence of autonomous foreign policy, the need to woo very small fractions of the electorate. Appropriate comparisons can be made with France or, even better, with Japan. In those two countries, the sizable left wing of the electorate has also been secluded, and the government parties have had no fears of losing elections. But the nonexistence of coalitions in Japan, and the Gaullist constitutional reform in France, have allowed the government party to go for big game in economic policy, to plan ambitious industrial strategies, to restrain consumption when it was necessary, and to be able to run autonomous foreign policies.

A comparison of these three countries brings out in crude relief the differences that exist between a monopoly and an oligopoly of power. And the importance of this distinction persists in the light of the fact that within the Italian government coalitions, the Christian Democratic Party has been by far the senior partner. As long as it remained in a situation of virtual monopoly (the Center Coalitions of the fifties) the Christian Democrats managed to administer and govern. When in 1963 they associated a large junior partner, the PSI, they became incapable of strategic planning and were confined to tactical maneuvering. Unfortunately, this coincided with an increasing need for strategy expressed by the Italian economy, as the latter was just beginning to feel the challenges and the strains of internal and international integration, the end of easy profit accumulation, the exhaustion of the first phase of postwar growth. It is indeed ironic to note that the socialists were associated to the power oligopoly because a part of the political and economic ruling elite thought a wider consensus was needed to meet exactly the challenges just mentioned. It is quite probable that the transformation of the power monopoly into an oligopoly took place in spite of the Christian Democrats' better advice, and after the aborted attempt at a Gaullist solution in 1960; it was virtually dictated by large-scale industry (both private and public) that had been disturbed by the wage explosion and that thought a policy of reforms paid by government money would have stemmed the tide of rising wages and reduced direct labor costs. No small amount of help was given in hatching the first center-left coalition by President Kennedy's and Pope John's benevolent attitude toward the Socialists.

As soon as the center-left coalition was formed, the Christian Democrats understood that to realize the reform program would have meant losing a considerable part of their votes to the Socialists, who appeared as the prophets of reform. It would have also meant losing part of their right-wing electorate, who would be hurt by reforms, to the Liberal Party and to even more conservative neo-Fascists and monarchists. In fact, just as much happened in the 1963 general elections. Once all this was absorbed by the Christian Democratic Party, the politics of statics was inaugurated, whose outcome has been the virtual stagnation of the Italian economy and in particular of Italian industry—stagnation only superficially hidden by the policy of redistribution effected mainly through the transformation of government expenditure into a mechanism of transfers from the government to private individuals and firms. In the Sea of Sargassus of Italian economic policy, since 1963 there has been place only for favors to particular groups, and all sense of direction has been lost. Being able to monopolize savings through the banking system, the government could satisfy everyone for about ten years, even allowing those who understood what this policy meant to export their savings to earn high interest rates abroad. Had U.S. inflation and the rise in raw material prices not intervened, the day of reckoning for the Italian economy would have been deferred by several more years. The government had in fact achieved a workable modus vivendi with the most irksome problems, mainly by permanently deflating investment, redirecting supply to the export market, and transferring income to consumers.

The rise of the U.S. inflation rate at the close of the sixties, the jump in interest rates that resulted from the American choice of a monetary policy that did not curb the money supply, abruptly awakened the Italian economy from its slump-flationary slumber. For almost a century, Italian authorities had been used to relying on a level of interest rates structurally higher in their country than abroad. In 1969 this changed radically, and the outflow of money from Italy turned into a flood. It became impossible to continue with stagflation at low cost. Deeper stagnation had to be combined with higher inflation. Labor costs were also thrown permanently out of equilibrium. And there was even less space for investment.

At the same time the capital account of the balance of payments—which in

Italy even more than elsewhere lives a life of its own detached from the current account—acquired an alarmingly large permanent deficit, which overflowed the borders of the previous stagflation equilibrium. On top of everything came the U.S. decisions of August 15, 1971. I shall say more later about their consequences for the Italian economy and for Italian economic policy.

Main Themes of Italian Foreign Economic Policy

Since the end of the Second World War the Italian political class, government and opposition, and economic leaders (large farmers and industrialists, trade unionists, financiers) have firmly and repeatedly expressed their preference for free trade and for the integration of Italy in a community of European nations. The opponents of these two fundamental choices have been few and remarkably uninfluential. Dissenting voices were heard at times on the left and extreme right, and even among certain anticapitalist Christian Democratic groups. But the widest possible consensus was reached very early in the postwar period on policies aimed at realizing the liberalization of internal and international trade. Such quasi-unanimity must be interpreted as a reaction to ten years of Fascist dirigism and corporatism, and to wartime economic controls. All these forms of economic organization were associated with the least popular phase of the Fascist regime and with the disastrous war it fought, which culminated in the first foreign invasion of the national territory since the unification of Italy.

Still it is remarkable how little effort the foreign paladins of free trade had to make in the immediate aftermath of the war to convince the Italian political class of the advantages of a liberal policy. While in France and the United Kingdom they met with organized resistance, double play, and deferment politics, in Italy they walked through open doors. In fact, it was in Italy that the Marshall Plan administrators had a memorable quarrel with the Italian economic authorities, and accused them of delaying the reconstruction of the country by their preference for balanced budgets, monetary reconstruction, balance-of-payments equilibrium, reserves accumulation, and other pre-Keynesian objectives. Interestingly enough, the Italian authorities prevailed on the U.S. local representatives, having secured the backing of the U.S. government and of top Marshall Fund administrators.[3]

At the very beginning of the fifties, Italy embarked on a very deliberate policy of trade liberalization. It was still at the time, at least on paper, the most *dirigiste* country in Europe. Most of the Fascist laws through which the corporate economy had been instituted were still in force. The government sector included already the greatest part of heavy industry and almost all banking, and the Banking Law of 1936 could be effectively used to silently plan the country's economic life.

Italy was also the most heavily protected economy in Europe. As said above, further protection was provided by the concentration of its industrial sector. Lastly, the level of wages was so low compared to those prevailing in the other European countries that Italian industry had little to fear from foreign competition. This was said very clearly by top Italian industrialists, especially by Fiat's Vittorio Valletta. Valletta even ventured to predict, in a parliamentary hearing as early as 1946, that Italian automobile exports would have a brilliant future; he affirmed that he did not fear European competition in small cars and had reached an understanding, long before the war, with the U.S. car producers on a policy of noninterference in their respective national markets.

Thus as early as 1947 the lira was stabilized by the drastic credit squeeze engineered by Luigi Einaudi, who firmly believed Italian industry, overprotected and overextended, had to be pruned severely by a dose of monetary restraint that would allow only the strongest to survive and face international competition. After a little adjustment of only 8 percent in 1949, following sterling devaluation, the lira-dollar rate remained untouched until the Smithsonian Agreement of December 1971, a prime witness of the Italians' belief in the Bretton Woods system.

By 1952, 70 percent of Italian imports were free from quantitative restrictions, compared to 4 percent in 1946. And Italy, according to the EPU in 1956, easily came out on top of other European countries in imports liberalization. Virtually all trade was by then free of quantitative restrictions.

These tough liberalization policies, inspired by the frank belief in economic liberalism, were accompanied by the country's early and disciplined association with the IMF and GATT. Italy was in fact one of the main prophets of what came to be known as "the IMF philosophy," based on reserves accumulation, balanced budgets, and a preference for a monetary policy with short-term stabilization purposes.

It was, however, in the process of European economic integration that the faith of the Italian economic authorities in economic liberalism shone most brightly. Already by 1952, the average tariff rate had come down to 6.5 percent from the 13.8 percent of 1938. But after the enthusiastic agreement given to the EEC, the Italian authorities proceeded fast in the demolition of trade barriers and effectively completed it in the early years of the Common Market.[4]

To keep the country on the liberalistic course, the Italian authorities had to repeatedly administer severe doses of credit deflation, in 1952-53, in 1958, and in 1963. This frequent recourse to deflation did achieve, until the middle sixties, the purposes intended by the Italian authorities: the logic of the cold war had very early convinced them of the need to reconvert the Italian economy in a way that would allow it to fend for itself in the Western markets. It must be remembered that Italian industry had until then considered the eastern and southeastern European markets as its "natural" markets. When international political developments closed them to Italian trade, Italian economic leaders understood that they had to find an *ubi consistam* for Italian exports in the most competitive markets of the world, those of Western Europe and the United States. That they succeeded in finding it, is clearly shown by Table 6-2. In this new international division of labor, Italy was able to increase its share of total trade, but at the cost of (1) not absorbing all its effectively and potentially available labor supply and (2) specializing in the production and export of light industrial products, thus crystallizing its labor force into a low productivity, low-income-per-head area.[a]

With the inception of the EEC, a further toll had to be paid: the Common Agricultural Policy (CAP) the EEC finally agreed on was naturally enough designed to promote northern European agriculture.[5] As a result, it effectively projected the northern part of Italian agriculture, which benefited from it, and the large cereal producers of southern Italy. But it did nothing for central and southern Italian agriculture based on Mediterranean products. The complement of the CAP, the Mansholt Plan, with its emphasis on reorganization of land tenure toward larger farms, gave Italian absentee landowners legal permission to evict their peasants. While the big spurt in Italian industrialization was taking place, the "liberated" peasants could find jobs in industry.

Table 6-2
Geographic Distribution of Italian Exports, 1951-1974

	1951	*1954*	*1958*	*1962*	*1965*	*1968*	*1970*	*1974*
Western Europe, *of which:*	54.5	54.9	52.7	61.2	65.3	62.7	63.7	64.4
EEC	–	–	24.0	33.7	40.2	40.1	42.9	45.4
West Germany	7.7	11.3	14.3	18.2	21.2	18.7	21.6	18.5
France	9.0	5.9	5.3	9.2	10.3	12.6	12.9	12.6
Belgium-Luxembourg	2.4	2.4	2.3	2.9	4.0	4.2	3.8	3.7
Netherlands	2.0	2.2	2.1	3.4	4.7	4.6	4.7	4.5
U.K.	13.5	7.9	6.8	6.0	4.7	4.4	3.8	5.2
Switzerland	5.6	7.2	7.0	7.1	5.4	4.5	4.7	4.2
Eastern Europe	4.0	3.5	3.5	5.2	4.6	5.4	5.4	5.5
U.S.A.	6.9	7.9	9.7	9.5	8.6	10.7	10.2	7.7
Canada and Japan	0.9	1.5	1.5	1.5	1.5	1.7	1.9	2.2
Middle East	(n.a.)	7.1	7.0	5.5	5.9	5.8	2.9	4.4
Latin America	(n.a.)	9.6	10.7	6.6	4.4	4.4	4.2	4.0
Other	(n.a.)	22.6	15.9	8.5	9.7	9.3	11.7	
Total		100.0	100.0	100.0	100.0	100.0	100.0	

Source: United Nations, *Commodity Trade Statistics. Series D* (New York, various issues).

[a]Even the Communist Party wholeheartedly agreed to Italy's role in the new international division of labor. As early as 1944 and 1945, Palmiro Togliatti repeatedly affirmed in his speeches that protectionism and autarky had to be abolished and that several of the most protected industrial sectors would have to be sacrificed in the name of the expansion of light industrial exports. See L. Barca (ed.), *I comunisti e l'economia* (Bari: De Donato, 1975).

By the middle sixties, however, the great industrial leap had occurred and job creation in industry ceased almost completely as the cold winds of competition began to blow on Italian industry. But the flow of people from the countryside to the cities continued unabated and even increased, as the logic of Sicco Mansholt's Plan worked itself through Italian agriculture. The labor that industry was no longer able to absorb had to be employed in makeshift, ill-planned jobs in the tertiary sector, which the government rushed to create, helped by the Reform Programme of the center-left coalition. This program tried to alleviate the inadequacy of Italian services, but it only yielded a services structure aimed at creating jobs much more than at efficiency. The workers who were not absorbed by the tertiary sector were induced to emigrate to the Western European countries. As not even this was enough to provide a politically acceptable level of employment, the school-leaving age was dramatically increased, and young people were further kept away from the labor market by the opening of thousands of new high schools and by the freeing of university education to all holders of a high school diploma. Today Italy has as many university students as Germany and a commensurate number of people in primary and secondary schools. Further measures to reduce the number of job seekers were introduced, by lowering the retirement age and by a generous disability pensions policy.[6]

None of these measures was particularly different from those implemented in the rest of Europe. They must be seen as a rapid catching up, on the part of Italy, with European social standards. The trouble is that they coincided with the end of the "easy" phase of Italian industrialization, so that they were used mainly to quickly relieve the labor market, overcrowded because of the fast decline of Italian traditional culture.

To complicate the picture even further, there was the Italian authorities' enthusiastic adherence to the principles of liberalism for what concerned outward and inward capital movements. This came as a necessary complement to their reliance on monetary policy for short-term stabilization purposes, in a world where the Eurodollar market was assuming its monster size and where interest rates were gradually lifted up by U.S. inflation.

As early as 1963 it had become clear that the use of monetary policy in the new international financial context implied capital shifts that compelled the Italian authorities to sacrifice either the rate of industrial expansion and the growth of domestic demand or balance-of-payments equilibrium. They might have come out of this vice by letting the lira float. But a downward float to reflate the economy would have enraged the Americans, who were then, as we may recall, altogether wed to fixed rates. Also, an upward float would have gained for the authorities the enmity of Italian exporters, who were then experiencing the full thrust of international competition. In addition, the Italian authorities knew that a floating rate would be extremely dangerous as it would reinforce the speculative habits of Italian industrialists, who have always shown a strong inclination to build up large stocks of raw materials.

Thus the Italian authorities were confined to greater reliance on monetary policy, whose asymmetrical impact, favoring large and penalizing small firms, favoring static and penalizing dynamic, entrepreneurs, could not fail to exert a strong negative influence on the structure of the Italian economy. It is interesting to note, however, that this policy has until quite recently gained the Italian authorities the applause of the international bodies—like the IMF, the OECD, the EEC Commission, and the B.I.S.—which preside over the working of the Western economy. They were even strongly advised, very often, to adopt those measures, and they could use such foreign admonitions to convince the Italian public of their inevitability. A little game could also be played, from time to time, by setting the U.S. against Italy's European partners to alleviate somewhat the monetary squeezes the deflation-inclined Europeans recommended. This was done in 1964 and again in 1974.

Between 1963 and 1969, the Italian authorities managed the socioeconomic stalemate into which their country had worked itself quite successfully. They oriented Italian industry toward foreign markets and thus balanced the imports account, which had been dramatically increased by the crisis of Italian agriculture, incapable of producing all the food Italians now required, and by the high import content of Italian industrial production. Exports were also enough to pay for the capital outflow engendered by the integration of financial markets, by the inability of Italian financial institutions to provide the assets that the new entrepreneurial class demanded to realize its profits, and particularly by the enormous weight of new public debt issued to finance the Reform Programme (necessary, as said above, to provide the jobs destroyed in agriculture and which industry, struggling with its structural crisis and pressed by international competition, could not provide).

By this policy, which lasted as long as foreign interest rates remained structurally lower than their Italian equivalent (and could be so easily conducted especially because the level of government indebtedness was so low to begin with after a wartime inflation that had destroyed the previously existing national debt and fifteen years of balanced budgets), the Italian authorities managed to satisfy Italy's international obligations, and on the whole to give a bigger share of national income to some of the workers. As noted above, without the inflationary consequences of the Vietnam War, it is even possible that the long-term implications of the economic policy dictated by the Italian stalemate would have taken much longer to come home to roost.

Conjectural history not being a very useful endeavor for the economist, this point must not be pressed any further; instead I will proceed to analyze how the Italian crisis was precipitated by the stormy climate through which the international economy has lived, especially since 1971.

What has basically happened since 1971 is the revelation of Italy's divergence from the rest of the EEC. Up to 1971 it had not been fully realized to what extent the course that the Italian economy had taken since 1963 had deviated from the courses taken by other EEC members. As said above, this divergence is best shown by the crucial data on industrial investment. In the boom years from 1958 to 1963, Italy had seemed capable of aligning itself to other fast-growing European countries and of generating a high rate of industrial investment. But after that happy phase was brought to an abrupt halt by the 1963-1964 credit squeeze, the Italian economy's equilibrium and the preservation of the delicate sociopolitical balance were achieved by sacrificing the generalized high investment rate, and reducing its permanence to large-scale industry. Thus while the rest of the EEC embarked on a decade of increasing substitution of capital for labor, achieved by high investment rates, and formalized a growth model based on cyclical recourse to Mediterranean labor and permanent full employment for their own nationals, Italy plunged more and more deeply into a vicious circle. I have already described that circle; its most important result was a growing inability for the Italian economy to march in step with the rest of the EEC. The EEC was proceeding toward greater integration and beginning to take a place in the international economy as a high-growth strong-currency bloc of countries that exported technically sophisticated products, long-term capital, and technology. They were also increasingly self-sufficient in agriculture and imported raw materials, light industrial products, cheap labor, and short-term capital.

These hard facts remained hidden until the 1971 monetary explosion began to reveal them in their glaring crudeness. When the dollar's gold convertibility was officially suspended, the lira was pushed up with the other developed countries' currencies. When in March 1972 the EEC Council of Finance Ministers agreed to further restrict the margins of fluctuation between member state currencies, Italy went along. In February 1973, however, when Belgium, Denmark, France, Germany, Luxembourg, and the Netherlands informed the IMF that their central banks would no longer intervene to hold the value of their currencies relative to the U.S. dollar, within the margins dictated by the December 1971 Smithsonian Agreement, Italy was no longer able to follow. Between the European joint float and the dollar, the lira had to choose the dollar as a reference. It was in fact the flight from the lira in early 1973 that precipitated the currency crisis that pushed up the Swiss franc and the Deutsche mark, and culminated in the dollar devaluation.

It was thus revealed that after almost fifteen years of European integration, the Italian economy remained, vis-à-vis its EEC partners, in the same position in which Southern Italy had remained with respect to Northern Italy in the same period. As in the latter case, the distance had grown rather than diminished. The Italian economy had become crucially dependent on foreign trade, but it was even less able to trade on its own terms than it had been in 1958. Italy now imported essential raw materials, fuels, agricultural products, high-technology investment goods, and it exported consumer durables, low-technology investment goods, labor, and capital. The dependence on imports had drastically increased and Italian exports had remained concentrated in sectors where competition from developing countries—in Southern and Eastern Europe, Latin America, and Asia—was growing all the time.

Nor had the country been able to exploit the Common Agricultural Policy to its benefit as France had done. After the French managed to convince the others on a price support policy for northern agricultural products, the Italians tried to have that mechanism extended to their own Mediterranean products, but with very little luck. Moreover, the process of integration had never gone as far as to include a regional policy worthy of the name, and the strong-currency partners had also balked at any notion of a common internal monetary policy, which may have served to finance the more inflationary countries.

As all this began to dawn on the Italians, the Arab-Israeli War came to expose in even sharper contrast the contradictions of the Italian international economic position. The Italians had managed to buy some breathing space by recourse to international credit in the Eurodollar market, which in 1972 and 1973 had been a buyers' market because of the private flight from the dollar. With the quadrupling of the fuel bill and the huge increase in raw material prices,[b] it was clear that a readjustment of the Western payments balances could

Table 6-3
Commodity Composition of Italian Foreign Trade, 1951-1975

<table>
<tr><th></th><th colspan="3">Imports</th><th colspan="3">Exports</th></tr>
<tr><th>Commodity Group</th><th>1951-55</th><th>1972</th><th>1975</th><th>1951-55</th><th>1972</th><th>1975</th></tr>
<tr><td>Raw materials</td><td>24.5</td><td>9.0</td><td>8.5</td><td>5.2</td><td>0.7</td><td>0.5</td></tr>
<tr><td>Auxiliary materials</td><td>23.2</td><td>22.7</td><td>32.6</td><td>13.0</td><td>9.0</td><td>11.3</td></tr>
<tr><td>fuel</td><td>19.2</td><td>14.9</td><td></td><td>7.7</td><td>4.2</td><td></td></tr>
<tr><td>other</td><td>4.0</td><td>7.8</td><td></td><td>5.3</td><td>4.8</td><td></td></tr>
<tr><td>Semifinished manufactures</td><td>15.8</td><td>15.1</td><td>13.0</td><td>13.2</td><td>12.2</td><td>14.8</td></tr>
<tr><td>Final consumption goods</td><td>24.4</td><td>35.7</td><td>31.1</td><td>51.7</td><td>48.0</td><td>44.9</td></tr>
<tr><td>food</td><td>18.1</td><td>20.5</td><td>17.7</td><td>22.7</td><td>8.8</td><td>8.1</td></tr>
<tr><td>other nondurable</td><td>3.1</td><td>5.4</td><td rowspan="2">13.4</td><td>19.5</td><td>21.3</td><td rowspan="2">36.8</td></tr>
<tr><td>durable</td><td>3.2</td><td>9.8</td><td>9.5</td><td>17.9</td></tr>
<tr><td>Final investment goods</td><td>12.1</td><td>17.5</td><td>14.8</td><td>16.9</td><td>30.1</td><td>28.5</td></tr>
<tr><td>plant, machinery, and equipment</td><td>9.5</td><td>13.7</td><td>11.7</td><td>11.9</td><td>23.9</td><td>22.7</td></tr>
<tr><td>industrial vehicles</td><td>1.8</td><td>2.6</td><td rowspan="2">3.1</td><td>3.8</td><td>4.4</td><td rowspan="2">5.8</td></tr>
<tr><td>other</td><td>0.8</td><td>1.2</td><td>1.2</td><td>1.8</td></tr>
<tr><td>Total</td><td>100.0</td><td>100.0</td><td>100.0</td><td>100.0</td><td>100.0</td><td>100.0</td></tr>
</table>

Source: Banca d'Italia, *Relazione Annuale* (Rome).

[b]As is shown in Table 6-3, auxiliary materials, which include fuels, jumped from 22 percent to 33 percent of total Italian imports from 1972 to 1975. Because of low oil prices in the 1960s and the lack of an alternative energy policy, the Italian economy has become completely dependent on imported oil and natural gas.

not happen by increased export volumes, but mainly by increased export prices, reduced import volumes, and capital imports. Export values were in fact increased by means of currency upvaluations generated by capital inflows, in addition to price raises. Italy was not able to attract short-term capital. It had to negotiate credits at government level. It was not able, as a consequence, to upvalue its currency. Having no control over the prices of its exports, Italy could not use that adjustment mechanism either. As a result, the Italian authorities had to rely as usual on a savage credit squeeze and an import deposit mechanism.

Being halfway between development and underdevelopment, Italy has not been able to manage its recent economic difficulties by determinate choice of either the "developed countries recipe"—which relies on the functioning of the international market, as the dominant position those countries have in it makes the latter work to their advantage—or of the "underdeveloped countries recipe"—which is based on direct controls, adopted because of the awareness those countries have of their weak position in the international market. The formal ties that link Italy to its EEC partners could not be severed when they were seen to be working to the detriment of the country's economic welfare. Besides, to attempt such a policy would have required the Italian government to act with firm equanimity with respect to the vested interests of many socioeconomic groups that have prospered within the context of the EEC. These range from large landowners to big industry, which participates in many European cartels. But they also include myriad small farmers, who have grown used to EEC protectionism, and myriad small exporters, who would not be able to face foreign retaliation.

Straight political corruption, on the other hand, explains the country's inability to have a national oil policy, after having invented it before most countries in Enrico Matteo's time.[7] And the same explanation must be given to justify Italy's extraordinary loss of pace in the use of nuclear energy for electricity in the sixties, again after a very brilliant start, and for abandoning studies on solar energy and on endogenous energy sources, all fields where Italian scientists had made, up to the early 1960s, brilliant advances. No Italian politicians were there to defend these sectors when oil made its onslaught on them in the sixties. All this had been conveniently forgotten as the country enjoyed the benefits of low oil prices; it was suddenly remembered in October 1973. Old scandals were unearthed and new ones exploded, but no new policies were initiated, which might indicate a will to amend past mistakes. At the International Energy Conference, for instance, Italy's voice was almost muted, except for a few squeals following Japan's example. The National Nuclear Power Plant Construction Plan has not taken off. The Italian government has not been able to follow France's example in negotiative bilateral deals with oil-producing countries, although ENI is by far the largest of the nationalized oil companies in the world and was the first to give better terms to oil-producing countries, as early as the 1950s.

Italy has not been able to negotiate with raw material and food producers either, although it is one of the largest world importers of these products.

Finally, although Italy's "Mediterranean role" is often evoked, no Italian policy exists vis-à-vis the Mediterranean countries.[8] The Italians did not participate in the work to reopen the Suez Canal. They entered into the SUMED pipeline contract only when Bechtel abandoned it. Italian policy vis-à-vis Libya is almost nonexistent, although Italy's share in Libyan imports is still the largest. Italy's relations with Tunisia are permanently hindered by a quarrel over fishing rights, where the Italian government insists in protecting the dubious rights of a notorious mafia-ridden industry, which does not employ many people anyway. Italy's relations with Algeria have recently improved (especially as a result of the Franco-Algerian quarrel) and the Transmediterranean pipeline, which will link Algerian oil fields to Sicily, is to be completed soon. With Middle Eastern countries economic relations are left to the fantasy of Italian entrepreneurs. A much-exalted state visit by the Italian president to South Arabia yielded no tangible economic results, while in the case of Iran, Italy secured a package deal involving the construction of a town, steelworks, a port, and a refinery, but it looks more and more as if the shah, as in many other instances, may have second thoughts.

In the case of Eastern European countries, the Italian government has been more active. Italian exports to these countries have grown rapidly, but so, unfortunately, have Italian credits to them. It is, at least superficially, quite strange to see a country get more and more into debt on the international market while at the same time conceding larger and larger credits to other countries. The explanation is quite simple: the Comecon countries have become the largest importers of what Italian industry manages to produce in the way of advanced technology investment goods, which are not very able to face competition in Western markets. In addition, large Italian corporations find Comecon countries a convenient dumping ground for their surplus products. All this is possible, however, only if generous credit terms are conceded. Bilateral trade is, moreover, notoriously full of snags, especially with Comecon countries. The Italian Central Bank, in an attempt to get rid of a part of these credits vis-à-vis Comecon countries, have proposed to make them assimilated to commercial paper, which means making them negotiable. Other Western governments seem to be tepid about this proposal, although it is quite reasonable. If applied on a world scale, it would give up to $30 billion liquidity to central banks.

Conclusion

This chapter has tried to show that since 1945 Italian foreign economic policy has followed a linear trend, indicated by the liberalization of trade and payments in the early fifties, and by the return to external convertibility and participation in the EEC in the late fifties. They were momentous political choices, and they were unanimously accepted by the entire Italian political spectrum. The presence of such a wide and unqualified political consensus makes it totally irrelevant to debate the appropriateness of those policy choices. Through their elected representatives, the Italian people clearly manifested their desire to take part in the world free trade and payments system and in the European Economic Community. The cost of these choices has been quite high, and it has been felt in the last decade. It must be noted, however, that, when Italy agreed to cofound the EEC, complete economic, financial, and monetary integration were considered as the ultimate objects of the exercise. The Italians had reason to expect that complete integration would also imply a strong regional policy and a decreased relevance of intra-Community balance-of-payments deficits. In other words, they expected that the nations of the EEC would become regions of an integrated Europe. They began to realize that it was not going to be so when the Common Agricultural Policy turned out to be a Franco-German compromise.

It can safely be said that the Italian political milieu understood its participation in the world free trade system and in the EEC as a preference for a quasi-automatic system, where the market mechanism would replace national policies. Consequently, they dismantled the bureaucratic apparatus that ought to have defended the national economy against dangerous trends originating in the international economy, and they did not construct a new bureaucratic apparatus capable of asserting Italian viewpoints in Brussels and in other international forums. As a result, Italian foreign economic policy, in specific instances, has been determined more by interested pressure groups than by the government or the state bureaucracy. The weakness of this approach was revealed in the seventies, when the dramatic increase in international negotiation found the Italian government totally unprepared to take part in it. The tools to conduct a positive foreign economic policy were just not there. The Italian Central Bank was asked more and more frequently to represent the government in international economic negotiation, and in international economic forums. But it never received a full mandate, and as a result it could never defend Italian interests effectively. Italian politicians, incapable of conducting foreign economic policy, remained ready to undo what the Central Bank had been doing, in the fear that it might alienate the favor of the United States or the major European partners.

That Italian representatives have no mandate to negotiate is a centuries-old tradition. Niccolo Machiavelli himself experienced the frustrations of it and bitterly complained about it. The reason for this tradition is that the Italian internal sociopolitical stalemate is also centuries old, and it can only generate day-to-day, last-minute foreign policy decisions, but certainly not the clear policy lines that allow professional negotiators and representatives to have full mandate.

Notes

1. The best book available in English on the Italian economy is K.J. Allen and A.A. Stevenson, *An Introduction to the Italian Economy* (London: Martin Robertson, 1975). It contains most of the relevant descriptive, analytical, and statistical material to which I refer in this chapter. It also offers a very discriminating and comprehensive list of specialist references on the subject.

2. See F.L. Cavazza and R.S. Graubard, *Il caso italiano* (Milan: Garzanti, 1974), which is a collection of generally very good articles by various authors, on Italy's sociopolitical structure, with a few interesting articles on the Italian economy as well.

3. On early postwar Italian choices, see my "Economic Policy in the Reconstruction Period," in S.J. Woolf (ed.), *The Rebirth of Italy* (London: Longman, 1973).

4. See F. Roy Willis, *Italy Chooses Europe* (New York: Oxford University Press, 1971).

5. On Italian agriculture and EEC agricultural policy, see R. Galli and S. Torcasio, *La partecipazione italiana alla politica agricola communitaria* (Bologna: Il Mulino, 1976).

6. On the economic events of the decade following 1963, see A. Graziani (ed.), *L'economia italiana, crisi e ristrutturazione* (Torino: Einaudi, 1974), and P. Ranci (ed.), *La congiuntura più lunga* (Bologna: Il Mulino, 1975).

7. On Eni and Italian oil policy, see S. Holland, *The State as Entrepreneur* (London: Weidenfeld and Nicholson, 1972).

8. See my own "Sulla vocazione mediterranea della economia italiana" in *Prospettive Settanta* (April-June 1975): 5-9.

7 Japan

Philip H. Trezise

The Structure of the Japanese Economy

There is no industrial country in which foreign economic policy can be considered to be separable from economic policy-making generally—or for that matter, separable from domestic politics. Japan is certainly no exception. Concern for foreign economic affairs preoccupies the principal Tokyo ministries, even those with basically domestic responsibilities. Politicians, businessmen, journalists, and academics are likely to have views and sometimes an impact on foreign economic policies. And a vigorous, widely read national press and other communications media make it the rule that plain citizens also are frequently aware of important economic developments affecting or believed to affect Japan's interests abroad.

This is not because Japan is particularly deeply involved in external economic matters, however. The proportion of Japan's economic effort that goes into foreign transactions in fact is small compared with nearly all other industrial powers. Exports of goods and services valued in current prices have been in the range of 10 to 12 percent of GNP since 1955,[1] a figure smaller than for any West European country (the United States, of course, is by far the lowest among industrial countries, at 5.6 percent in 1973).[2] In constant prices—i.e., in volume—the percentage is higher because export prices have risen more slowly than prices generally. To be sure, the figure is higher for exports in relation to goods output generally, much higher in relation to manufacturing output, and higher still for some export-oriented industries. But this kind of pattern is found in all industrial states. The basic point is that relatively few Japanese citizens are directly engaged in producing for foreign account.

Nor have Japanese been foreign investors of consequence until very recently, and then briefly. Over most of the postwar period, capital outflows were closely and carefully rationed. Only after large surpluses appeared in Japan's balance of payments in the late 1960s were capital outflow restrictions relaxed, then to be tightened again in the aftermath of the 1973 oil crisis. Japan's current holdings of assets abroad is not known exactly, but in direct investment the total is lower than those of Canada and less than 5 percent of those of the United States.[3]

The yen has not been an international currency except in a severely limited sense. Most transactions between Japan and other countries are carried on in dollars, and even the nations that do most of their trade with Japan continue to peg their currencies to the U.S. dollar. No one pegs to the yen, which is still subject to extensive exchange controls.

Thus while Japan is the world's third most productive economy as measured in GNP, according to some of the major indicators, its international interests are comparatively small. This judgment changes quite radically, however, when we consider Japan as an importer. It is an old story that Japan depends heavily on imports for industrial raw materials and for primary commodities in general. But the degree of Japan's reliance on external supplies has increased sharply with economic growth. In 1955, Japan could provide from domestic sources more than 75 percent of its energy consumption, 60 percent of its coking coal, 60 percent of its copper, all its nickel, half its lead, and so on. By the end of the 1960s each of these domestic shares had changed dramatically: down to 25 percent for energy, 20 percent for coking coal, 15 percent for copper, 60 percent for nickel, and 30 percent for lead.[4] The trends are uniformly in the direction of eventual near-total dependence on other countries for the materials essential to the operation of Japan's industrial economy.

What is true for industrial raw materials is in only somewhat lesser measure true for food. Japan is already the world's largest national import market for wheat, soybeans, and coarse grains. As Japanese incomes rise and the consequent shift toward an increased consumption of animal protein continues, Japan will become an even greater purchaser of the basic cereals and oilseeds in world markets. A 1972 estimate by Japan's Ministry of Agriculture was that imports of animal and poultry feed might reach almost 30 million tons within ten years,[5] which would make Japan a dominant force in world trade in the coarse grains and oilseeds. In the most bitter extremity, of course, Japan could retreat to a severely restricted diet and relative self-sufficiency in food, but this could never be a freely made choice.

It was this basic and inexorably growing dependence on imports that brought a Ministry of International Trade and Industry official to say in 1970 to the OECD, "The Japanese economy cannot escape its destiny of having to import raw materials and foodstuffs and to export processed goods. For a long while, Japan has been unable to escape the nightmare choice of either exporting or perishing."[6] The choice of words conveys something of Japanese policymakers' traditional and obsessive concern with the country's external position, a concern that is rooted in considerations of national livelihood and, in the end, of national existence as a modern state. For Japan, international trade has been more than a way of improving what might otherwise be an acceptable standard of living, as in effect is true for the United States. Instead trade was looked upon as being crucial to Japan's ability to escape from the poverty and stagnation that afflicts much of the rest of Asia.

Japan Incorporated?

Both in popular writings and in scholarly works, Japan's economic decisionmaking has customarily been described as a tripodal system in which big business, politicians, and civil servants have collaborated to prosecute the primary objective of economic growth and the associated objective of promoting the export trade.[7] Because these were in fact well publicized as national objectives and because progress toward reaching them was very rapid, it was perhaps natural that the triad of business, politics, and the bureaucracy had ascribed to it, by Japanese as well as foreigners, unusual capacities for making best choices cooperatively and then acting decisively and coherently on them. Some observers attached special weight to one or another of the elements in the structure—the London *Economist* once called Japan's "the most intelligent bureaucracy"[8]—but in the main, the characterization of Japan's policy-making was one of an intimate linkage between elected legislators and political leaders, appointed officials, and private businessmen, and eventually it was summed up by the catchphrase "Japan, Incorporated."

This view of Japan has a good many elements of reality. Big business has had a close affiliation with the Liberal Democratic Party, which has been the standard bearer for the cause of order, private property, profits, and other conservative values, including the important relationship of Japan with the United States. The LDP has depended heavily on business and business organizations for its finances. The civil service, in Japan's parliamentary government, has traditionally had an important role not only in carrying out policy but in helping to shape it. And in the postwar period, with government intervention in day-to-day economic affairs a standard operating procedure, senior and not-so-senior officials were given wide scope for making definitive judgments on matters that in many other countries would have been left to private determination. National economic "plans" were being drafted even during the occupation—at the instance of the occupation authorities initially—and the procedure was continued, elaborated, and in a way politicized once independence has been regained. The private sector was represented in the planning process, as it was in other governmental activities, through another legacy of the occupation, the advisory council technique. Literally hundreds of councils, made up of distinguished persons and also of persons with interests in what government might decide, were created to advise the political leadership and the Tokyo ministries and bureaus on policy problems. Through these and other channels, formal and informal, opportunities flourished for exchanges of views and information between business and the several levels and institutions of government.

Still, as with simplistic interpretations of policy-making anywhere, the Japan, Inc., approach has its many limitations as an explanation for what happened or did not happen in postwar Japan.

For one thing, the picture of a conservative political party slavishly devoted to advancing either economic growth of the interests of big business leaves out of consideration the people who vote. The core of Liberal Democratic Party electoral strength has been in rural Japan, among farmers and their families and neighbors. Small business has been a second center of conservative political support. The LDP could ignore these and other sources of votes only at peril to its very existence. It can be argued, indeed, that its most signal service to economic growth in Japan may have been its espousal of policies that paradoxically worked to slow the movement of people out of low-productivity agriculture and from rural areas into factories and urban centers; social change might have run explosively fast if the rural sector's fate had been left wholly to market forces. Big business had no option but to accept the farm policy and its adverse direct impact on industrial expansion, as it also accepted policies that provided subsidies and other aids to small business. The politicians, not the businessmen, decided these matters on political, not economic, grounds.

By the same token, the LDP was not in monolithic control of the political scene. To be sure the opposition has been and remains fragmented and, like the LDP itself, faction-ridden, and it has shown little capacity for presenting plausible alternative policies to the country. Nonetheless the LDP has undergone a slow erosion of its voting strength. It has been a minority party since the 1960s, holding its commanding Diet position principally through an electoral district system that is heavily biased in favor of representation for the rural voter. In these circumstances the political opposition must be taken seriously. Concessions must be made to keep crucial voting blocs from further shifts to the Japan Socialist Party or to other parties. In the Diet, legislation is normally the product of compromise between the LDP and the Socialists rather than of a steamroller conservative majority.

The national press, with its huge readership, is a further check on the LDP and the government. Editorially, the mass circulation newspapers are habitually hypercritical of politicians and the government. No prime minister and no cabinet can expect tender treatment from the media on governmental policies and none get it.

As for the power of big business, there is the obvious question: Who speaks for business? In popular commentaries, it is the *zaikai*, a term applied to a body of elder business leaders who are able and willing to devote a good deal of time to discussing public policy. But Japanese business is not a single entity. The body of common interest is there, of course—most if not all businessmen favor low taxes, an orderly society, and checks on trade unionism—but wide differences can appear on other matters. A reading of the pronouncements of the leading business organizations—where the *zaikai* are dominant—would have led to the conclusion that liberalization of trade and investment was coming fast in the latter part of the 1960s. In fact, it came slowly because many other people in business and the government saw hazards for particular interests in too rapid a change. Bitter struggles to hold or expand market shares always have colored the views of individual firms or groups of firms on government policies—not in the direction of unanimity. Or on the broad issue of economic expansion, the banking community has regularly warned against the inflation bias of monetary policy without much affecting the Ministry of Finance.

"Planning" in Japan, which has so impressed some foreign observers, has been of two kinds. There have been the national plans, nominally drafted by the prime minister's Economic Deliberation Council, which are supposed to set general economic policy guidelines for a fixed period ahead. The 1973-1977 plan—the seventh since 1955—has had many of its premises upset by the violent inflation of 1973-1974, and it can hardly have had even a remote relationship to events, but that is not an unusual development. The plans are vehicles for presenting general policy ideas, and thus they take on some of the features of political manifestos on the part of the prime minister in power. But they are drawn in very general terms (actually by the staff of the Economic Planning Agency), their binding force on the operating ministries and agencies of government is nil, and their impact on economic life has been indirect and probably modest.

Another variety of planning goes on in the ministries—Finance, International Trade and Industry, Agriculture, Transport, Construction, and so on. These are the "home" ministries for industrial sectors. The banks are Finance's responsibility; much of manufacturing is subject to MITI's regulations and guidance; agriculture and fisheries are looked after by the Ministry of Agriculture; and shipping, shipbuilding, the railways, and the airlines are the Transport Ministry's domain. Through regulatory, tax, and subsidy powers, and through the less formal authority known as administrative guidance, the ministries can and do influence industrial decisions and actions in some detail. In the more mythical expositions of Japanese policy-making, all this makes a neat and coherent whole. The national effort and the national resources have been carefully guided into their most productive uses, conflicts of interest have been avoided, and economic growth and exports have been systematically fostered by an elite corps of bureaucrats operating in league with the business community and conservative politicians.

The truth of course is that the Japanese ministries resemble bureaucratic agencies elsewhere. They defend their prerogatives with great zeal, they persistently seek to expand their own authority and power, and they resist coordination and control from outside. It may even be that in Japan's "vertical society"[9]—where loyalty up, to the organization, is supposedly an unusually compelling social force—interministry struggles are waged more fiercely and central control over policy is more difficult to achieve than in other nations. When an issue engages the interests and responsibilities of more than one ministry, the policy answer must be worked out through the process of interministry discussion and negotiation, and the outcome normally will be a compromise reflecting the common denominator of agreement possible among the disparate interests involved. The Japanese method of resolving interministry differences is as time-consuming and, for the participants, as frustrating as that found anywhere.

Thus there is no special magic attached to the Japanese civil service. Its career personnel have the strengths of a rather rigorously selected group, but they also suffer from the weaknesses that afflict all civil services, or, one might say, all bureaucracies public or private. To the extent that Japanese bureaucrats exercise power (and they do), they make both good and bad choices, usually with caution and if the matter engages other bureaucrats after all due consultation and clearances.

So setting aside the tripodal model as interesting but without much general applicability, it is useful to consider next the broad characteristics of Japan's postwar foreign economic policy, which can be identified quite readily.

Japan's Postwar Growth

The policy lines that were followed, after the occupation had ended in 1952, to cope with Japan's extraordinary reliance on the outer world were both bold and cautious, inward-looking and externally oriented. Domestic policy was quite consistently aggressively expansionist. Easy money and administered low interest rates helped an activist-minded business community to build plant and equipment at a pace that astonished everyone in and out of Japan. Precepts of "sound" financing were tacitly ignored. Japanese industry grew mainly on the strength of bank credit rather than equity investment, with business taking full advantage of the leverage offered by debt financing in a rapidly growing economy.

As seen in Tokyo, the chief constraint on the growth process was to be found in the balance of payments. As the economy grew, so did inescapable import needs. Periodically, the bill for imports outran earnings from exports. At these points the cure was to tighten monetary policy enough to curb new investment and thus to slow down the growth of domestic demand until exports had caught up with payments for imports. Until well into the 1960s, Japan's thin foreign exchange reserves provided only a limited cushion to fall back on. In a sense the country's economic managers lived constantly with a narrow margin of maneuver. Yet the choice was regularly made to opt for domestic expansion up to the point that the balance-of-payments position seemed clearly so dangerous that action to check economic growth could not be postponed.

In contrast with the risk-taking tenor of domestic policy, external transactions were handled with an excess of prudence. Part of the heritage of the U.S. occupation was a full complement of controls on foreign exchange expenditures. Imports, including imports of technology, were carefully managed, outward investment was controlled, and inward investment discouraged. This was a regime that had what seemed a fully adequate theoretical justification in the supposedly precarious state of Japan's balance of payments. It also satisfied a number of specific domestic interests. Japanese industry, whether infant or otherwise, enjoyed a very large measure of protection from import competition. Foreign direct investment in Japan, which was viewed with much suspicion, not to say xenophobia, could be held within narrow limits. Governmental intervention in foreign transactions could sometimes give the Japanese participants a bargaining advantage, or so it was believed.

There were costs, of course. Wholesale protectionism meant that sick industries were propped up along with the promising new industries. The restraints on foreign investment not only deprived the country of capital inflows but also may have perpetuated industrial bottlenecks longer than necessary. Controls on technology imports often led to expensive delays in obtaining the knowhow that Japan was lacking in the wake of the war. But the sweep of the domestic economic expansion proved to be so broad and strong that these costs could be absorbed without much notice being given them. From the Tokyo perspective the system was quite defensible on both practical and theoretical grounds.

Exports were pushed vigorously. Tax benefits went to exporters and export industries. The Export-Import Bank provided favorable financing for sales abroad. Trade promotion programs had high priority in budget-making. Above all, the need for export expansion was discussed incessantly, so that exporting seemed to be equated with patriotic behavior.

This mix of domestic and export growthmanship, together with a barebones policy toward transactions requiring the spending of foreign exchange, was applied in a world that had several features favorable to Japan. For one thing, the relative prices of Japan's indispensable primary commodity imports declined more or less steadily from the end of the Korean War boom (in 1951, actually) until late in the 1960s. For another, export markets for Japanese goods were buoyant, as economic growth in the world greatly surpassed the expectations of observers who had been conditioned by memories of the depression. Also, since Japan's place in the world economy was modest, outside pressures to modify the restrictive import and foreign exchange policies were slow to make themselves felt. In 1962, Japanese GNP (which had doubled in seven years) was a little more than 10 percent of the U.S. GNP, and its exports were 3.5 percent of the world total. On a per capita basis, it lagged behind, mostly well behind, the other industrial countries. While the country's economic achievements had attracted attention abroad, the tendency was to be somewhat tolerant of Japanese shortcomings—the more so because in Europe and elsewhere a large measure of systematic discrimination against Japan's exports persisted in spite of the general liberalization of international trade.

This tolerance could hardly last indefinitely, and as the sixties went on the volume and acerbity of the complaints from other countries, most of all the United States, grew steadily. Nonetheless, and despite the formal acceptance of yen convertibility in 1964, the apparatus of control over Japan's foreign transactions was modified only slowly and modestly. The failure to liberalize more rapidly was perhaps the major foreign economic policy issue confronting Japan up until 1972-1973.

It is worth stressing that the general line of foreign economic policy in the 1950s and 1960s was associated with success, success beyond any and all expectations. The domestic boom was matched by booming exports. Markets for Japanese goods expanded. Foreign trade barriers were lowered in the Kennedy Round, to Japan's export advantage. The balance-of-payments constraint on domestic policy was eased until in the late sixties it temporarily disappeared as a problem.

The vested interests and the habits of thought formed during the period when everything was going well must have acquired a powerful hold on those who made or contributed to foreign policies. For a number of industries, led by agriculture, a protective regime seemed not only desirable but the natural state of affairs. Even those sectors adversely affected by import controls—electric power, for example—became accustomed to living with policies that raised costs, given the expansionary environment that prevailed. Restrictions on inward direct investment appealed to all the firms liable to being exposed to new competition but they had a wider appeal as well in a country that has a very full share of insular attitudes.

Bureaucracy and the Policy-Making Process

All the considerations of self-interest and attachment to standard procedures were necessarily effective within the official foreign policy structure. A bureau director whose entire career had been spent in an environment of import and foreign exchange controls was not likely to agree quickly that the system could safely be altered in substantial ways. If his responsibilities were to advance the well-being of an industry of an industrial sector, the more reason for him to oppose changes in policies that were understood and seemed to have worked well. Obviously there were countervailing forces to stand-pattism within and outside the government, but their strengths were inevitably limited.

Foreign economic policy responsibilities are divided in Japan much as they are in the United States. The Ministry of Foreign Affairs (read Department of State) has a broad grant of overall policy authority and is normally but not uniformly the spokesman for the government with other governments; lacking any private domestic constituency and by mandate concerned with maintaining good relations with other nations, it usually has the most forward position on external policy questions; also it is usually cast in the thankless role of an organizer of the necessary interministry concords on the Japanese response to particular issues.

The Ministry of Finance (read Treasury) has a final bureaucratic say on external monetary questions. Like the Treasury, it has its representatives abroad, in the embassies and in the international financial institutions, and it speaks for Japan on international monetary matters. As the coordinating agency for economic policy generally, and as the budget-making ministry, it has great bureaucratic power that it guards with much jealousy and skill. The principal industry coming under its wing is banking, and this has tended to give the MOF a relatively liberal cast of mind in relation to import protectionism but not necessarily toward other controls.

The Ministry of International Trade and Industry (MITI) (read Commerce) has a mandate of sorts in international trade policy, including especially export promotion, but its abiding interests have been in mothering those domestic industrial sectors that fall within the domain of its industrial bureaus. The Agriculture Ministry, unsurprisingly given the handicaps under which Japanese farming had operated, has held strongly protectionist views about agricultural trade, and has pressed them effectively on the other ministries.[a] Both MITI and Agriculture have the closest of connections with major domestic interest groups, whose fortunes they naturally seek to protect and advance. A fifth ministry, Transport, has within its charter the responsibility for international aviation and shipping and for an important export industry, shipbuilding.

A senior politician from the ruling Liberal Democratic Party presides over each of these ministries. At least one but probably two or three of these ministers will control LDP factions of their own, that is, different from the faction headed by the prime minister. Some of them will have ambitions to succeed the incumbent prime minister and each will have at a minimum a concern for keeping his personal faction alive and well. The prime minister (who is by custom the elected president of the LDP) in turn will owe his preeminence to votes from factions additional to his own, so that while he is first among equals his power ultimately to decide has to be diluted by the need to take account of (a) his debts to his (often temporary) allies and (b) the threat to his tenure or his reelection posed by his factional rivals in the cabinet.

It hardly requires arguing that neither the bureaucratic structure nor its political directorate, the cabinet, are conducive to easily reached decisions. The Japanese may well have an ingrained national attachment to consensus, or an aversion to unilateral decision-making. But even without this attitude, the policy-making system is one in which compromise is always desirable and most often necessary. A consequential issue coming up through the bureaucracy is not likely to be decided by a single minister, or by the prime minister, but rather by the process, not unheard of in other governments, of lengthy discussion and mutual adjustment coming in the end to some limited area of agreement—or, not infrequently, to a tacit agreement to postpone a decision.

In the policy process, the domestic interests immediately concerned will have adequate channels to present their views. Most direct would be through the ministries themselves, where individual bureaus or sections have responsibilities

---

[a]The U.S. Department of Agriculture is of course far more foreign trade minded, as befits the agency concerned with the U.S.'s greatest export industry, although it too is devotedly protective of certain farm sectors.

for the welfare of particular economic sectors, such as textiles or steel or automobiles. Pressures can be brought to bear as well through Diet members, who are naturally susceptible to constituency claims. And ministers, who are also Diet members, have frequently proved to be most effectively solicitous of interests, sometimes of a very localized character.

By contrast, less parochial groups have the usual problem of contesting for general principles against specific and well-defined interests or demands. The Ministry of Foreign Affairs commonly finds itself in this position, and so have academic experts and spokesmen for the business organizations. In the long struggle over the modification of Japan's basic foreign economic policy, the forces favoring liberalization were typically at a disadvantage.

Foreign Economic Policy Issues: Import Liberalization, Yen Revaluation, and Textiles

In retrospect, most of the 1960s can be seen as having been a period of internal and external conflict over the pace of change in Japanese foreign economic policy. In the latter 1950s, Japanese public pronouncements had begun to recognize that external liberalization was required. Japan had been accepted as a contracting party of the General Agreement on Tariffs and Trade and as a member of the International Monetary Fund. These entailed obligations as well as rights (although in truth Japan was initially accorded less than full rights in the case of the GATT). There was ample precedent for delaying compliance with the rules of these institutions, but delay obviously could not go on without end.

Inside Japan, the Ministry of Foreign Affairs took the leadership for change, with occasional help from the Ministry of Finance—and in a public relations sense at least, from the Economic Planning Agency. Big business was at first a cautious and gradually a more outspoken voice for liberalization. But on the other side were ranged such powerful ministries as Agriculture and MITI, and a host of political interests with a stake, fancied or real, in the maximum feasible degree of gradualism.

As a predictable outcome, the rate of progress was slow. A limited measure of import liberalization in the early 1960s was followed by yen convertibility in 1964. Thereafter little forward movement took place for several years, even though the balance of payments began to move into strong surplus after 1965. Indeed, it was not until 1971-1972, when an embarrassingly large payments surplus made action unavoidable, that import and investment liberalization was substantially stepped up.

The effect of all this, unintended and even perplexing so far as Tokyo was concerned, was to put strains on Japan's foreign relations, most particularly on relations with the United States. With Japanese GNP growing at 11-plus percent annually and exports growing faster still, there was understandable impatience abroad at the grudging changes made in the structure of import and investment controls. Inside Japan, however, there was somebody to object to every proposed action: this industry was not yet competitive, the state of the balance of payments was still in doubt, the giant foreign multinationals threatened to swallow up Japan's industries. All these propositions could find supporters within the factionally divided political leadership (as for the opposition, it was by far more restrictionist than the party in power) and among the chief domestic ministries. There was no place in this diffused power system where the conventional go-slow wisdom could be challenged effectively.

It was in part because of this laggard response to the pressures for liberalization that the Japanese government found itself confronted with the critical problem of yen revaluation in 1971-1972.

The first signs that the yen might be moving toward undervaluation came in the mid-1960s when the balance of payments shifted into surplus. This could be overlooked initially—indeed it was scarcely noticed—so fixed was the conviction that Japan's external position was doomed to be chronically on the margin. By 1968-1969, however, the indications of a structural Japanese surplus—"fundamental disequilibrium" in the IMF sense—had become too apparent to be entirely ignored. At this point Japan had several policy options. One was an all-out drive for import liberalization that, while it might not have reduced the external surplus quickly, would have begun the process and earned favorable notice abroad. Another was to stimulate further the domestic economy so as to attract imports and discourage exports; this alternative could be called the inflationary choice. A third was to revalue the yen, thus taking the real income gains that were to be gleaned from cheaper imports and dearer exports.

In practice, a fourth choice was made: effectively to do nothing. Or rather, when wholesale prices showed a slight tendency to rise, the decision was taken in late 1969 to dampen the growth of the domestic economy. As was to be expected, the slowdown at home gave added impetus to exports and pushed the external surplus toward unmanageable levels. This was a major factor in the background for the international monetary upheavals that culminated in the abrupt U.S. action to abandon dollar convertibility in August 1971.

Now revaluation could be avoided only by official intervention in the foreign exchange market. For two weeks after the U.S. move, the Bank of Japan bought dollars to support the 360-yen-to-the-dollar rate. When this excessively costly experiment had to be given up, the next line of defense was to seek to minimize the amount of the now unavoidable December 1971 revaluation. And afterward, in 1972, when upward pressure on the yen was resumed, the political leadership went out of its way to promise that another revaluation would never happen. Not until 1973, and then under duress from outside, was the definitive policy shift made.

The price is still being paid for this stubborn and in the end fruitless resistance to a policy choice that most economists would have recommended at an early point. Defending the old yen value required heavy foreign exchange purchases by the central bank, making the private business sector unaccustomedly liquid. Then in a further effort to ward off revaluation, the tight money experiment of 1969-1970 was replaced by highly stimulative monetary and fiscal policies. The foundations for the subsequent violent inflation were thus established through what now can be labeled only a series of mistaken choices.

Why was this allowed to happen? One argument was wrongly drawn from history. In 1930, in different circumstances, a Japanese government had elected to raise the external value of the yen, and it and the country had suffered a political disaster. A second factor was the prevailing mind set of senior officials whose experience of twenty years argued for standing pat. Export interests, and those in small business particularly, were strongly opposed to revaluation; and the then MITI minister's home constituency included the export-oriented, small-firm, cutlery industry. The political opposition and the trade unions could be counted on to attack revaluation. No strong body of opinion favored it. Decisions were taken, or not taken, for reasons that were understandable. It was the results that were unexpected, and bad.

No other foreign economic policy question in Japan's postwar history has had the importance of the issues of trade and investment liberalization and then the revaluation of the yen. These were matters that touched pervasively on the whole of the domestic economy. They also affected, mostly adversely, the country's external political relations, notably those with the guarantor of Japan's security and its indispensable trading partner, the United States. Only the 1969-1971 textile dispute with the United States had a remotely comparable impact on Japan's foreign relations (its domestic economic importance was small), and that to some extent because of considerations peculiar to the case.

To dwell briefly on the textile episode, the issue was put to Japan by the new U.S. administration in 1969 quite starkly, even brutally: would Japan agree to restrain exports to the United States of synthetic fiber and woolen textiles according to procedures and guidelines laid down by the United States? The Japanese textile industry, which carried a grievance stemming from the operations of an earlier export restraint arrangement on cotton textiles, was quick to call for resistance. It was able to get passed without difficulty a Diet resolution opposing acceptance of the U.S. demand, and it mobilized a good deal of public sentiment on behalf of its position. What might have been a relatively manageable issue–though not so easily handled as some of the new administration's people hoped would be the case–became something of a national cause in Japan.

The late Prime Minister Eisaku Sato was anything but anxious to have a row with the United States over textiles. His overriding foreign policy objective was to get the Nixon administration's assent to the prompt restoration of Okinawa to Japanese political control and administration. Anything likely to get in the way of that objective was undesirable. Negotiations on the Okinawa question went smoothly and successfully, with the U.S. side, at least, expecting that a textile understanding would soon follow in spite of the poor start that had been made. Unhappily for all the principals concerned, this proved to be impossible to achieve. After more than two years of sporadic "negotiations," it took a U.S. threat in October 1971 to impose unilateral restrictions on textiles from Japan to conclude the matter. This threat came after an impressive showing in former President Nixon's August decisions of the U.S.'s readiness to take matters into its own hands, whatever the views of its friends and allies. It undoubtedly was entirely credible in Tokyo.

There is something to be said for the proposition that nobody came out ahead in the textile controversy. In the end—and after severe strains had been put on a crucial foreign relationship—the Japanese government and industry accepted what were essentially the original U.S. demands. The United States, for a sizable political price in Japan, obtained controls on Japan's textile exports after those exports had begun to recede anyway in the face of competition from newer suppliers. Two years after the imposed agreement, the two countries had their representatives in Geneva negotiating a full-scale agreement designed to slow the growth of textile exports from the developing world into advanced industrial countries like the United States and Japan.

One conclusion, presumably, is that none of the participants in this affair was especially farsighted. Another, however, is that it was pressures from public opinion, the legislature, and from one sector of industry that on this occasion effectively stymied the policy-making process in Japan. Here was a situation in which the interests of an unusually successful, long-tenure prime minister, the basic interests of the ruling conservative party, and the interests of the big business community were arguably aligned in favor of a prompt resolution of the textile dispute. The return of Okinawa and the continuation of close relations with the United States were policy goals having far more substance than was involved in an extension of already existing restrictions on the textile trade. There were of course intragovernmental divisions on the issue, between Foreign Affairs and MITI. But MITI's inflexibility reflected the textile industry's attitudes, not the more cautious views of big business as a whole. Still literally no decision could be reached in the course of almost thirty months. If any corrective is needed for the notion that the gears of Japan's policy machine always mesh smoothly and effectively, the textile case ought to be it.

Japan's Vulnerability in the Oil and Raw Materials Crises

Since 1971, when some of the fundamentals of the nation's foreign economic policy were shattered, Japan has been through the oil crisis and raw materials inflation of 1973-1974 and the first genuine recession of the postwar era. Its vulnerability to external events was dramatically underlined by the OPEC oil embargo, by U.S. restrictions on soybean exports, and by the explosion of raw materials and food prices. The recession, too, had some of its origins in developments outside Japan and these, naturally enough, have been given special emphasis by Japanese observers. In this period of unusual vicissitudes and uncertainties, Japan's external policies conceivably might have been expected to shift in a nationalist, *sauve qui peut* direction, with stress on bilateral deals, subsidized exports, and restored controls on imports.

This has not happened. The first reaction to the oil crisis saw a spate of Japanese missions, overlapping those from Western Europe, to the Middle East oil-producing countries in search of "secure" supplies. But the results for the Japanese were discouraging, as they were for others, and Japan put aside its misgivings about its relations with the OPEC nations and helped in framing the International Energy Agency as an undisguised consumers' protective association. Along with other advanced industrial countries it has pledged itself to avoid beggar-thy-neighbor trade policies in coping with the impact of higher oil prices. There is no real indication that the pledge has been fudged upon; rather, the authorities have intervened in the exchange market to check the depreciation of the yen, this notwithstanding a disturbing decline of exports. The import and inward investment liberalization steps of 1972-1973 have not been reversed, and Japan appears to be as dedicated as anyone to the slowly ongoing Tokyo Round of negotiations in Geneva designed to further reduce barriers to trade.

All this goes to suggest that Tokyo has assessed Japan's external economic interests as being bound up with those of the United States and Western Europe in a search for workable multilateral arrangements to help reduce the prevailing uncertainties and dangers in the world. If so, it would seem to be a rational assessment. Japan clearly cannot cope on its own with its nearly absolute vulnerability, in the worst case, to the decisions of people who control supplies of food and raw materials. Similarly, markets abroad will not be kept open simply because Japan needs access to them. And Japanese investments in the developing world are no less exposed to nationalist political currents than are U.S. or European investments. Anything that can be done better to assure an orderly and open world economy will be to Japan's advantage. As the former Indonesian ambassador to the United States, Soedjatmoko, has said, "More than with any other major power Japan's security and basic interests depend on the viability of the political and economic international order."[10]

There are of course counterpressures in Japan to multilateralism and particularly to the idea of sharing responsibilities trilaterally with the United States and Europe. Any suggestion of confrontation with the Third World, or portions of it, generates unease. Saburo Okita expresses a general view in his aphorism "Japan is defenseless on all sides."[11] A widely held attitude is that links with Southeast Asia should be given priority in foreign economic policy. Trade and economic relations with mainland China are given special importance in some quarters, as witness the 1974 agreement with Peking that predictably cost Japan Airlines dearly. Considerations such as these, taken together with Japan's abiding concern for having a diversity of markets and sources of supply, make it probable that foreign economic policies will not be expressed or managed with the utmost of clarity and singlemindedness. Nonetheless the broad directions of Japan's policy are not likely to move very far from their multilateral, advanced industrial country focus unless and until decisions and actions in Washington and Brussels prove conclusively that Japan is to be treated as odd man out in the industrial world.

Notes

1. Bank of Japan, *Economic Statistics Annuals*, Tokyo. GATT, *Japan's Economic Expansion and Foreign Trade, 1955-1970*, Geneva, July 1971.

2. European data are from European Free Trade Association, *EFTA Trade*, Geneva, April 1974.

3. Bank of Japan data are as carried in the *Japan Economic Journal*, October 13, 1974, p. 4.

4. *Japan's Economy in 1985*, Japan Economic Research Center, Tokyo, April 1971, p. 34.

5. FAO, *International Agricultural Adjustment, Japan* (Rome, 1973).

6. *The Industrial Policy of Japan*, OECD, Paris, 1972, p. 16.

7. Harohiro Fukui, "Foreign Policy Making in Japan," a paper given at the 1974 annual meeting of the Association for Asian Studies (Boston, April 1-3, 1974) cited the large number of Japanese and U.S. scholars, including himself, sharing this view (pp. 5-8).

8. Vol. 223, May 27, 1967, p. ix.

9. This concept has been presented in fullest form, I believe, in Professor Chie Nakane's *Japanese Society* (London: Weidenfeld and Nicolson, 1970).

10. The Tokyo Colloquium, "Views on the Future Perspectives of the Asian-Pacific Region," June 1974 (mimeographed), p. 125.

11. "Natural Resource Dependency and Japanese Foreign Policy," *Foreign Affairs*, July 1974, p. 123.

8 Canada

H. Edward English

The distinctive characteristics of Canada that explain the nature of the country's historical role in international economic relationships are: (1) the great relative importance of natural resources, most of them requiring capital-intensive exploitation; (2) the relatively small size of Canada's population, relative, that is, to the size of Canadian resources and to the populations of most other industrially advanced countries; and (3) the close cultural and geographic association of Canada with the foremost industrial powers of the nineteenth and twentieth centuries.

To these basic economic and social factors might also be added the political contribution of early leaders of the Canadian confederation, national transportation and industrial protection policies designed to tie the country together politically and to provide a basis for more advanced stages of processing and manufacturing activity without seriously handicapping the international competitiveness of the products of the resource industries.

These elements continue to have a major influence on Canadian roles and attitudes, particularly dependence on external markets for the sale of resource-based products, on external sources for some of the finance capital required to exploit these resources and transport them to market, and on the technology that, along with capital, is so readily accessible from English-language centers of industrial research and management training.

Major Domestic Issues Affecting Foreign Economic Policies

Since 1945, and partly as a consequence of the war, there have been significant changes in the domestic economy that bear on Canada's international relations. These changes largely relate to the size of the Canadian domestic market and of domestic savings. The Canadian population reached 20 million in the early 1960s (compared to only 10 million in the late 1920s), by that time with a per capita income second only to the United States and more than double the level of the 1920s. As a consequence of these changes, by the 1960s the Canadian domestic market for many manufactures was large enough to absorb the product of plants of sufficient scale to be internationally competitive. This made it politically as well as economically feasible to dismantle the traditional policies of protection of manufacturing that were so resented by consumers, particularly in the outlying provinces whose economies relied mainly on resource industries and who had tolerated protection of manufacturing activity located mainly in Ontario and Quebec as a concession to national unity.

However, it was discovered that for most manufacturing industries these economies of scale were not being achieved because the protection of the market had permitted the establishment and survival of too many plants, and in many of these production that is too diversified. The explanation for this situation is to be found in two main factors:

1. The tariff and other instruments of protection without which it would not be possible for manufacturers to avoid import competition and to continue charging the higher prices that are necessary to sustain inefficiently small and excessively diversified plants
2. The forms of oligopolistic competition that occur in a relatively smaller national market. In these circumstances price competition can be avoided by conventions such as price leadership by the larger firms, in the Canadian case often based on a price just low enough to preclude large-scale import competition (i.e., near the level of import price plus Canadian tariff). Such conventional pricing leaves oligopolistic rivals to contend among themselves over market shares by employing elaborate marketing strategies, style changes, and even industrial research and development of minor product modifications—all designed to maintain loyalties, using what would otherwise be short-term profits that might encourage price wars and the entry of new competitors.[1]

It has sometimes been suggested that this industrial structure problem in Canada that affects the ability of Canadian industry and Canadian government to move to much more comprehensive dismantling of trade barriers is the consequence of foreign ownership of Canadian manufacturing firms. It is true that many of the industrial sectors that have experienced the structural inefficiency here described are mainly composed of subsidiaries of companies with foreign head offices, and there is no doubt that the international operations of these companies depend heavily on consumers' familiarity with the well-known names of their products as well as their established supply and service facilities. But there are industries in which the same structural problem has occurred that are not "dominated" by foreign-owned firms, such as the fine papers industry. One must conclude that the most fundamental determinant of the structural inefficiency problem, the segregation of the Canadian market by Canadian trade policies (and to a lesser extent by those of other countries) is a necessary condition of the higher-cost manufacturing activity and of the oligopolistic industrial organization and behavior. There is nevertheless sufficient involvement of multinational corporations in these situations that the policies of the government toward such enterprises become a part of the effort to deal with the industrial rationalization problem.

Possibly the best example of a unique international economic policy reflecting these newly perceived circumstances is the Canada-U.S. automotive products agreement of 1965, which was a move toward free trade in such products together with an agreement between the Canadian government and U.S.-based companies for the purpose of assuring that the rationalization of the industry would occur through larger-scale, more specialized production in Canada and a volume of exports necessary to achieving those production economies for all the firms involved. The result was a massive expansion of Canadian exports of such products so that in some years they exceeded the already high and growing level of imports. Most costs were brought down as intended. The rest of the economy, however, did not fully share in the benefits of the arrangement because tariffs on consumer imports of automobiles were not removed, so market prices in Canada remained above those in the United States. Furthermore, the consequent higher level of potential profits made possible a more rapid increase in wages to the highly organized auto workers, putting upward pressure on wages in labor markets supplying other manufacturing industries that have not experienced the same cost-reducing rationalization process. This experience illustrates most of the new postwar concerns about the structure of the Canadian domestic economy. It also reflects both the advantages and disadvantages of at least one of the policy approaches adopted—sectoral bilateral integration.[2]

The other major change in the postwar period has been the shift in Canadian attitudes toward reliance on foreign sources of capital. Until the early 1950s there was seldom any objection expressed concerning heavy reliance on foreign capital. The basic nature of the Canadian economy described at the start of this chapter guaranteed a massive need for imported capital to finance the infrastructure and later the processing stages in a capital-intensive system of exploiting a large stock of natural resources with a small labor force.[3] Even in the first decade after the war, the needs of the rapidly expanding petroleum industry and of other mineral industries generated a larger inflow of capital, and the share of Canadian mining and manufacturing controlled by nonresidents reached a new peak. Following this boom there was a recession in the late 1950s and from then on the growth of nonresident investment was matched by a growth of domestic-owned investment and the relative size of the former has changed very little. Furthermore, the relative size of investment by United States residents declined somewhat as more of the external funds came from Europe and Japan. Increasingly in recent years the view has been expressed that Canada need not rely so much on foreign capital. The maturing of the Canadian economy, it is said, has meant that a much higher level of savings was being generated within Canada. It has also become more popular to question the need for a very high growth rate, and to argue for redistribution policies and a larger role for government. Even the structural problem discussed earlier pointed to the wastefulness of much previous investment. Comparisons between Canadian and

U.S. capital-output ratios in manufacturing have shown a higher ratio in Canada, largely it appears because of much less efficient use of capital.

On the other hand, events have repeatedly cast doubt on the possibility for a significant decline in reliance on foreign capital. The high rate of growth of the labor force particularly during the early 1970s pointed to high levels of investment as an essential support for adequate growth of employment opportunities. With the anticipated exhaustion of cheaper energy sources, higher capital investment is forecast as essential to the development and more distant and unconventional energy sources such as Arctic petroleum and natural gas, the Athabasca tar sands and coal gasification. The size of capital requirements make it seem likely that at least in absolute terms, larger amounts of foreign capital will still be required for some time even if a lower-growth option is chosen by future Canadian governments.[4]

This discussion of changing postwar economic conditions in Canada leaves little doubt that whatever the ebb and flow of nationalist sentiments, Canadians as a whole will continue to favor international institutions and policies that permit the continued marketing of the products of their natural wealth, the rationalization of their manufacturing industries, and the financing of these activities by foreign capital to the extent required by claims made on domestic savings. No one expects that Canada will soon cease to rely on foreign trade for the sale of nearly half its commodity production nor that Canadians will be prepared to sacrifice the substantial contribution of imports to their high material standard of living.

Canada's Role in International Economic Policy-Making

The foregoing discussion explains why Canada is deeply committed to the support of economic interdependence. However, the postwar period has seen a substantial change in Canada's role in forming international policies. It may be said that the economic world during the period from 1945 to the end of the 1950s was dominated by North America, while the 1960s saw the return of Western Europe and Japan to full strength, and the 1970s have witnessed the increased importance and influence of the developing countries, particularly those with mineral wealth. While the United States is still the greatest single economic power, Canada, which was second only to the U.S. in the non-Communist world in 1945, has sunk to a much lower rank, falling behind Japan, West Germany, France, and Britain at least. But what does this ranking really mean? Circumstances differ from one international economic arena to another. In trade and monetary negotiations, Canada probably ranks fourth in economic influence after the United States, the European Economic Community, and Japan, yet Canada remains the U.S.'s most important single trading partner and has usually held closely parallel views in monetary negotiations. Thus Canadian importance to the United States in international policy-making gives the country a substantial continuing influence. However, both North American nations must now accommodate the much larger role of the European Economic Community, Japan—and more recently, the OPEC members of the Third World group.

On the foreign investment issues there are no really multilateral institutions and few multilateral negotiations affecting private investment, although guidelines or codes of behavior have been discussed in OECD and UNCTAD. Canada, as the nation with more foreign direct investment than any other nation in absolute as well as relative terms, is likely to play an important role in the formulation of such codes if and as they become more widely applied. But in this sort of policy development the developing countries and many other OECD countries will share an interest in the kind of code adopted. Some of these countries—e.g., Japan and Sweden—have a longer tradition of screening or other means of foreign investment regulation.

External aid policies are also coordinated in the OECD, by the Development Assistance Committee. Canada is not a leading donor either in absolute or relative terms, but it does have a distinctive role. It is the largest country in the group that has neither great power status nor an imperial tradition. While this suggests a distinctive perspective, it does not mean that Canada is likely to influence the other members greatly.

The Postwar Record of Canadian External Policies

It is not easy to generalize about the major themes of Canadian postwar policy. They may perhaps be summarized as follows:

1. support of multilateral trading arrangements based on GATT and UNCTAD, but with notable bilateral deals and accommodations primarily but not exclusively involving the United States
2. support of multilateral monetary arrangements based on the IMF, but insistence on a flexible exchange rate for the Canadian dollar for over half the period since the IMF was founded
3. support of relatively free flow of private capital until 1963, and thereafter experimentation with various incentive and regulatory policies
4. participation in external aid for the developing countries, with particular emphasis on the Commonwealth and French Community countries and some institutional innovation since the mid-1960s.

The major events of the postwar period are sufficiently unique to each economic policy that it becomes more convenient to treat trade, monetary, and investment and aid policies separately.

Trade Policy

In trade policy the first three years after the war witnessed the negotiations leading to the establishment of GATT and toward the aborted International Trade Organization. Canada in these negotiations supported the principles of nondiscrimination in international trade but at the same time insisted on the preservation of the Commonwealth preferential system, though along with Britain it did agree that no new preferences should be permitted.

All the early rounds of negotiations, including the initial Geneva Conference in 1947, took place during the period of European and Japanese reconstruction and the practical implication of concessions, except for those by Canada, and the United States was limited by the overriding effects of exchange controls. Exchange convertibility was achieved only at the end of the 1950s.

The other event of this period, a proposal to form a Canada-United States free trade area is significant in this context. The idea was raised in 1948, and after extended consideration and perception of feasibility at the technical economic level, it was shelved by Prime Minister Mackenzie King, who was then about to retire and apparently reluctant to identify himself at that stage in his career with a venture of uncertain immediate political consequences for his party. It is unfortunate in retrospect that he and his associates were not more courageous at that time, because it would have been good timing for such an arrangement, when the postwar pattern of industrial development had not crystallized and both North America and the overseas markets greatly exceeded supply. The problem of Canadian industrial structure, including the wasteful forms of foreign direct investment in manufacturing, almost certainly could have been avoided or corrected before it was compounded. Two decades later when these issues were better understood, it had become politically more difficult to achieve the restructuring needed in the Canadian manufacturing sector.

The second phase of Canadian trade policy began with the establishment of the European Economic Community. The issue was how to react to regional integration in Europe and how to participate in GATT negotiations involving the fully recovered and integrating continent. In 1956 the British proposed an industrial free trade area including all European countries, which would have suited Canada well as it would have retained access to the British market for Canadian agricultural products and other raw materials and even many manufactures. But a few months later, in March 1957, the Rome Treaty was signed by the original Six of the Common Market, and shortly after de Gaulle returned to power in 1958, the French discontinued all further consideration of European industrial free trade association. In this period Canada played a modest role, while the U.S. favored the Common Market in Europe and was distinctly lukewarm toward the larger, looser, and more open free trade arrangement. This apparently illogical U.S. position was explained by Washington's preoccupation with political unity as a source of strategic strength. Subsequent events raise grave doubts about the reality of U.S. expectations that a moderately closer economic unit would make a significant net contribution to European security over that which any form of trade liberalization would make possible. But whatever the merits of that argument, it is clear that Canadian efforts directed toward getting U.S. acceptance of the British proposal were either minimal or ineffective.

Once the Common Market was established, the key questions for Canada were two: Would Britain, at that time Canada's second largest trading partner, enter the Community? And what common external policy could emerge? With respect to the former, the Canadian government showed no concern until 1961 when Britain first announced its intent to apply for membership. The government then sought to make its case and to join with other Commonwealth countries in defense of the preferences or to design some special relationship to preserve access to the British market.

The focus soon switched to the U.S. Trade Expansion Act of 1962 as a means of negotiating with the EEC and encouraging the acceptance of Britain as a member, while dismantling trade barriers between the Community and other GATT members. Here again the Canadian government had an opportunity to influence events but failed to exploit that opportunity effectively. The U.S. government included a provision in the Trade Expansion Act that became known as the "dominant supplier authority," under which the U.S. negotiations were to be given authority to reduce to zero U.S. tariff rates on those categories of commodities (Standard International Trade Classification three-digit commodity groupings) in which the United States and all countries of the European Community accounted for 80 percent or more of the total non-Communist world trade. As the general negotiating authority under the act was for 50-percent reduction, this additional special authority might have brought about a substantial increase in the scope for negotiations, but this depended on the number of countries who were members of the EEC at the time of the negotiations. If only the six members were included, only two or three insignificant categories could be covered and the dominant supplier authority could mean almost nothing. If, however, Britain and its principal EFTA partners who were interested in joining the EEC had become members by the time of the GATT negotiations, about twenty-five categories of commodities could have been eligible for tariff removal by the U.S. negotiating authority. This considerable extra scope for negotiation was clearly intended as the U.S. government's inducement to the EEC to expand its membership, based on the belief that the Community would value highly the additional opportunity for negotiating access to the United States market. Events proved that the Kennedy administration had overestimated de Gaulle's interest in exports to the United States and underestimated his determination to keep Britain out of the Community.

But the important point for Canadian policy was that the Canadian government failed to play a role in encouraging the most liberal and expansive scope for U.S. legislation. As it happened, there was a rare opportunity for Canada to do so because the Congress (perhaps more realistic about the U.S. administration's leverage on the EEC and particularly on the French president) passed an amendment expanding the 80-percent categories to cover the trade of EFTA countries as well as EEC countries, thus making EEC membership unnecessary to the application of the dominant supplier authority on a wide range of commodities. Unhappily, the administration persuaded Congress to remove this generous amendment before the final vote on the legislation, presumably because of its mistaken belief in the increased political leverage on EEC membership it might thereby exert. Had the Canadian government or its representatives been effective at that time in persuading the U.S. administration to accept the generous version of the law Congress had approved, both Canada and the United States would have entered the Kennedy Round with substantially greater scope for the removal of trade barriers.[5] Unfortunately, at the time relations were strained between the Canadian and U.S. governments. There is no evidence that any significant representation was made by the Canadian government.

The subsequent position of the Canadian negotiators at the Kennedy Round further supports the impression that Canada suffered from the lack of scope for complete tariff removal in the United States Trade Expansion Act. The Canadian government claimed that it could not make as substantial cuts as the U.S. or EEC within the general authority for 50-percent reductions because Canadian industry could not attain internationally competitive cost levels within the Canadian market (given the oligopolistic structure of most industries). Since the attainment of such unit costs would depend on specialization and export, 50-percent reduction would leave producers operating in the Canadian market with duties to absorb a larger proportion of their output than those already producing primarily for and within the United States or Western Europe. This type of argument makes it all the more regrettable that Canada was unable or unwilling to lobby for the liberal version of the Trade Expansion Act.

The Kennedy Round of GATT negotiations that ended in 1967 was the last multilateral bargain completed. The current Tokyo Round gives little indication of providing a new solution to the problem of rationalization of Canadian manufacturing industries. So far as is possible to detect the Canadian position, the emphasis appears to be on obtaining better access in external markets for more processed forms of Canadian natural products. A principal means of achieving this, cited by Canadian spokesmen, is sector deals that would eliminate duties and any relevant nontariff barriers on primary and processed (including fully processed) forms of broad commodity categories. One might speculate on the application of this approach to nonferrous metals, pulp and paper, or petrochemicals. In the last two cases the comprehensive reduction of tariffs and other barriers might indeed assist the rationalization of production, but the prospect of achieving such an objective is severely constrained by the limited interest so far evident in the U.S. and Europe, particularly if the Canadian requirement is for completely free access for the sectors concerned.

It is too early to evaluate the prospects of the Tokyo Round, but the unique requirements of the Canadian economy and the much less compelling interests of the larger trading units make it unlikely that the Tokyo Round will bring an outcome well suited to Canadian needs.

Other Canadian trade policy activities in the postwar years have been mainly of two kinds:

1. Efforts to improve the selling activities of Canadian industry especially in overseas markets, primarily by expanding and upgrading the services provided by the Trade Commissioner Service (administered by the Department of Industry, Trade, and Commerce).
2. Various supports for particular sectors, both those under import competition pressure and those believed capable of expanded export activity. Examples of these latter policies included:
    a. Production-sharing arrangements for defense industries, under which Canadian firms are afforded specific opportunities to obtain U.S. defense contracts as part of the general integration of defense production capabilities
    b. Voluntary export restraints negotiated with countries, mainly suppliers of labor-intensive products such as textiles and footwear that threaten to undermine particularly weak sectors in the Canadian economy
    c. Sector arrangements such as the Canada-United States automotive products agreement already mentioned; other sectoral arrangements have been considered for the paper, chemicals, and industrial machinery industries, but none of these has been put into effect

For the most part it has been considered necessary to approach sectoral arrangements with caution in view of the resistance to further bilateral deals in both Ottawa and Washington. As a consequence of the automotive agreement, some U.S. congressmen and business and labor interests question the value to the United States of schemes apparently designed to use access to the U.S. market in a project whose operating conditions are defined in Ottawa to achieve the objective of improving the effectiveness of Canadian production and the volume of Canadian trade.

Since the end of 1972 a new theme has been introduced in Canadian external policies that has particular importance for Canadian-U.S. trade—the so-called third option. In an article in the autumn of 1972, Minister of External Affairs Mitchell Sharp stated that there were three basic options in Canada-U.S. relations: the status quo, closer economic integration, or the substitution for the international market mechanism in North America of a domestic policy strategy designed to achieve Canada's long-term economic needs. The minister indicated that the government favored the third option.[6] Two differing but perhaps complementary implications have subsequently been drawn from this choice. The most logical interpretation of the third option as originally stated by Sharp is that the government intended henceforth to base policy for Canada's economic and social development on a kind of national economic planning not so fundamentally dependent on the competitive pressures or opportunities of external markets. In subsequent debates about the third option, however, government spokesmen including the prime minister have interpreted it to suggest that the government was seeking to expand its economic relations with other countries, notably those of the European Community and Japan, but also with the Communist bloc, China, and the developing world, as counterweights to the U.S.'s preponderant economic influence. The Sharp article indicates that the third option is not incompatible with a generally liberal trade pattern and should not depend on it.

During 1975 the government paid considerable attention to a new "contractual arrangement," or "link," with the European Economic Community. The prime minister and other senior ministers and officials made several trips to European capitals to obtain some specific European recognition of Canada's separate identity as an economic partner. Most observers, including government officials in Ottawa, regard the results of these exercises with counterweights as largely rhetorical, but they are not without political effect, as they may satisfy some Canadian nationalists that the government is doing whatever it can to improve communications with overseas economic partners so that access to those markets is as close to equivalent to the access already enjoyed to the North American market as can be achieved without substantive changes in the remaining formal trade barriers. These barriers are at present in the hands of the GATT negotiators for the Tokyo Round, since Canada continues to pursue the traditional multilateral approach to trade liberalization. One thing is clear, however: neither the third option nor the extent of trade liberalization at present considered probable via the Tokyo Round is likely to contribute greatly to the solution of the structural efficiency problem described in the early part of this chapter. One need only compare the effect of the automotive agreement with the effect of the whole Kennedy Round negotiation to observe how much more significant a contribution to economic efficiency and growth is made by a policy with for the most part sharply defined direction and appropriate (if overgenerous) transitional arrangements. It is primarily for this reason that the Economic Council of Canada in its recent publication *Looking Outward* supported a much more vigorous and comprehensive use of commercial policy liberalization.[7]

In the period since the food and petroleum price increases of 1973-1974 and the oil embargo, Canada, like other Western countries has had to reappraise its domestic and international policies on raw materials. Unlike most other Western countries, however, Canada's interests have been complicated by the country's perception of its role as producer as well as consumer of such products. Considerable attention has been given to the optimistic view that Canada is relatively well endowed with natural resources and that its competitive position internationally ought to be improved if there were to be more effective (i.e., price-raising) cartels or producer-oriented commodity agreements. While such expectations are not entirely invalid, many Canadian policy-makers and analysts argue that Canada cannot afford to rely on the asymmetrical distribution of resources. In the first place it is not clear that cartels and like arrangements can be successfully established for many of the raw materials in which Canada is especially rich. For example, Canada is a processor of bauxite, not a significant producer of the raw material. There are a sufficient number of copper producers that efforts to achieve collusion among them have not to date succeeded in stabilizing higher price levels. Unpredictability of production conditions and policies, notably but not exclusively in the Soviet Union, have constrained efforts to stabilize wheat and other cereal prices at higher levels, and so on.

However, it is in the energy sector that the main lessons have been learned. Canada has dreamed of being a producer of large exportable petroleum and natural gas surpluses, but as long as Middle Eastern supplies were available at the pre-1973 prices, it was not economic to supply Canadian oil in the most easterly part of Canada, and western production was in part exported to the midwestern U.S. market while eastern Canada (Montreal and beyond) was supplied from overseas sources, such as Venezuela. When the price of Middle Eastern oil was raised, it became clearly economical for the first time for Canada to supply its most easterly provinces, but the pipeline necessary to achieve objectives remained to be built. In the meantime it became necessary to decide whether the traditional midcontinent markets (on both sides of the Canada-U.S. border) should be supplied at world prices. It was decided to move in steps toward world prices for the Canadian consumer, subsidizing the eastern consumers for a time to ensure that their prices would be no higher (on a well-head basis) than the oil supplied from Canadian wells to western consumers. The subsidy was to be financed by an export levy on oil exported to the U.S. midwest, bringing that oil to world prices. This move was resisted by several groups—some midwestern U.S. consumers and their congressional representatives, and the governments of western producer provinces. The former mistakenly thought that the Canadian government was discriminating against them. In the absence of the export levy, the oil companies could have been able to capture the whole windfall gain in the U.S. market. The western provinces, on the other hand, believed that they should have a substantial share of such gains through royalties. For a time the federal government refused to allow the companies to deduct provincial royalty payments in the calculation of federal tax liabilities, and the companies feared total profit confiscation. Thus the short-term effect was to disrupt trading and investor relations with the United States, but the price issue faded as it was belatedly explained to the U.S. interests, and discussions between Alberta and federal governments resolved the most serious of the "double taxation" problems. Nevertheless, to some extent international investors remain uneasy about the possibility of the recurrence of problems arising out of federal-provincial conflict.

A longer-term legacy of both the food and energy price situations of recent years has been the attitude of many Canadians (as well as many Americans) that self-sufficiency is a desirable and meaningful goal with respect to major sectors of food and raw materials production. Happily for a healthy and efficient international allocation of resources, this obsession with self-sufficiency is being revealed as unrealistic. In Canada it is dying more slowly partly because it has been used by economic nationalists as a symbol of independence from the United States. Some of the more protectionist-minded agricultural interests have also exploited the occasion to press for additional subsidies from the federal minister of agriculture. The whole episode, it is hoped, may yet teach policy-makers useful lessons about the scope and limitations of economic independence for a country that continues to depend heavily on export markets for many natural products as the source of its high standard of living.

International Monetary Policy–Canada's Unique Role

The postwar evolution of international monetary policy also can be divided into several stages. The first stage is closely parallel to that for trade policy, namely, institution building. This was completed even before the war's end with the establishment of the International Monetary Fund in 1944. Canadian officials Louis Rasminsky, later governor of the Bank of Canada, and A. Wynne Plumptre, later assistant deputy minister of finance, were two of the major contributors and were active along with their British and U.S. colleagues in the IMF's design. All were influenced by the 1930s experience with competitive devaluations and other manipulations of exchanges, and selected a fixed but adjustable rate system for the postwar world. In retrospect, this was an overreaction, but it is easily understandable on the basis of past experience. In any case, during the reconstruction phase a flexible rate system would have raised the costs and uncertainties substantially. Until 1959, exchange rate changes were permitted to play only a limited role, and nonconvertibility and exchange controls were accepted. This left the main emphasis in the IMF on short-term liquidity arrangements.

Canada played a unique role in this period. While continuing to participate in the IMF in all other respects, Canada with the IMF's grudging acceptance adopted a flexible exchange rate policy in 1950. The immediate circumstances that led to that decision were associated with effect of the outbreak of war in Korea, leading to a new burst of demand for Canada's mineral and other resources and a related large-scale inflow of capital. The Canadian government had devalued the dollar by 10 percent only a year earlier when the 30-percent British devaluation occurred. Upward speculative pressure became extreme in the summer of 1950 and threatened to pay off handsomely. Freeing the dollar limited the payoff and allowed the government time to determine at what level a new fixed rate might be established. Events demonstrated that a flexible rate with relatively modest short-term exchange stabilization activity could result in stable rates, largely because of the huge and economically sound Canada-U.S. trade and investment-related transactions. The flexible rate has subsequently worked very well, except for the one period when the Canadian government for a time pursued an inappropriately tight monetary policy through its central bank, and even then it may be said that the overvalued exchange rate appropriately signaled that policy's folly. In 1962, after the management of the Bank of Canada had been changed, the government was confronted just before an election by new speculation on the dollar, brought on in large part by the government's announcing its intention to drive down the currency's foreign exchange value. The government felt compelled to abandon the flexible rate.

Beginning in the early 1960s, or perhaps with the convertibility of overseas currencies after 1959, the international monetary system entered a new stage. If in the previous period the system may be said to have had a liquidity orientation, it became adjustment-oriented in the 1960s and 1970s. The problems of the 1960s were manifested in the U.S. balance-of-payments situation. Although it was not at first recognized publicly as a problem requiring attention to the adjustment mechanism, that is what it was. Western Europe and Japan had recovered but refused to revalue or to permit a U.S. devaluation to reflect that recovery, thus revealing one of the main practical weaknesses of the IMF system, the great resistance to an explicit policy change that weakens export strength. The refusal to accept exchange rate changes meant that inflation rates in Europe and Japan had to exceed those in North America. This was accepted until the financing of the Vietnam War generated higher rates of U.S. inflation, prolonging the balance-of-payments problem and resulting in greater dissatisfaction in overseas capitals. Nevertheless it was not until August 1971 that the resistance to substantial shifts in exchange values was overcome, then only after unusually vigorous U.S. policy moves. The much modified system that emerged from the negotiations of the next two years has incorporated exchange flexibility and has worked very well, particularly considering the historically unique peacetime shock delivered to the international monetary system by the petroleum cartel in 1973-1974.

Canada's role in this period was largely reactive. In most respects Canada has operated within the system since 1962, adjusting to the shocks delivered by shifts in U.S. balance-of-payments policy, especially those designed to discourage or limit the effects of U.S. capital export. Canada obtained exemptions (complete or partial) but agreed to limit the growth of Canadian foreign exchange reserves and the "pass through" of capital to the Eurodollar market. There was growing uneasiness in Canada about the consequences of the widely recognized undervaluation of the dollar (which remained fixed at 92.5¢ U.S.) and about the necessity of the exchange reserves limitation commitment to the United States. Eventually, in May 1970, the Canadian government elected to return to a floating rate and the dollar rose quickly to over 97¢ U.S. and thereafter edged toward equality with the U.S. dollar. But this time Canada was out of line with IMF practice for a comparatively short time, since following the Smithsonian Agreement in December 1971 the other industrially advanced countries moved toward exchange adjustment and in 1973 to a high degree of exchange flexibility.

The Canadian preoccupation after 1971 was closely parallel to that of other industrially advanced states, and particularly with the United States. The object was to make the revised IMF system work and, after 1973 particularly, to accommodate the effects of severe sectoral price shocks in world food, raw material, and energy markets and the resulting balance-of-payments difficulties of the poorer Third World states. The former Canadian Minister of Finance, John Turner, and his officials played an important role in these efforts. There is little that now separates Canada from the main trends of international monetary arrangements, though it may be said that these trends have moved more toward positions Canada adopted in its own particular interest twice before its main partners decided to veer to the same course.[8]

International Investment and Aid

The institution-building phase in international investment at first paralleled that in the international monetary system. Formally, it centered on the founding of the International Bank for Reconstruction and Development in 1944, though of course the World Bank does not dominate in its sphere as the IMF does in its. Fundamentally, as its name implies, there were two spheres of activity—the postwar reconstruction of the economies of the industrialized states, and the development of the Third World economies. In the former activity the Bank was complemented by the Marshall Plan and the OEEC established in 1948. In the latter activity, there have emerged other institutions within the World Bank and U.N. family, e.g., the International Development Association, the U.N. Development Program, and the regional development banks (the Inter-American, the Asian, and the African). There have been the DAC of the OECD and numerous bilateral and subregional groupings. Canada is involved as a U.N. and OECD member in all these activities, and more directly in most of them.

In general the reconstruction stage of postwar experience ended in about 1960, as already mentioned in connection with the trade and monetary policy discussion. Canada participated fully in this phase, with massive official loans to

Britain and Europe in the early postwar years and active support of U.S. efforts through the OEEC, though admittedly considerably less involvement in the later private investment stage of European recovery. Canada's domestic capital needs made it a huge net importer in the 1950s.

Nevertheless Canada began to participate in aid to the Third World on a bilateral as well as multilateral basis as early as 1950. The major effort of the early years were directed to the Asian Commonwealth countries (under the Colombo Plan). In 1958 the Canada-West Indian Aid Program began, and in 1961 a program was established in Commonwealth Africa. In the mid-1960s aid to the French Community countries in Africa was initiated. More general technical assistance, and refugee and food aid programs also were initiated in this period as well as contributions to the IBRD, IDA, and IFC, and U.N. technical assistance. But for the first fifteen years of Canada's development aid, the Colombo Plan and food aid to the same countries together constituted almost 80 percent of all Canadian aid. Most of the remainder was channeled through United Nations agencies including the IBRD, the main share being to the IDA and to refugee programs. The total for this period was less than $700 million.

Since the mid-1960s the Canadian government has given a higher priority to external assistance and tried to raise the proportion of its GNP that has gone into external aid. Although it still falls well short of the 1 percent of GNP goal that was highlighted at the time of the Pearson Commission Report, it has increased—and perhaps more important, it has been in some respects more innovative. For example, in 1970 the government established the International Development Research Centre "to initiate, encourage, support and conduct research into the problems of the developing regions of the world, and into the means for applying and adapting scientific technical and other knowledge to the economic and social advancement of those regions." More important than its purpose is its method of operating. The IDRC is governed by a half-Canadian, half-international board, and in selecting projects it emphasizes the requirements of developing country governments and institutions and the management and research capacities of the developing countries. Furthermore it underwrites more risky research enterprises in the belief that they are less likely to be supported by national aid agencies under closer political surveillance. In its first five years it has approved projects exceeding $50 million in value, about 40 percent devoted to research in agriculture, food, and nutrition sciences, 20 percent to social science research, and the rest to human resources and the research of population and health sciences and information sciences.

The main themes of Canadian aid that distinguish it from that of some other countries may be summarized as follows:

1. There has been a greater emphasis on those regions that linguistically and culturally share similar historical roots—the Commonwealth countries and the French Community

2. There has been, especially in recent years, some interest in innovative forms of assistance, notably through the IDRC, designed to develop the capacity of developing countries to help themselves and one another.

In addition, Canada has incorporated in its aid program little of the military or security-oriented aid that is more characteristic of the great powers and little of the administrative assistance characteristic of such former colonial powers as France. Nevertheless Canadian aid programs under the Canadian International Development Agency have many of the characteristics of bilateral aid programs elsewhere. For example, much Canadian aid has been tied for commercial reasons or has provided incidental support for Canadian professionals in the technical assistance program. Multilateral aid remains a small part of the total. Shifting domestic priorities and turnover of senior administrators has led to costly reviews. Political influences also have been strong in the choice of top administrators. The fact that the electorate and Canadian political leadership of all parties have been generally supportive of external aid programs might lead one to expect a somewhat less politically motivated program, and it does at least in the IDRC. There is now increasing sentiment for a higher proportion of aid to be channeled through multilateral agencies, but such changes are not high priorities. Some of those who resist this shift probably exert more influence at times of decision-making, while the electorate is permissive but not activist.

There are indications that Canada's interest in the developing countries extends beyond development assistance. There is, of course, the need to respond to the demands mainly through UNCTAD for commodity arrangements and tariff preferences in industrial goods. In these matters Canada has shown sympathy and has offered concessions similar to those of other developed countries, but nothing particularly distinctive. In other contexts, such as the conferences on the law of the sea, there has been some effort to relate Canadian interests to those of the developing countries. Occasionally there has been mention of Canada's possible role as a leader or interpreter of developing country interests. There is no doubt that Canada as a smaller industrialized country with no colonial power history, a good record as a peacekeeper, and an average record in development assistance has a generally favorable reputation in the Third World. But it seems unlikely that Canadian political leaders will place much emphasis on Third World relations as a counterweight to those with the United States, or as a complement to those with Europe or Japan. The developing countries are increasingly capable of representing their own interests effectively and clearly prefer to do so. However, if Canada is able to devise distinctive ideas or arrangements relating to the trade policy interests of the Third World, or on the policy environment in which private investment and the transfer of technology function, then Canadian influence in the developing countries indeed may be enhanced.

The other side of the investment balance concerns the inflow of private capital. Here Canada's record as the world's largest single importer and major recipient of direct investment might indicate a capacity to provide some leadership in international efforts to ensure that the benefits to the recipient or host country are expanded without undermining economically sound private investment patterns. In fact, until the mid 1960s Canada adopted a free market approach to international investment flows.

What is the purpose of regulating foreign direct investment or the multinational enterprise, once established? The growing Canadian conviction that some intervention may be necessary is based on several contentions:

1. The desirability of controlling investment decisions to ensure the fulfillment of national plans or at least of certain specified priorities. This is the operative factor in the case of the countries that have screened foreign investment longest, such as Japan, Sweden, and France.
2. The desirability of capturing economic rents, particularly from resource industries, while ensuring that investment in such industries is maintained at a socially desirable level, given longer-term considerations such as conservation of the resource concerned. This phenomenon has become important for many developing countries as well as resource-rich developed countries such as Canada.
3. The desirability of controlling or limiting the oligopolistic effects often associated with the structure and behavior of large multinationals, especially in manufacturing industries. This is a quite general concern now that research findings of recent years have indicated the wider incidence of oligopoly in national markets segregated by trade barriers as well as certain international markets.[9]

The Canadian studies of multinational enterprises to date have pointed to the need for better information about the structure of industries, and for increased attention to national tariffs, patents, trademarks, and so forth, that restrict competition possible in national markets and result in oligopolistic behavior, misdirection of resources, and sometimes excessive profits of larger enterprises of all kinds, including the multinationals that are often the leading two or three firms in such industries.

The more specific measures by the Canadian government on the control of foreign direct investment have been of two kinds:

1. the exclusion of foreign-controlled firms from certain key sectors of the economy that are believed to be politically (or culturally) sensitive—e.g., the media—or important to macroeconomic policy—e.g., the banks and other major financial institutions
2. the screening of new takeovers and of foreign direct investment in new lines of business—the designated areas of activity covered by the new Foreign Investment Review Agency

Neither of these policies was adopted on the basis of a systematic empirical examination of the consequences of foreign enterprises in such sectors. The former seems to have arisen from the experience and basic convictions of the political leadership and bureaucracy concerning those sectors, while the screening activity was adopted as a way of getting information and developing criteria for relating that information to the broad criterion of "substantial benefit to Canada." There is considerable evidence from the experience that the government was not well informed in advance about the complexity of the field of activity it was about to enter or of the substance of the benefits that could be derived from screening.[10]

The report of the Task Force on the Structure of Canadian Industry in 1967, which was the government's first substantial effort to assess the impact of the multinationals on the operation of the Canadian economy, stressed the importance of improving on the disclosure requirements of the government and strengthening the competitive forces in the economy both by trade liberalization and by the improvement of competition laws. There have been some moves in these directions, minor modification of disclosure laws, and some substantial amendments to competition legislation. However, those amendments of competition legislation that have most bearing on the sectors in which multinationals are most prevalent are the provisions not yet enacted or even fully drafted, e.g., those that relate to mergers, specialization agreements, and export agreements.[11] Very little has been done to increase competitiveness by trade barrier reduction.

In general, the Canadian government did not adopt this broadly based approach to improving the operations of the market system. Instead, after some years the government adopted the screening approach. Even now that this approach is applied to both takeovers and foreign direct investments in new lines of business, it will not have any marked effect on the well-established multinational firms that play a predominant role in many mining and manufacturing industries. Possibly this is just as well, since the cost of screening and applying the long list of criteria now being used by the Foreign Investment Review Agency to all the substantive investments by most of the leading manufacturing firms in Canada could be a very costly procedure.

It is regrettable that the government did not see fit to pursue the more comprehensive disclosure and structural policies suggested by the task force. The tendency now to go into detailed review of certain investment activities and the practice of price review now being adopted in connection with wages and price controls may lead to a new and bureaucratically very costly interventional phase. It will be particularly unfortunate if a new tradition of intervention becomes buttressed with a rationale that the market system is permeated with oligopoly when perfectly straightforward policies had been suggested to the government by its own task force eight years ago (as well as many economists and others outside government), but were never seriously applied.

Canada's foreign economic policies in the investment sphere are of interest to the developing countries who are trying to work out arrangements for acquiring capital technology and managerial skills without the costs associated with imported or "home-grown" oligopolistic market structures. One can hope such host countries will learn all the available lessons from Canadian experience and will pay adequate attention not only to possible terms of agreements with multinationals but also to the national policy framework within which such firms operate. A protective framework militates against competition and allocative efficiency in a segregated national market and encourages the oligopolistic practices, transfer price systems, and other noneconomic effects that are so difficult to identify and control.

Political and Bureaucratic Factors in Canadian Foreign Economic Policies

In analyzing Canadian foreign economic policy since the war, it is useful to briefly sketch the policy-making process and the kind of political alignments that affect policy choices. The policy-making process with respect to foreign economic policies is relatively simple. Canada is a federal state, and for many policy areas, federal activity is circumscribed by the constitutional prerogatives of the provinces. In general, foreign economic policy is wholly federal. Provincial governments have no direct role in trade policy, exchange rate and other aspects of international monetary relationships, and aid policies. To be sure, there is nothing to prevent provincial governments from supporting external selling activities of enterprises resident within their borders, or from offering aid to developing countries—and so they have done both of these things. Since strictly speaking, diplomatic representation abroad is a federal responsibility, the presence of a B.C. or Ontario House in London or a Quebec representative in Paris depends on Ottawa's sufferance and, preferably, formal approval.

The federal-provincial question becomes more vital in matters of foreign investment. Under the Canadian constitution, property and civil rights and domestic trade within a province are subject to provincial control. The provinces have their own corporation law and their own right to regulate the purchase and sale of corporate securities and related activities. The more the federal government seeks to regulate foreign investment, the more likely its activity will be to conflict with that of the provinces. This is particularly true because the provinces have generally welcomed foreign investment in the past. In any event, it is only in this sector that constitutional considerations give the provinces a significant role.[12]

Within the federal structure the responsibilities of foreign economic policy are distributed unevenly among three departments, and agencies responsible to them.

1. For all international policies the Department of External Affairs has a general coordinative role and participates in all negotiations it does not wish to delegate. But its role is greater for some policy issues than for others, the degree depending on the technical complexity of the subject and the extent to which other departments have established roles and independent functions.

Among the foreign economic policy subjects here discussed, foreign aid is most completely within the authority of External Affairs, but the administration of aid is the responsibility of the Canadian International Development Agency. Although this agency reports to the minister of external affairs, the fact that it spends substantial sums of money means that there is likely to be considerable cabinet-level discussion of the parameters of aid policy, and of significant new expenditure items. The practice of tying aid engages the Department of Industry Trade and Commerce in this policy area.

2. For trade policy the lines are clear but the responsibility is nevertheless sharply divided. The Department of Finance, because of its responsibility for tax policy, controls the tariff and at one time played a much larger role in the nontariff aspects of trade policy. In recent years most of these, along with the promotion of exports by the trade commissioner service and by other forms of direct assistance to industry, have become the responsibility of the Department of Industry, Trade, and Commerce. Most trade policy issues involve active participation by representatives at the assistant deputy minister level or lower in interdepartmental groups or committees, with the leadership being taken normally by Finance or by Industry, Trade, and Commerce. In a matter relating to agricultural trade, the Department of Agriculture will be very active since nontariff policies of that department are often the subject of negotiation. In energy matters the National Energy Board will play a leading role, but generally, at least in recent years, only within the policy framework established by the cabinet with the full involvement of the ministries already cited and, of course, the Department of Energy, Mines, and Resources.

3. In matters relating to international monetary arrangements the Department of Finance has virtually exclusive jurisdiction, though the Bank of Canada, the domestic monetary authority that reports to the Department of Finance, always will be involved in exchange stabilization.

4. In matters relating to foreign investment in Canada, the lines have not been so clear, since until recently there was little in the way of comprehensive policy. When issues relating to key enterprise takeover have arisen as in the case of the Mercantile Bank, it rapidly becomes a cabinet matter but with the Department of Finance giving the main guidance. In the case of media policy the Department of Communications and the secretary of state (who is concerned with publications policy) are active.

The question of the screening agency raised a new issue: What department should be charged with responsibility for the legislation defining the agency and its functions? The decision to give the responsibility for the agency to the

Department of Industry, Trade, and Commerce was plausible on the grounds that this department was accustomed to dealing with industry but questionable on the equally good grounds that the process involved was regulatory whereas most of the department's other activity is dedicated to promoting industry. The department with the most expertise on the evaluation of the social performance of an industry is probably the Department of Consumer and Corporate Affairs. However, it is apparent that the preferences in cabinet and between the ministers of the departments in question played a major role in determining the assignment of this agency.

For all these foreign economic policy matters there have been important interdepartmental arrangements. In the past a group of senior deputy ministers exercised an informal coordinating function. These included the deputy ministers of the Departments of Finance; Industry, Trade, and Commerce; and External Affairs, and depending on the issue might involve the secretary of the treasury board and secretary of the cabinet and possibly senior-level representatives from relevant departments such as Agriculture; Energy, Mines, and Resources; and Consumer and Corporate Affairs. These were the well-known "Mandarin" group, whose particular assignments were at times less important than their general prestige in the public service.

In the last few years the shift to a more systematic cabinet committee arrangement has somewhat altered as was intended, the role of the senior bureaucracy in relation to the cabinet. The cabinet has become much more involved in the formation of policy, especially as the members have their senior officials with them in cabinet committee and these are often cross-questioned by other cabinet members. In international matters, the arrangement has some advantages since the cabinet members usually have less direct familiarity with the subject matter of these issues. The cabinet committee meeting thus becomes both educational for the cabinet and a genuine consensus-forming unit. Of course the positions that cabinet ministers take should be traced to their regional and party origins and perhaps to the kind of clientele they served as lawyers in private practice. In more fully identifying attitudes to international economic policy issues, the relevant characteristics of Canada's principal political parties will be explained, followed by a brief review of regional and functional groups.

The Liberal Party has been in power federally since 1935 except for the period from 1957 to 1963 when the Progressive Conservative Party was in office. However from 1957 to 1958, 1962 to 1968, and 1972 to 1974, there were minority governments. These minority governments meant that policies became relatively short-sighted and that bold initiatives were rarely considered on international issues.

The differences between political parties on international issues have been related to regional strengths. But the latter have shifted in the past fifteen years and have somewhat affected certain international policy attitudes. For example, from the war until 1957 the Liberal Party was a party with substantial support in the western provinces and from the province of Quebec with more fluctuating support from Ontario and the Atlantic Provinces. The Progressive Conservative Party usually had a majority of Ontario seats, including most of the rural seats, good representation from the Atlantic provinces, and a minority of members from the west. Most of the members of the CCF (Corporative Commonwealth Federation), in 1960 renamed the New Democratic Party, have come from Saskatchewan and from certain urban centers, namely, Vancouver, Winnipeg, and Toronto; a few are from mining and forest industry constituencies in British Columbia and Ontario.

Since 1958, when the Progressive Conservatives swept to power with the largest majority in history, the prairie provinces became an important area of strength for them under the strong personality of the western Prime Minister John Diefenbaker and his colleague Alvin Hamilton who, as Minister of Agriculture, claimed the credit for the first large wheat sales to mainland China. Ever since then, although the same selling policies have been maintained by successive liberal governments, the west has remained mainly loyal to the conservatives. This left both major parties struggling for a majority in most years with the two liberal majority governments (1968-1972 and after 1974) depending on a virtual sweep of Quebec seats, some strength in the Atlantic provinces, and a good showing in Ontario.

The effect of these shifts on policy attitudes can be summarized as follows. The Liberals had been the traditional "free trade" party in the years before the First World War; their commitment on this issue was based on the vital importance of overseas markets for wheat and other natural resource products and the obvious economy to be derived by purchasing manufactured products from Britain, the world's lowest cost supplier of so many of these products. But the years between the wars undermined confidence in the international market and Liberal party leaders became somewhat self-conscious about their identification with free trade, perhaps because of their desire to appeal more to Ontario interests and because of mixed views in Quebec. The large share of Quebec province that relies on natural resource industries is also oriented toward free trade but important sections, notably in textiles (east and southeast of Montreal in the eastern townships), are protectionist. Agricultural protection is also important in both Quebec and Ontario. Although the rank and file of the Liberal Party continue to espouse a free trade policy especially in the west and the Atlantic provinces, these elements have less influence on Liberal Party discussions than they used to. Then too, among the younger generation of voters, the rise of nationalism has had some influence on the attitudes toward any trend to international interdependence involving closer integration with the United States. These elements are particularly vocal in important urban centers, especially in Toronto and Ottawa, but also in the west. The Liberal Party continues to support multilateral trade liberalization in principle, and it initiated the automotive agreement with the United States in 1965, but today it is led by elements that are not hostile to international interdependence but are generally reluctant to consider any bold moves especially of a bilateral nature with the United States (such as a broad industrial or sectoral free trade arrangement).

The Progressive Conservative Party has been the traditional party of "protection," especially in Ontario. However, Diefenbaker conservatism being based in the prairies is affected by traditional free trade sentiments of western grain and cattle farmers, and this has left the party with more mixed views in this area. Hence this party is likely to go along with general liberalization, is particularly anxious to maintain overseas trade links with Commonwealth countries, and perhaps is a little more protectionist but not more nationalistic toward the bilateral links with the United States. However, in the John A. Macdonald tradition of pragmatic use of commercial policy for economic development, it is entirely possible that a Conservative leader might have fewer inhibitions than the Liberals concerning a Canada-U.S. free trade arrangement accompanied by suitable transitional safeguards.

The New Democratic Party, also based in part in the west, has not dissimilar trade ideas, but it is somewhat more nationalist thanks to greater support from urban votes and notably those who are both younger and more left-wing in this sector. However, its economic nationalism is more clearly focused on foreign investment than on trade issues. The New Democratic Party and the left wing of the Liberal Party are influenced in these views by recently expressed criticism of the market economy, including those of John Kenneth Galbraith. They have come to believe that the predominance of large enterprises in major industrial sectors is well enough established to warrant the conclusion that market forces, including international market forces, no longer operate effectively to control the market power of the largest enterprises, and have hastened to the conclusion that many had already espoused sentimentally, namely, that direct "planning" is the only intellectually satisfactory means of attaining national objectives. Of course, to draw this conclusion without reference to the effects of segregation of national markets by international trade restrictions trade policies is unwarranted.

As already suggested, these political views have affected the attitude toward both foreign investment and foreign trade; however, it is the former that generated the most political debate. In fact, the political argument on foreign investment has often been used as a reason for restraint on policies for trade liberalization, especially vis-à-vis the United States. This view neglects the evidence generally available from economic studies that foreign direct investment has been promoted by trade barriers and that many of the most criticized features of foreign enterprise operations are directly traced to protectionist policies of the host government. This confusion clearly illustrates how strong are the purely political arguments for some nationalistic policies.

All three major political parties have paid some attention to foreign investment control. The Liberal government has tried a number of approaches—tax incentives for the promotion of minority share holdings in wholly owned subsidiaries and appointment of Canadians to management positions; funding of a Canada Development Corporation to encourage greater Canadian participation in dynamic sectors of the economy; direct restriction or fiscal disincentives to foreign ownership of firms in key sectors such as banking and the media; and of course the screening agency. These policies have generally been supported by both other parties, though more critically by the Progressive Conservatives. A Conservative provincial government in Ontario has sponsored studies of the effects of foreign control on Ontario industry and culture, but this had not resulted in significant specific policy initiatives in the province.

In spite of all this debate, foreign investment has never become a significant electoral issue, and within government the variety of both political and bureaucratic views has meant that the application of policy ideas for the control of foreign investment activity has been generally cautious and moderate.

Conclusions

Canada's foreign economic policy record has been a function of four main factors:

1. A high level of interdependence in the world economy associated with the combination of a relatively small population and a high per capita income
2. A decline in influence from one of unusual status as senior partner to the major power at the end of World War II to that of relatively weak fourth among market economies
3. A uniquely close relationship to the world's greatest economic and political power
4. An internal economic structure based on a highly individual form of the dualistic economy, where the weaker sector is enslaved not to traditional noncapitalist institutions or groups but rather to traditional capitalist policies allied with persistent nationalistic sentiments of varying political coloration

This combination explains the peculiar combination of conservatism and liberalism in the pattern of Canada's international economic policies. Trade policy embodies a long liberal tradition with a distinctly inconsistent protection that in the postwar years has been under severe attack as its traditional intellectual foundation has crumbled, but that survives tentatively with a new noneconomic rationale. Monetary policy fortunately does not require the same awkward compromise. Canada has been too conservative to attempt multiple exchange rates but has chosen a different kind of compromise—formal adherence to rules of the international system but for much of the postwar period a unique practice of exchange flexibility. It was accepted internationally precisely because

Canada was so effectively integrated into the world economy and its institutions of management, but in Canada its ultimate rationale, like that of commercial policy, lay in the limited economic necessity and the apparently greater political necessity for devices that leave (or appear to leave) some scope for the independence of Canadian economic policies from those of its neighbor.

Finally, policies relating to international capital flows have reflected the same factors, but here the traditions are much newer. Until the past decade Canada simply accepted interdependence, but like many other countries, the control of investment inflows has become another issue reflecting the reaction to North American interdependence together with a reaction to the effects of the Canadian version of dual economy that have been attributed to foreign direct investment rather than the protectionist policies that largely explain why some industries are less efficient performers than others.

Policies affecting outflow of capital, mainly foreign aid policies, are less influenced by the economic factors listed than the other external economic policies, but these do reflect to some extent both the attempt to support the dual economy and the value, albeit limited, of foreign aid policy as a political counterweight to North American integrative links.

In the circumstances of the 1970s Canadian political leaders have, for understandable but nonetheless regrettable reasons, permitted themselves to drift into a position that precludes the use of major trade policy changes as a means of correcting the problems of the dual economy and are seeking instead to attack some of the macroeconomic consequences of their policies by more direct intervention in the control of markets. If, as is all too probable, these policies (wage and price controls, etc.) are mere palliatives that are not accompanied by any fundamental strengthening of the weaker sector of the dual economy, then the other international economic policy instrument will come into play, and flexible exchange rates will lead to depreciation as a substitute for the rationalization of the protected sector.

So long as Canada is unable to find a substitute for protectionist economic policies as a perceived necessity in the maintenance of a separate Canadian identity, Canadian international economic policies will remain in a measure incoherent, and Canada will benefit from only part of the benefits of international economic interdependence. This is not an intolerable inefficiency to an already wealthy country, but it may be less acceptable both economically and politically in a world where the major market economies are already beneficiaries of substantially free access to one another's markets. Both Canadian and foreign investors are likely more often to reject Canadian opportunities as second best. Domestically, it could also mean that the costs and uneven regional burden of unique levels of protection will have to be borne by compensating subsidies from Canadian governments, using finances that could be employed better elsewhere in the political and social system rather than an incomplete substitute to the international market system.

Notes

1. These phenomena have been extensively examined in Canadian economic studies over the past ten to fifteen years. Among the more general studies are: H. Edward English, *Industrial Structure in Canada's International Competitive Position* (Montreal: Private Planning Association of Canada, 1964); and D.J. Daly et al., *Scale and Specialization in Canadian Manufacturing* (Ottawa: Economic Council of Canada, Staff Study no. 21, 1968). Particular industries having many of these characteristics have been examined in greater detail, e.g., by the Royal Commission on Automotive Products and Royal Commission on Farm Machinery.

2. Carl E. Beigie, *The Canada-U.S. Automotive Agreement: An Evaluation* (Montreal: Canadian-American Committee, 1970).

3. Hugh G. Aitken, *American Capital and Canadian Resources* (Cambridge, Mass.: Harvard University Press, 1961).

4. Economic Council of Canada, *Twelfth Annual Review* (Ottawa: Information Canada, 1975).

5. Howard S. Piquet, *The U.S. Trade Expansion Act of 1962: How Will It Affect Canadian-American Trade?* (Washington, D.C.: Canadian-American Committee, 1963).

6. Mitchell Sharp, "Canada-U.S. Relations: Options for the Future," *International Perspectives* (Autumn 1972): 1-24.

7. Economic Council of Canada, *Looking Outward* (Ottawa: Information Canada, 1975).

8. Canadian postwar experience with flexible exchanges has been detailed in Paul Wonnacott, *The Floating Canadian Dollar: Exchange, Flexibility and Monetary Independence* (Washington, D.C.: American Enterprise Institute, 1972) and Robert Dunn, *Canada's Experience with Fixed and Flexible Exchange Rates in a North American Capital Market* (Montreal and Washington, D.C.: Canadian-American Committee, 1971). The relation of this to capital flows and macroeconomic policies has been further examined in Richard E. Caves and Grant L. Reuber, *Canadian Economic Policy and the Impact of International Capital Flows* (Private Planning Association of Canada and University of Toronto Press, 1969).

9. David Schwartzman, *Oligopoly in the Farm Machinery Industry* for the Royal Commission on Farm Machinery (Ottawa: Information Canada, 1970), and *Report of the Royal Commission on Farm Machinery* (Ottawa: Information Canada, 1971).

10. *Foreign Direct Investment in Canada* (Ottawa: Government of Canada, 1972), Chap. 25.

11. Lawrence Skeoch and Bruce McDonald (in consultation with Michael Belanger, Reubin M. Bromstein, and William Twaits), *Dynamic Change and*

Accountability in a Canadian Market Economy for the Department of Consumer and Corporate Affairs (Ottawa: Queen's Printer, Catalogue RG 5210, 1976).

12. Eugene Forsey, "Constitutional Aspects of the Canadian Economy," in *Canada-United States Relations*, ed. H. Edward English, *Proceedings of the Academy of Political Science*, vol. 32, no. 2 (New York, 1976).

9 The European Community

Geoffrey Denton
and Theo Peeters

In the conduct of its foreign economic policies the European Community is confronted with a rather unique situation. In economic terms it is often characterized as a superpower, and there is reason to agree with such a statement, as Table 9-1 sufficiently demonstrates. But it is a superpower with a rather limited capacity to act. The EC is in fact a "self-restricted giant."

Foreign economic policy embraces at least four major areas of policy actions: concerning trade, aid, investment, and financial matters. Only in one of these areas, trade, has the Community an explicit authority and responsibility for the conduct of external relations. In the other areas either the Community is absent or it can formulate an external policy only after a common internal policy has been established and common interests identified. The Community's machinery is designed principally to promote the harmonization of the member states' *internal* policies. Except for commercial matters–and even here important limitations remain–the harmonization of *external* relations needs an additional development of political intention. Although potentially a supranational decision-making body, the Community is essentially an intergovernmental organization, as it is likely to remain for several years. Member states can only be expected to entrust it with power over limited areas of policy. Divergence of national interests and ambitions, rather than the driving force of a common purpose, is characteristic for the Community. Evidence for this is to be found at the heart of its power structure.

How else could one explain the simultaneous existence of the objective of a so-called global Mediterranean policy with the careful division of authority between the British member of the commission responsible for external relations (including relations with the northern Mediterranean) and his French colleague responsible for developing countries enjoying special relations with the Community (including the southern Mediterranean).

Even if the Community were to become entrusted, either at the initiative of the commission or by a council decision, with major additional powers in foreign economic relations, the fact remains that the manpower resources at the Community's disposal are too limited for any large-scale administrative or executive operation. With a total staff smaller than medium-sized government departments in the larger member countries, and with virtually no diplomatic representation in the countries with which it deals, common external policy must still depend on intergovernmental rather than Community action.

Another particular feature of a Community foreign economic policy is that

Table 9-1
Size of the European Community Compared with Other Major Countries, 1974

	EC(nine)	*U.S.A.*	*USSR*	*Japan*
Population (thousands)	257,700	211,910	252,060	109,670
GNP[a] ($ million)	1179.2	1397.4	467.2[b]	451.7
GNP per capita ($)	4,576	6,594	1,854	4,119
Imports ($ million)	293,568	100,972	24,880	62,110
Imports (% of world total)	35.2	12.1	3	7.5
Imports excluding intra-EEC ($ million)	153,963	100,972	24,880	62,110
Imports (% of world total)[c]	22.2	14.5	3.6	9
Exports ($ million)	275,099	98,506	27,395	55,536
Exports (% of world total)	32.9	11.8	3.3	6.6
Exports excluding intra-EEC ($ million)	136,071	98,506	27,395	55,536
Exports (% of world total)[c]	19.5	14.1	3.9	8
International Reserves ($ million)	69.634	16.058	–	13.519
International Reserves (% of world total)	31.6	7.3	–	6.1

Sources: I.M.F., *International Financial Statistics*; O.E.C.D., *Statistics of Foreign Trade*; U.N., *Monthly Bulletin of Statistics.*

[a]Gross National Product at Current Prices and Exchange Rates

[b]Net Material Product

[c]Excluding intra-E.E.C.-Trade

it has to operate outside an explicit general foreign policy framework, notwithstanding the proposals for greater political cooperation and the Davignon Committee. The Community's foreign relations, therefore, will continue to be dominated by economic issues: trade (including industrial policy and other nontariff questions), external ramifications of agricultural policy, aid, and monetary relations. The other main component of foreign policy, security, is in the hand of national governments or of another international organization, NATO. There is therefore a real danger that economic issues may become divorced from security issues and from what have been traditionally considered "high politics." The varying degree of transatlantic linkages that have been established in the recent past between trade policy, international monetary reform, foreign investments, aid, and balance-of-payments adjustment on the one hand, and burden-sharing of military expenditures and military strategy on the other, have blurred the distinction between "technical" economic decisions and "political" strategic decisions. Foreign economic policy is increasingly elevated from the level of "low policy" to the forefront of "high policy." But the Community is in no position to deal with a situation where GATT, UNCTAD, IMF, and NATO are mixed up at the same time, since a delicate balancing act is involved between Community action and the national diplomacy of member countries.

A further complication for a Community foreign economic policy arises from the profoundly different views held on important issues by the different member states. The situation is further complicated by the different styles of policy-making in different areas of activity. Not only do the influence and the power of pressure groups vary substantially between countries; the situation may be different even within the same country—between, say, monetary and commercial policy.

Community foreign economic policy will unavoidably reflect divergences of interest between member countries. Failure to agree on some aspect of internal policy has rendered the Community incapable of functioning effectively in important aspects of its external relations; energy and monetary questions are particularly revealing examples (see pp. 206-208). Member countries are also still commercial competitors, even if they agree at the Community level on the broad principles governing particular areas of a common commercial policy. Geographically differentiated trading interests need to be accommodated if a policy is to be developed. The same is true for member countries who conduct substantially different percentages of their total trade with countries inside or outside the Community. The contrasting situation of Germany and the United Kingdom in terms of monetary reserves and balance-of-payments prospects explains many of the differences in their attitudes toward world monetary reform. Thus Community foreign economic policy can be expected to concentrate on and to be most successful in areas where a common interest dominates over national self-interest. The division of responsibility between the Community and the national level depends inter alia on national governments' perceptions of when they expect to benefit from their own conduct of policy in respect to when they think the Community can handle things better. At the same time it remains true that the member countries of the European Community have made the fundamental decision that they have more important interests in common than those that separate them. To the extent that they increasingly succeed in agreeing on "Community solutions" over significant areas in their economic decision-making, a growing harmonization of their external repercussions will result.

A discussion of the EEC's foreign economic policy therefore must be even more complex than a discussion of such policies in individual countries. To all the conflicting policy objectives, pressures and interests, and practical constraints that make up the shifting policies of each of the member states is added a set of new variables that immensely complicate the picture. Among the most significant are: changes in the economic and political parameters of each member state vis-à-vis both the partners and third countries, caused by the

Community's initial policies and rules regarding trade and monetary questions and the like; the development of common policies that have repercussions on the interests of members and third countries; and the development of a common commercial policy toward third countries that replaces or constrains the member countries' individual policies.

In seeking the economic and political advantages of regional cooperation, the EC had serious repercussions on affairs in other parts of the world, and accommodation to the new situation after 1958 required a major adaptation of the GATT system. Although the EEC was established under the provisions of Article 24 of the GATT, the repercussions it produced were hardly envisaged when this general permission excluding the creation of free trade areas and customs unions from the general rule of nondiscrimination had been inserted. The consequences for third countries were mixed: positive in that further trade liberalization in Western Europe, beyond that achieved in the 1950s, stimulated further worldwide liberalization, implemented in the Kennedy Round; negative in that the inevitable trade diversion effects of discriminatory regional tariff removal harmed third country interests and tended to provoke protectionist reactions. The consequences of the initial provisions of the Rome Treaty in this direction were slight, in view of the strongly trade-creating, and minimally trade-diverting, character of the Six, and the coincidence of its early years with a period of rapid and sustained growth in the members' economies, which increased total imports from third countries by more than enough to outweigh such trade diversions as did occur. Nevertheless, third countries were concerned; this concern was acknowledged and two early concessions included the extension of two early stages of tariff cuts to third countries on a most-favored-nation basis, and the initiation of the Kennedy Round negotiations.

The Community's extension to the internal markets for agricultural products after 1966, unifying the national support policies pursued by member states (as by all advanced industrial countries), raised more acute problems. It revealed a phenomenon latent in any regional economic unification—namely, that policies applied by a block with a powerful bargaining position, though no more protectionist than those employed by individual members before integration, may nevertheless be more harmful to third country interests.

Similar external effects of common policies also would have applied in managed markets, or in industries enjoying government aid, producing a wide range of industrial products, especially in the advanced technology areas. The Community failed in practice to make significant progress in developing common policies in these industries. Yet in principle, member states accepted the desirability of such policies, and the fear of the effects of such common policies on the export trade of other countries was an element in the reaction, especially of the United States, toward the Community as a protectionist bloc. That common interventionist policies to support such industries would merely be giving the Community the kind of advantages already enjoyed by the U.S.

(because of its vast unified market and powerful governmental support for industrial development) could not overcome the natural antagonism to the change that would be brought about in the relative commercial strength of the EC, and the threatened disruption of existing trade relations based on the relatively weak industrial competitiveness of the member countries individually.

The Community Authority for External Economic Policy

In the Treaty of Paris, which created the ECSC, a common external policy is explicitly outside Community competence. Despite its supranational character, the absence of a Community authority over external commercial policy in the ECSC treaty makes it resemble a free trade area more than a truly common market in its external relations. The power to conclude commercial agreements with third countries remains with the member countries.

In the Treaty of Rome the common commercial policy is the logical result of the Community's having developed into a full-fledged customs union. There is a short but important part on the association of overseas countries and territories; references to trade exist in the part on agriculture; and Articles 110 to 116 concern a common commercial policy. Along with Article 238, which provides for "association" agreements concluded by the Community, since the end of the transition period on 1 January 1970, Article 113 has been the most important single basis for the EC's external relations. Association agreements, of which the precise content is not specified in Article 238, can be concluded between the Community and third countries, a union of countries, or even international organizations. They can in fact take all possible forms ranging between full membership and simple commercial agreements. And it is the Community, not the member states, that has the treaty-making power. The Council of Ministers concludes association agreements after the commission negotiates on the basis of a mandate approved by the council.

However, no stipulation in the Treaty of Rome precisely defines Community competence in common commercial policy. The treaty specifies neither the instruments at the Community's disposal for executing its commercial policy, nor its substance. As far as the instruments are concerned, Article 113 defines the commercial policy as including "in particular" matters of tariffs, quantitative restrictions, antidumping measures, a common regime for export incentives, and the authority to conclude commercial agreements. The enumeration is meant to be illustrative, but the member states have always insisted on a restrictive interpretation. Instruments not mentioned are considered to fall outside the specific Community competence and to remain under the competence of the member countries.

The restrictive interpretation of Community authority over external commercial relations no longer fits the requirements of a modern commercial policy.

Modern commercial policy is necessarily concerned not only with regulating the flow of already existing trade, but with creating trade and promoting economic interchange in general. International investment becomes more and more a substitute for trade. Industrial cooperation, including the setting up of joint ventures and the exchange of technological information and know-how, gains in importance over trade in relations with both state trading countries and developing countries.

The EC's creation has in no way affected its members' legal position in international organizations; they continue to exercise their rights as individual members. However, the Community's functioning requires a concerted action of the member countries in international economic organizations. Article 116 stipulates that the member countries must defend a common position in international organizations, either through a common delegation or through a Community representative, whenever the subject discussed touches on the particular interests of the Common Market. The object and the nature of this common position can vary according to the importance of the subject matter, considerations of political opportunity, and the particular degree of each member's participation in the operations of international organizations. There is thus no uniform pattern for Community participation in these organizations.

In general, the Community attends the international economic organizations alongside the member countries as an observer with the right to speak but not to vote. This is the case, for example, in the United Nations and its specialized agencies, in the GATT, IMF, and OECD. But whenever matters under the competence of the Community are discussed, the Community takes a more active role. This is particularly true for commercial negotiations within the GATT framework, where the commission acts as negotiator vis-à-vis third countries and the council concludes the commercial agreements. Within GATT the Community therefore usually occupies an ad hoc position that goes beyond the position of a simple observer. Despite its considerable activities within this organization, however, it is not an autonomous contracting party. Only the member countries are contracting parties and recognized as such.

Whereas in the commercial policy field the Treaty of Rome at least imposes a Community approach vis-à-vis the rest of the world, the power of Community institutions in the external aspects of other economic policy problems are at best restricted to coordinating the national actions of the member countries.

Ambivalence and a lack of coherence in the Community's external economic relations should hardly come as a surprise. There exists a serious gap between the apparent importance of the Community as an actor on foreign economic policy and its actual capacity to act. In the words of Dahrendorf, "There is an almost absurd disproportion between the expectations of the European Community's partners in the world, and the instruments which the Community has at its disposal in order to respond to these expectations."[1]

The Procedures for Negotiating and Concluding Commercial Agreements

Article 113 (paragraph 3) defines the procedure for negotiating commercial agreements:

> Where agreements with third countries need to be negotiated, the Commission shall make recommendations to the Council, which shall authorize the Commission to open the necessary negotiations. The Commission shall conduct these negotiations in consultation with a Special Committee appointed by the Council to assist the Commission in this task and within the framework of such directives as the Council may issue to it.

The commission enjoys the right of initiative (*droit d'initiative*), conducts exploratory talks, and can submit proposals for the opening of negotiations. It also has the right to negotiate. The council decides on the appropriateness of the commission's proposals and addresses its directives for negotiations to the commission. The council in the end concludes agreements in the Community's name. Competence is thus shared between two major institutions: on the one hand, the commission, as a pure Community body, is in permanent contact with the outside world and negotiates the content of agreements; on the other hand, the council, which is both a Community and an intergovernmental body, takes the decisions.

In all trade negotiations the commission is assisted by a special committee that emanates from the council. Following a council decision of 5 February 1970, the "113 Committee" replaced the Article 111 Special Committee set up for the transitional period. The 113 Committee is composed of representatives of the member states, chaired by the country holding the chairmanship of the council, and its secretariat is provided by the council secretariat. Since the great international trade negotiations–e.g., the Kennedy Round–the status of this committee has been enhanced because it defines and adapts the commission's mandate on the basis of the broad outlines drawn by the council. This special committee's role is to discuss with the commission the member countries' respective commercial interests and to submit the national positions. It assists in seeking an overall technical solution applicable to the text of a future commercial agreement. It is the role of the commission to synthesize the different national positions thus formulated in order to arrive at a common negotiating position. The 113 Committee as an advisory body should facilitate the commission's task by formulating recommendations that are not binding. Since it represents the national interests and its members are nominated by the council, the commission is well advised to take the recommendations from the committee seriously to avoid disagreement in the council at the moment of concluding the negotiations. In fact, each member of the committee takes part personally in the development of the negotiations. Thus even if the commission has the authority to negotiate, at this stage the member states are also constantly present as watchdogs.[a]

The Committee of Permanent Representatives (COREPER) does not interfere during the negotiations. But in its role of preparing the council meetings it elaborates the directives that the council will address to the commission in the form of a mandate for the negotiations.

The decision-making process to arrive at a negotiation mandate thus operates, on the basis of concrete proposals by the commission, at three different levels: (1) the work of the specialized committee and subcommittees of the council for the technical examinations by national experts; (2) arbitrage and general orientation in the COREPER group; and (3) final decisions taken by the council either through formal adoption of the options of the COREPER or through ultimate arbitrage during the council meeting.

Between these three stages a decision-making "elevator" is constantly operating either because *des préalables* have to be settled or because isolated sectoral problems need to be solved.

Since any mandate for negotiations necessarily includes tactical positions and since every detail of the development of negotiations cannot be foreseen in advance, the original mandate will hardly allow the negotiations to be concluded. Continuing adjustment is necessary by the "elevator" technique functioning between the negotiation conference, the 113 Committee assisting the commission, the Committee of Permanent Representatives, and the council. The mechanism of this "elevator" is rigid because the delegation of power between the different stages is generally very limited.

From what has been said so far it is obviously a slight overstatement to say that the commission negotiates on behalf of the Community. The commission is subject to rather strict instructions. When it is acting as spokesman for the Community, the "observers" of the member states are constantly present, and its positions are constantly supervised through the 113 Committee's coordination sessions. It is hardly surprising that the Community's negotiating machinery functions rather slowly and takes time to react to new developments, and that the commission's role is more often that of a broker between the divergent interests of the member states, trying to preserve the Community interest, than that of an independent negotiator with Third World countries.

A last complication results from the fact that the COREPER or the council functions only after a very careful process of filtering the technical difficulties at the expert level. In the work of the expert committees or subcommittees, the representatives of the technical ministries interested in a particular question

[a]In certain cases the negotiations for commercial agreements have been conducted by a mixed delegation composed of representatives of the Community and the member states. The commission assumes the presidency of the delegation whereas the vice-president is the representative of the member state presiding over the council at that moment. The commission is still the chief negotiator; the national representatives assist as observers.

from nine different capitals normally participate. The pressures coming from different lobbies in nine capitals are thus felt from the start. Under these circumstances the council runs a great risk of losing contact with the reality of the negotiation in the process between the initial option to start the procedure leading to the opening of a negotiation and the final decision on a mandate for these negotiations. The result is an inadequate and/or too vaguely formulated mandate, which requires updating and more precisely elaborating the directives for the commission at an advanced stage of the negotiations. Trade negotiations with the Community are inevitably prolonged.

The Community Position in Tariff Negotiations in the Tokyo Round

A joint declaration in February 1972 by the U.S., Japan, and the EC recognized the need for proceeding with a comprehensive review of international economic relations. To this end, a new round of multilateral trade negotiations in the framework of GATT was launched officially at the GATT Ministerial Meeting in Tokyo in September 1973. These negotiations are dominated once more by two major protagonists—the United States and the European Community—with Japan as the most important outsider. Because of the Community's enlargement, the nominally multilateral negotiations are in fact a U.S.-Community bilateral negotiation, even more than during the Kennedy Round. Unless a bargain can be struck between them, no bargain appears to be possible at all. From what is known so far about the respective negotiating positions, bargaining will again be hard. A close look at the Community views will provide some insight on the major divergences.

Since the opening of the GATT negotiations in 1973 the international economic climate has changed drastically, although judging from official declarations, it has not undermined the will to expand free trade. The climate of economic euphoria resulting from strong growth of production and exports has nevertheless been wrecked by the oil crisis. International monetary instability and huge current deficits for the Community as a whole, together with high rises in unemployment and inflation, create a particularly unfavorable environment. The Trade Negotiations Committee, comprising negotiators from some eighty industrial and developing countries, has nevertheless begun substantive discussions involving the establishment of working groups on the various questions of tariffs, nontariff barriers, safeguards, agriculture, tropical products, and the sectoral approach to trade liberalization.

A debate on which time was spent during the Kennedy Round is bound to emerge once more in tariff negotiations on industrial products. The U.S. Trade Act of 1974 authorizes linear across-the-board tariff cuts of up to 60 percent for duties higher than 5 percent ad valorem, while duties of 5 percent ad valorem or less can be eliminated. The Community directives, on the contrary, aim at a harmonization of tariffs whereby countries with high rates of duty in their tariff schedules would be required to make larger concessions than countries with more even rates of duty in order to overcome the problem of tariff disparities. The Community's official position considers harmonization to be the only approach that will make it possible to arrive at a fair and balanced result, the argument being that the average level of the EC customs tariff for industrial products is the lowest among the principal participants and its profile extremely homogeneous. Harmonization to achieve a greater similarity in the tariff profiles for industrial products of the major developed countries should be arrived at through a substantial diminution of present tariffs of the major participants on the basis of a generally applicable formula (excluding agricultural products), combining the objectives of harmonization and substantial tariff reductions. In the EC's view, duties of over 20 percent should no longer be applied. But below a specified minimum duties would not be reduced, in order to maintain a margin for future negotiations. The fear exists that linear tariff cuts, short of complete elimination, would leave the Community with some duties that lose all real value for future negotiations, while only eliminating really excessive protection in the high tariff rates of some other countries.

The initial starting positions of the EC and the U.S. appear to be almost diametrically opposed. The U.S. aims for complete elimination of lower duties (5 percent and less), which the EC does not want to reduce at all. The EC insists on the principle that the reduction of duties should be graduated according to the existing duty level, while the U.S. is offering only a linear cut of 60 percent. But there is room for negotiation in between, with a compromise formula being once more the key issue.

While harmonization appears attractive at first sight, its logic is open to question. As a protectionist device, a tariff system should recognize the relative competitiveness of a domestic industry and its foreign competitors. It should not be expected that an equal degree of protection will be appropriate or necessary in all countries industry by industry. It is implicit in the EC position that the high peaks in a country's tariff schedule can easily be bargained for, short of total elimination, without substantially affecting the competitive position of the protected industry. It would have been in the logic of the Community argument to propose a formula that includes, however remotely and gradually, automatic progress to zero tariffs for industrial products (and raw materials), possibly on a conditional MFN basis using GATT Article 24. The negotiation would then focus on the timetable of the progressive, automatic reductions and the exceptions for some industries that need a longer transition period in which to adjust to international competition.

However, this approach has in fact been rejected by the Community for the Tokyo Round although the relevant reference was dropped in the final draft of the Community's initial bargaining position adopted by the council. In the widely disseminated commission document,[2] tariff-free trade was rejected as unrealistic: first, because customs duties in some countries and for some products protect economic sectors that are already experiencing real difficulties in facing up to competition; and second, because there is a lack of international harmonization of national policies concerning taxation, social legislation, and measures to stimulate economic development. Neither argument is convincing. The first concerns the necessary exceptions to be negotiated. The second argument is even more shaky if it is meant to imply that all competitive conditions are to be equalized before free trade can be allowed; if that were the case no division of labor through trade could take place. International trade depends on relative cost differences. Conceptually there is a clear distinction between (1) ruling out distortions to competitive conditions resulting from government interventions, which would fall into the group of nontariff barriers, and (2) ruling out differences, in competitive conditions due to a lack of harmonization of taxation, social security systems, economic development policies, and so on. The first is a feasible and necessary part of any attempt to liberalize international trade. The second is neither feasible nor necessary among countries not aiming at economic and political union.[3]

Underlying this distrust of free trade in industrial products is the fear that the customs union, which is the living element of the Common Market, would thus be diluted. The external tariff has become a symbol of European unity as well as the element binding the member countries together. Whereas this was certainly a forceful and respectable consideration during the 1960s, it has lost much of its credibility by the 1970s, since the Community countries have given themselves the objective of building an economic and monetary union that would go far beyond the limited aims of the customs union. Failure to make progress with economic and monetary union, however, may explain why the need to preserve some external symbol of the customs union is still so strongly felt. The customs union is indeed mentioned explicitly with the Common Commercial Policy and the Common Agricultural Policy, among the elements basic to the unity of the European Community, which may not be called in question.

The Community is nevertheless prepared to envisage in the context of specific agreements a total elimination of duties in a limited number of cases when economic circumstances justify it. It appears that the aeronautics industry might be one of these cases. On the other hand, in some cases that involve products supplied mainly by developing countries that benefit from generalized preferences, the Community wishes to discuss the possibility of not reducing existing duties to maintain preference margins, or of reducing them but on a different time scale. The argument once more is hardly convincing and carries with it the danger of being in fact a distinguished protective device. Most of the imports presently benefiting from generalized preferences are imported under schemes that limit preferential entry by tariff quotas and ceilings. Where preferential entry is unlimited in principle, the donor country retains the right to invoke a special escape clause. Developing countries would benefit more from unlimited nonpreferential access at *lower* MFN duties, combined with existing generalized preference schemes, than from the maintenance of preferential quotas with *unchanged* MFN duty rates. A reduction of the MFN tariff represents a net benefit to the exporting developing countries, not an erosion of preferential advantage.

Although without great enthusiasm, the Community does subscribe to the aim expressed in the Tokyo declaration following a Canadian suggestion that the negotiations should include an examination of the possibilities for a coordinated reduction or elimination of all barriers to trade in selected sectors. The Community insists only that sectoral negotiations should be a complementary technique and does not oppose methodological, economic, and statistical studies in this field. But according to the spokesman at the opening session of the Trade Negotiations Committee, one should envisage resorting to this technique only after discussions have progressed sufficiently on general formulas for tariff reduction, and only a limited number of sectors will lend themselves to this exercise. This statement should be considered together with a passage from the Overall Approach document, which states, "While recognising that mutual advantage and reciprocity must be sought in the overall outcome of the whole range of the negotiations, the aim should be to seek, so far as possible, reciprocity in each individual field, in particular as far as tariffs are concerned." The statement indicates a clear reluctance to trade tariff concessions on industrial products for concessions in the agricultural sector, a particularly sensitive issue in the Community position. The abortive deal during the Kennedy Round of trading tariff concessions on chemical products in exchange for the abolition of a particularly protectionist nontariff barrier–namely, the U.S. American Selling Price system–apparently is still remembered.

Nontariff Barriers

Because of the progressive reduction of tariffs, there is an intensified concentration of interest on nontariff barriers to trade. They cover a very large variety of practices, many of which are not in fact "barriers" but stimulants, though of a kind generally condemned as internationally discreditable, such as export or production subsidies. The diversity and complexity in this area is generally recognized, together with the consequent difficulty of any comprehensive or general approach to mounting reciprocal bargaining on any kind of quantitative basis. Negotiations case by case are therefore almost unavoidable. In fact, the Community itself is still struggling very hard to attack these barriers to its internal trade. Tackling them in multilateral negotiations will be a highly technical and time-consuming process. A long and probably slow move toward creating international order in this field should be envisaged.

Where many countries use similar measures, the Community favors multilateral solutions, whether by abolition or amendment of existing practices or by creating harmony or discipline through explanatory notes to the existing provision of the General Agreement or through the establishment of general principles or codes of conduct. Advantages that might derive from solutions comprising obligations going beyond the present GATT rules should be accepted only in relation to countries that themselves accept and abide by the same obligations. In other words, the principle of conditional MFN treatment should be applied in those cases. The antidumping code negotiated during the Kennedy Round already applied this principle.

The Community envisages that appropriate machinery for consultation and the settlement of disputes should be established together with some mechanism for applying sanctions in appropriate cases. The arrangements would not only deal with interpretative questions arising from the agreement but provide a permanent mechanism to continue unfinished business related to existing matters not dealt with in the negotiations or new issues arising subsequently.

With a view of securing the future, the Community wishes to set up a procedure for discussion and consultation to avoid or minimize the effects on trade flows of future legislative actions. Environmental protection, a legitimate and well-intentioned objective, is specifically mentioned for its indirect but nonetheless significant and serious trade-hampering effects. The interests of the European car industry and Concorde are of course directly at stake.

Difficulties may arise in this area with respect to the commission's role as spokesman for the Community and the member states individually. The Member states might think some of the issues are not covered by the Common Commercial Policy as it is currently interpreted and for which the commission has negotiating authority. Some hesitation is also bound to arise in the negotiations from the stipulation in the U.S. Trade Act stating that before trade agreements covering nontariff barriers become effective in the United States the president must notify Congress of his intention to enter into negotiations at least ninety days in advance, showing how the agreements would benefit the U.S. economy and how they would be made effective. The Community, on the contrary, can negotiate without being obliged to cope with a parliamentary procedure.

The Community document also raises the demand for all the contracting parties to cease to benefit from the exception provided by the GATT protocol of provisional application.

There will certainly be plenty of major issues for this part of the negotiations, given the traditional U.S. antipathy to export subsidies and consequent antidumping action, together with the parallel EC dislike of the way countervailing and antidumping duties have been applied in the past, not to speak of pressure that is bound to be exerted on the Community to trim its residual quantitative import restrictions. Customs valuation procedures, standards, and public procurement policies are also on the Community priority list.

Export restrictions and access to supplies have come to the forefront since several raw material-producing countries tried to follow the OPEC model for such basic raw materials as iron ore, copper, tin, bauxite, and phosphate. Concern is shared by the major industrialized countries (the U.S., the EC, and Japan), but there is harmony of interests. Some industrialized countries like Canada and Australia have clearly divergent interests. It may be sufficient also to mention the word *soya*, or the differences of approach between the U.S. and the EC in standing up to the OPEC. The Community is in a weaker position compared to the U.S., depending much more on outside raw material supplies. The risks involved in a policy of confrontation with the raw material-producing countries are much greater for the Community than for the U.S.

Americans, Europeans, and Japanese together agree on the need for internationally accepted rules on supply restrictions. The complexity of the problems is at the same time recognized, given the existing lack of international discipline, the variety of situations product by product or country by country, and perhaps most of all the desire of the developing countries to add value to their raw materials by processing on the spot. At the UNIDO conference in Lima, the industrialized countries had to recognize the right of developing countries to form export cartels.

In this respect the Community favors once more a step-by-step pragmatic approach. As a starting point, the international rules and disciplines applicable to import restrictions should by analogy also apply to export restrictions. Whereas import restrictions to connect domestic unemployment are forbidden under GATT rules, with the exception provided for as a general safeguard in the case of market disruption, the same principle should apply to export restrictions as an instrument against domestic inflation. In cases of emergency and as part of a domestic price control program, supply-sharing arrangements comparable to orderly marketing arrangements on imports, to avoid sudden and arbitrary interruptions of trade flows, are necessary. In other words, an effective multilateral safeguard mechanism has become indispensable on the export side too. A common set of rules of conduct, and notification and consultation commitments, on restrictions of access to supplies should be explored.

Safeguards

The Community accepts an examination of the adequacy of the multilateral safeguard system during the negotiations and in particular GATT Article 19. Given the paradox of opening negotiations to liberalize international trade in a climate of economic recession and latent commercial protectionism, it is hardly surprising that particular attention is being paid to the need for an effective and practicable, internationally agreed-upon and enforceable safeguard mechanism. Possibly the negotiations will not be so much bargaining for liberalization as finding an internationally acceptable system of emergency trade restrictions.

The provisions for temporary import relief in the U.S. Trade Act, however, are regarded with great suspicion on the European side of the Atlantic, whereas safeguards in general have traditionally been anathema to the developing countries and Japan. The EC remains attached to the present provisions of the General Agreement, while it is admitted that the modalities of application of Article 19 could be improved. The Community supports a more flexible mechanism that could be applied selectively to contain imports from specific geographical sources, rather than the currently imposed nondiscriminatory application, along with better international surveillance and discipline. This is a shift away from an earlier council position that rejected discriminatory action. Strong multilateral control could also avoid the need to give compensation or suffer generalized retaliation as is the current practice under Article 19.

Differences of opinion among the member countries do exist even more than on other issues. The Germans, for example, fear that a selective application might be to the detriment of their dynamic exporters; the French are not very keen to have an international control authority looking at their policies in certain sectors. For the commission, however, a renewal of international emergency protection would be one means of reestablishing its full control over a common EC trade policy, a control that has been steadily eroded by the voluntary restraint arrangements concluded between Japan and a variety of European industries (steel, ball bearings, electronic equipment, televisions, and so forth).

Agricultural Policy

The EC's Common Agricultural Policy has without doubt created the most serious external commercial policy issues. Seen from the Third World's point of view, it combines two of the most unpopular protective devices: the variable levy, which increases the protection to match any attempt by foreign exporters to absorb the tariff and continue to export by reducing their returns, and the export restitution, which subsidizes exports of surplus of some products from the proceeds of the levies on imports of other products. The Community readily accepts that the variable levy is maintaining a target domestic price level for EC producers such as other countries maintain by producer subsidies or other devices, and that the export restitutions are necessary to achieve a structure of effective protection that does not drive meat and dairy farmers out of production by raising the prices of feeding stuffs. Such justifications are not so convincing to third countries, however. The common policies are also not distinctly more protectionist than the national policies they replaced, whether these were the continental systems relying on tariffs, or the U.K. system relying on deficiency payments (subsidies). The major impact of the common policy in replacing the national policies was to increase the effective protection by the unification of the previously separate protected markets in Western Europe.

Access to the German market increased French farmers' advantage over third country exporters, and the effective protection was greatly enhanced by the enlargement of the Community in 1973 to include the vast import market of the U.K., as well as two further agricultural exporters, Denmark and Eire. The total U.S. exports to the EC increased in volume through the 1960s, and even that U.S. exports of some agricultural products not subject to CAP levies also increased, did not disarm the criticism that the value of U.S. exports of agricultural products subject to the levies fell by about 33 percent between 1966 and 1969, following the introduction of the CAP.

Although the United States was the most vigorous complainant, the problems created were probably more serious for the countries of Eastern Europe, who relied on agricultural exports to develop their trade with the West. Since the EC could benefit from industrial exports to these countries, the CAP had unfortunate economic effects for both sides, in addition to the serious political implications.

Moreover, the Community's attitude on the agricultural issue was for some years insensitive. The EC relied on the argument that other countries, including the U.S. also protected and subsidized their agriculture, and it refused to recognize that a new structure of regional protection, disrupting trade flows that had accommodated to previously existing structures, was bound to provoke reactions in other countries.

The insensitivity was directly related to the CAP's political importance within the structure of EC integration. The major beneficiary and protagonist of the policy was France, and the policy was an integral part of the bargain by which France accepted industrial free trade; the Netherlands also derived great benefits, however, and other members' farming communities exerted strong pressure in favor of the policy. Concessions on external commercial policy in this area therefore could have jeopardized the whole structure of the EC.

While the agricultural policy has thus been a major issue in the EC's commercial history over the past ten years, it is likely to diminish in importance during the next decade. European agriculture is in rapid transition; the number of farmers is declining rapidly, productivity is growing fast, and the real CAP price level fell by about 2 percent per annum in the 1960s and is expected to go on falling. Combined with a probable continuation of higher prices in world markets for agricultural products, these developments will eventually close the gap between CAP and world food prices, which was dramatically reduced and even reversed for some products in 1973-1974. While by the 1980s the EC probably will not be importing large quantities of agricultural products, neither will it require a highly protectionist policy to keep the products out; it is not easy to forecast whether a high degree of protection will reemerge temporarily in the late 1970s, given the uncertainty about world food price trends over the next few years.

Changes in the world economy since the Kennedy Round, which left agricultural products well alone, make predictions extremely hazardous as regards developments in the Tokyo Round trade talks. While continual changes do not provide a firm basis for multilateral negotiation, the current situation seems to offer a better opportunity for mutually satisfactory settlements than ever before. From the old dispute of the Kennedy Round negotiations over "access to markets" versus "*montant de soutien,*" there is apparently some shift toward a common concern by the EC as well as the U.S. to create conditions for a better adapted supply and more stable markets in agricultural products. The possibility of negotiation will nevertheless depend on the final political will of the principal participants.

Given that the principles of the existing Common Agricultural Policy are not called into question, the Community is prepared to contribute to a more satisfactory evolution of world markets both for importers and exporters. This ought to be achieved, first, through the implementation of the resolutions of the recent World Food Conference for a commonly operated monitoring system of world production and consumption on the basis of a systematic and regular exchange of information, so that each government can draw for itself the necessary indications for the conduct of its own policy. Second, for the main products in human food consumption—such as cereals, rice, sugar, and the most homogeneous dairy products—the Community proposes international commodity agreements covering international price-fixing, market-sharing, and stockpiling policies. Such commodity agreements also would facilitate the implementation of food aid programs. It is for this "philanthropic" part of world trade that the Americans have lent qualified support to international agreements in the context of the FAO Food Conference in Rome. For the rest it is still to be expected that the U.S. will come to Geneva as a firm believer in free trade in agriculture and consequently with an outspoken feeling against the type of international economic interventionism implicit in world commodity arrangements and a not unfounded skepticism about the effectiveness of these mechanisms. The EC position is not so monolithic as might appear either. The Germans have repeatedly expressed their lack of enthusiasm for the financial consequences of internationally managed stocks (e.g., for sugar and rice) as compared to concerted national storage policies (such as for cereals).

Finally, the Community does not envisage negotiating exclusively international agreements. For products not likely to be covered by international agreements, concerted disciplines should be negotiated between exporters and importers to ensure orderly markets. The commission view in this respect has finally prevailed since the member states at some point wanted a reference only to concerted action among exporting countries. For products that are protected only by tariffs, reciprocal tariff reductions will have to be negotiated.

The major weakness of the approach outlined so far is apparently that some of the fundamental problems of agricultural trade that accompany the different support policies pursued by all industrialized countries are once more not going to be dealt with at all. The implicit objective of most commodity agreements traditionally has been to maintain the status quo. Organization of markets is one thing; liberalization of agricultural trade by carrying further the *montant de soutien* proposals made by the European Community at the time of the Kennedy Round is another. What is important in this respect is not agreement about appropriate or inappropriate *methods* of support but the support *levels.* Once these have been made transparent and comparable, negotiations, first to consolidate the existing levels and afterward gradually to reduce them, become possible.

Mainly under French pressure, the Community has, so far successfully, resisted the U.S. demand to link the negotiations on agricultural and industrial products. The negotiations are in fact conducted in separate groups. Although not stated explicitly in the trade bill, the U.S. would have preferred not to give special treatment to agricultural products. The American dislike for public interventionism, together with international stockpiling arrangements, is one of the most thorny issues of the Tokyo Round, along with the formula for tariff negotiations and the Community preoccupation with the trade bill stipulation that every agreement on nontariff barriers still needs congressional approval.

Monetary Integration

Exchange rate regimes are intimately connected with the commercial policy questions since parity depreciation can readily substitute for more complex policies of tariff or nontariff protection, while the fixing or rigidity of parities is in turn a major incentive to the adoption of protectionist trade policies. In the late 1960s the European Community was an influence for rigidity in monetary arrangements because of its concern to reduce the degree of uncertainty in internal markets. In particular, the agricultural policy was held to require that exchange rates remain interlocked since parity changes would destroy the common pricing structure based on the unit of account. As parity changes were forced on the individual members in 1969 (and thereafter with increasing frequency), the CAP was kept going by temporary compensatory payments and taxes, and the Community adopted plans for the gradual creation of a monetary union, including in the short term a narrowing of the permitted bands of fluctuation around the central peg rates of exchange.

The desire to avoid changes in relative parities inside the EC was an important element in the pressure put on the United States to solve its payments problems by devaluing the dollar rather than expecting other countries to make the necessary adjustments. In this way desiderata for the internal construction of the EC again created external issues. But even after events had forced the depreciation of the dollar, as of the yen, differences in the rates of inflation, and in other variables affecting the relative payments balances among the EC members, forced further changes in exchange rates.

The failure of EC efforts at monetary integration was finally sealed by the floating of the French franc in January 1974. The country that had been most insistent on monetary unification, because of its attachment to the agricultural policy, was forced to accept that reducing even the short-term parity fluctuations was, for the moment, impossible given the very different structures of the member economies. The "snake" has continued since 1974 to be an uncertain centerpiece of the efforts toward monetary union. The recommendation in the Tindemans Report on Economic Union in January 1976 that the "snake" should be "consolidated" but with a recognition of the necessity to accept for some time a "two-tier" system in which the weaker currencies—sterling and the lira—would remain outside, appears to be rather an expression of the sad political reality than of faith that monetary union can really be achieved.

Apart from the requirements of internal policy objectives, a strong element in the EC approach to the problem of reestablishing a new world monetary order has undoubtedly been an opposition to what was perceived as the dollar's dominance in the 1950s and 1960s. The attitudes of the various EC members have of course varied considerably on this issue, and some have changed their policy in the light of events and changes in their own economic fortunes and interests. It is impossible in the space of a few comments on monetary aspects of external economic policy to give an adequate account of all the twists and turns of national policies. But the outcome of the confused events in the monetary world up to 1976 appears to be the emergence of a new consensus about the broad lines of a new monetary order. While that is still considerable disagreement on the role of gold, or SDRs, there is a general acceptance on both sides of the Atlantic that a new system must be based on more than one key currency. In view of the importance of Western Europe in world trade, it is also necessary that it should take on some of the burden of supporting a new system, and this in turn implies that the creation of an integrated monetary system in the EC, and possible more widely in Western Europe, will be an essential part of the creation of a new multicentered world monetary system. Thus from being a disruptive force in the world system a few years ago, the Community's efforts at internal monetary integration have come to be accepted as having a more positive role.

Since October 1973 the monetary issue has been dominated by the question of how best to "recycle" the oil surpluses. Once more a conflict or rivalry has appeared between the U.S. desire for a world solution under its leadership, and the EC's desire to avoid allowing the U.S. to dominate. But in practice the EC has been divided, with each country seeking its own arrangements with the oil producers. Thus despite agreement on a relatively small EC loan of $3 billion in 1974, the initiative appears to have passed to the U.S., which has taken the lead in the creation of the International Energy Agency, and in the OECD financial facility (the "safety net"). Concerning the IEA, the U.K., as a future oil exporter, for a long time insisted on having a separate seat, while France was reluctant to accept the basic principle of a floor price for oil. Finally both gave way and there is a kind of EC policy, although France is not a formal member of the IEA. There is also, of course, the question of arrangements with the oil producers themselves, who are not prepared to accept passively whatever arrangements the West, through various institutions, may reach. Multiple methods for achieving the immense monetary transfers the oil price situation has required should be accepted, including private commercial deals by firms and banks, intergovernmental bilateral deals, arrangements by area groupings such as the EC, and more comprehensive arrangements at the level of world institutions.

But in these developments the EC appears to have been missing an opportunity to assist its members, especially those in the greatest difficulty, and at the same time to promote its own monetary and economic unification. For a really major intervention by the Community in the problem of recycling could be a powerful instrument for the furthering of monetary union. In view of the much greater dependence of Western Europe than of the U.S. on oil imports, a more positive Community policy in this area would also, following the earlier reasoning, have been a valuable contribution to the reestablishment of world monetary stability.

The interdependence of trade and monetary matters, on which the Community already insisted before the oil crisis, is perhaps the major unknown in the Tokyo Round. Indeed, it was stated in the Tokyo declaration as follows:

> The policy of liberalizing world trade cannot be carried out successfully in the absence of parallel efforts to set up a monetary system which shields the world economy from the shocks and imbalances which have previously occurred. The Ministers will not lose sight of the fact that the efforts which are to be made in the trade field imply continuing efforts to maintain orderly conditions and to establish a durable and equitable monetary system.

The official view of the Community is that "the trade negotiations presuppose that prospects exist for the establishment of a fair and durable monetary system based on the principles listed in paragraph 4 of the Paris communique"[b] [Summit Conference held in October 1972], and that "the Community will assess the progress of these negotiations in the light of the progress made in the monetary field."[4]

With the end of the review of the international monetary system, after the Kingston Agreement, it seems that for the moment at least, some of the heat may have gone out of this discussion. Nevertheless, toward the end of 1974 it was feared that some member countries (Italy and France) might question the whole principle of the trade negotiations by insisting that further trade

[b]Namely, fixed but adjustable parities, general convertibility of currencies, effective international regulation of the world supply of liquidities, reduction in the role of national currencies as reserve instruments, effective and equitable functioning of the adjustment process, equal rights and duties for all participants in the system, the need to lessen the destabilizing effects of short-term capital movements, taking into account the interests of the developing countries.

liberalization was not conceivable without the restoration of a more stable international monetary order.

Association Agreements

Some of the most contentious issues deriving from the discriminatory tariff removal within the EC have concerned the consequential special arrangements made with countries whose trade has been affected. And in no area is the distinction so hard to make between sensitive adjustments of trading policies to meet the needs of third countries in the new situation and exploitation of the new bargaining power of the regional bloc created in the EC. Following its formation, the EC found itself involved in meeting the problems created for a large number of countries whose traditional trading links, often supported by some kind of special relationship with one of the member countries, were threatened by the new mutual preference granted within the Community. Southern Europe's important exports of Mediterranean-type agricultural products were threatened by the inclusion of Italy, but not other Mediterranean countries, in the Community. The countries in question could not accept free trade in industrial products, and there were in some cases political inhibitions on their acceptance as members by the EC. So in the 1960s special individual association agreements were negotiated with these countries, to assure their markets for agricultural exports while at the same time gradually liberalizing their own imports of industrial products, in some cases with a specified transitional period intended to lead eventually to full membership (in the cases of Greece and Turkey).

Similarly, colonial and ex-colonial territories attached to member countries, (especially France) by strong commercial and other links faced the possibility of exclusion from the preferential access previously accorded them by the "mother" country. In these cases also, special arrangements were negotiated in the two Yaounde Agreements, effectively extending to the whole Community market the special status previously enjoyed by these countries in the markets of the mother country. Seen from the Community's point of view, these agreements could be interpreted as sympathetic and sensitive adjustments of commercial policy to ensure that the interests of these countries were not harmed in the process of creating the EC. But seen from the point of view of other trading partners of the developing countries in question, these arrangements were a case of the Community's using its bargaining strength to negotiate tough conditions for preserving some of the commercial advantages previously enjoyed by countries. Especially harmful, at least psychologically, was the insertion in these agreements of the notorious reverse preferences, the preferential access for EC exports to the developing countries granted in return for access to the EC market for their exports. The United States and other countries regarded these preferences as discrimination against their exports to the LDC markets, and the rationalization that these reverse preferences were needed both to comply with the GATT rules under Article 24 and to make the Yaounde Agreements true commercial agreements between equals rather than unilateral concessions maintaining a colonial status for the LDCs was not convincing, even to many Europeans. True sensitivity to the problems of Third World countries, it was thought, would have taken an expression less harmful to the commercial interests both of the LDCs and of their Third World suppliers.

The enlargement of the Community to include the United Kingdom, Denmark, and Eire from January 1973 created new problems of adjustment for Third World countries. The most urgent issues concerned the remaining members of the EFTA, and the Commonwealth countries that had had special arrangements with the U.K. under the system of Commonwealth preferences. Once more the Community had to undertake a set of negotiations to adjust the commercial relations with these two groups. So far as the EFTA countries were concerned, the outcome was the creation of what many had aimed for since the mid- and late 1950s, effectively a European free trade area in industrial products covering the whole of Western Europe (but not yet all of Southern or Eastern Europe). Two of the new members, the U.K. and Denmark, had a special interest in this outcome, since they had already developed their trade with these countries within the EFTA, and while they were far less important than the other EC countries as trading partners, it would have been harmful to British and Danish commercial interests if this trade had been disrupted by the reimposition of tariff barriers.[c] Thus after the enlargement there was a strong pressure within the EC for a liberal external commercial policy. The U.K. represented similarly a self-interested force for liberal arrangements with the Commonwealth countries, along the lines of those made in the 1960s with the Yaounde Associates.

The Community entered into negotiations [with forty-six African, Caribbean, and Pacific (ACP) countries, including members of the existing Association of African States and Madagascar (AASM), as well as British Commonwealth countries] that resulted in a new agreement's coming into force in February 1975 for a period extending until 1980.

The Lomé Convention, which replaced the second Yaounde Convention that expired at the end of January 1975, was a notable advance on earlier arrangements. It is not only geographically much larger, but being a Cooperation Agreement, it also establishes also a new model of relationships between developed and developing countries, relationships based on the principles of equal partnership and international solidarity.

---

[c]Though some temporary reimposition of tariffs was required between the U.K. and EFTA countries in the case of some "sensitive" products—including paper and aluminum—the EC was not prepared to concede duty-free entry to EFTA exports immediately. So the U.K. had to reimpose tariffs by stages on these products for several years, after which they would be removed again as the full free trade arrangement was finally applied to these products by the whole Community.

The convention consists of two parts: trade cooperation and financial assistance. The trade concessions include access for industrial products to the EC free of tariffs and quantitative import restrictions. The same applies for 96 percent of ACP agricultural exports to the EC. The remaining 4 percent–which include such products as corn, rice, and meat–still benefit from tariff reductions. For sugar the agreement includes an EC access guarantee for a quantity of 1.4 million tons at a price related to the price that the EC guarantees to its own sugar producers. No preferential access to ACP markets is asked as a counterpart. A major bone of contention between the EC and the U.S.–namely, reverse preferences–has thus been removed. The ACP countries only guarantee the EC a nondiscriminatory status of most favored nation vis-à-vis other industrialized countries, but not with regard to developing countries. The trade cooperation also includes a number of initiatives to promote ACP exports to the EC. But the major breakthrough in the Lomé Convention is its scheme for the stabilization of the export earnings of the ACP countries for twelve primary products (Stabex). If the exports of one of these products represents more than 7.5 percent of the total export earnings of the producing country, this country receives compensation from the Stabex fund if its export earnings from this product fall by 7.5 percent. This compensation is repaid if the market situation improves. But for thirty-four countries, which include the least developed, the above percentages are reduced to 2.5 percent. These countries are also not expected to repay the compensations they will receive. Much more than has ever been the case, the industrial cooperation provisions rely on the role to be played by the ACP countries, thus reflecting the changes that have occurred toward more equality between the partners in the economic relationships.

The financial resources available under the Lomé Convention amount to 3.39 billion units of account, 3.7 times more than under Yaounde Convention. They represent currently an average 20 percent of the total development aid given annually by the Community member countries.

Changes in the World Economic Situation

Since the enlargement, major changes in the world economic structure have altered the parameters of the Community's external commercial relations. First, the effectiveness in 1973-1975 of the oil producers' cartel has created a new bloc of rich developing countries with powerful bargaining weapons vis-à-vis the EC, which depends more on oil imports than any other part of the world except Japan. So far these countries are not exporters of industrial products, and the problems for the EC concern financial and monetary matters in dealing with the oil payments, and the development of markets in these countries for the EC exports needed if the oil is to be paid for by goods rather than indefinitely financed by monetary transfers. Second, the bargaining power of many other countries who export commodities to the EC has been enhanced in the conditions of 1973-1975; they also have succeeded in exercising some cartel power. This has been most marked in the case of sugar supplies to the U.K. from Commonwealth cane sugar producers. Indeed, this increase in the bargaining power of LDCs was an important determinant of the outcome of the ACP negotiations. These events raise the possibility of a major clash in the EC's commercial relations, with a possibility that the Community, from being a powerful bloc operating in a world of mostly small trading partners, will become one of a number of blocs carrying on world trade under quite different conditions than those in which it was carried out during the period when the GATT was in its heyday. In such a trading world, the EC would cease to be on the defensive as a regional grouping creating problems for other countries, and would come to be seen much more as a necessary cooperation to increase the bargaining power of its members in the face of strong pressures from outside suppliers on whom it depends critically for its vital energy and materials supplies.

A more offensive commercial policy, asserting the Community's self-interest rather than being concerned about not hurting others, would be appropriate.

But such reasoning could not apply equally to all parts of the world. Many of the poorest LDCs continue to have little with which to bargain. Far from having export commodities they can exploit in EC markets, they have themselves suffered, and relatively far more, from the increase in energy and raw materials prices in other LDCs. Thus a more complex commercial policy may emerge, distinguishing the LDCs that can now be regarded as commercial equals from those that are still obviously in need of gentler treatment. But it was not clear how permanent the new structure of bargaining power in world trade would be. While in the case of foodstuffs and some materials there is evidence that the structural conditions may have changed permanently so that a return to the terms of trade that prevailed in the 1960s between industrialized and developing countries is not to be expected, in other products the elasticities of supply and of demand may be sufficiently great to restore the pre-1973 relationships. Clearly, until the situation is clarified, the Community will require a flexible position with regard to its relations with nonindustrialized countries.

Notes

1. Ralf Dahrendorf, "External Relations of the European Community," in Hugh Corbet and Robert Jackson (eds.), *In Search of a New World Economic Order* (London: Croom Helm, 1974), p. 65.

2. "Development of an Overall Approach to Trade in View of the Coming Multilateral Negotiations in GATT," document of the Commission of the European Community, COM (73) 556, Brussels, 4 April 1973.

3. Alec Cairncross, Herbert Giersch, Alexandre Lamfalussy, Giuseppe Petrilli, Pierre Uri, *Economic Policy for the European Community: The Way Forward* (London: Macmillan, 1974), pp. 195-196.

4. "Development of an Overall Approach," EC Commission document, cited.

10 The Industrial States and the Third World: The Political Economy of North-South Relations

Roger D. Hansen

Each contributor to this volume probably has a somewhat idiosyncratic definition of the term "political economy." Tedious to the reader as such definitional problems might be, they are crucial to our understanding of the nexus between political and economic issues within states. And between states—the focus of this chapter—the removal of definitional ambiguities is the sine qua non of any further clarification of issues involved in the complex set of political and economic relationships that bind the world's industrialized and developing states in overlapping patterns of cooperation and conflict.[a]

Within states—let alone the international system—the problems of political economy are difficult to analyze. Yet for most national systems of political economy, one major distinguishing factor somewhat simplifies the analysis—a set of political mechanisms that operate with a constantly shifting but generally low degree of coercion and a relatively high degree of legitimacy to perform the

[a]In this chapter the term "North" will be used as shorthand for the world's rich industrial states. They include most European countries, the United States, Canada, Japan, Australia, and New Zealand. Most are members of the Organization for Economic Cooperation and Development (OECD), and I will occasionally refer to them as "the OECD countries." Average per capita income in these countries generally exceeds $2000.

The term "South" will be used as shorthand for the world's "less developed" or "developing" states, ranging from the suddenly rich but yet-to-industrialize oil states of the Middle East to the so-called "Fourth World" states—the poorest countries of the globe located for the most part on the Indian subcontinent, in Africa, and in the Caribbean region. Most of the population of the poorest stratum of countries is located in India, Pakistan, Bangladesh, and Sri Lanka, where upwards of three-quarters of the population have per capita incomes of less than $75. Average per capita incomes for the Fourth World as a whole are under $150.

Between the Fourth World and the suddenly wealthy oil countries is the so-called Third World, encompassing most Latin American countries and others from Asia and Africa. Many of these states are at least semi-industrialized, and have average per capita incomes in the $400-$800 range.

To cover this heterogeneous grouping of over 100 states, the single label "South" may seem terribly imprecise and misleading. However, as this chapter will demonstrate, there is at least a twenty-year history of bargaining between these countries on the one hand and the industrialized countries on the other, which has given more than minimal empirical content to the term. How much content there is, and how committed these countries are to organizing and operating as a bloc of states in negotiations with the industrial world, is one of the issues I will explore at length.

Time and space do not permit an examination of the interactions between the South and the North on the one hand and the "East," or "Communist countries," or "command economies," on the other. Since these latter countries have participated only marginally in the international economic system analyzed in this chapter, the omission is not important for its purposes.

ultimate functions of a political system: to allocate values authoritatively, or in simpler terms, to determine who gets what and when and how. Obviously the range of use of coercion is broad. Some developing countries (and a few developed countries) have high coercion systems; political systems in most developed countries are characterized by governmental structures and societal problem-solving mechanisms whose "legitimacy" is accepted by the citizenry to the point where coercion is of marginal necessity for system maintenance.

Within such national social systems, political choices, generally acceptable to their citizens, are made at various times concerning the fundamental structure of the national economic system. It is basically capitalist, basically socialist, or (gradually and increasingly) somewhere between those extremes. In relatively stable national political systems, issues concerning the basic structure and norms of the economic system have demonstrated a tendency to remain relatively depoliticized for very extended periods.

In contrast, marginal changes in the economic *process* are frequent, even in the most stable of societies. Included in this process category are changes in such issue areas as tax law, tariff law, and a host of sectoral policies (e.g., agricultural price supports and stockpiling arrangements) and other public expenditure programs (such as education, welfare, defense, and research and development) that constantly alter the payoff matrix of the political economy in an incremental manner. At the process level, fights over who gets what, when and how tend to be institutionalized. They are played out in labor-management negotiations, in local and national legislative and executive branches of government, and occasionally in independent or semi-independent judicial systems.

Every economic system has its own "natural" income distribution pattern attributable to its structure and norms; and every political system redistributes income at the process level to some degree in responding to "mass" or "elite" pressures for altered rewards.[b] The basic choice as to type of economic system and the ever-changing laws, regulations, and norms that together determine modes of production and the distribution of income, wealth, and "life chances" within such a system constitute the essence of political economy as interpreted here.

If the task of analyzing the structure and processes of political economy is difficult within a single society, it is even more complex at the international level. In addition to the increased number of variables and interactions that must be understood, the major reason is that there exists no counterpart of the state

[b]Capitalist and socialist systems allocate economic and status rewards on a different scale. For example, income distribution within socialist states is significantly more egalitarian than it is in capitalist states. Presumably much of this difference reflects the fact that income from the ownership of capital does not in most cases accrue as income to individuals. For a recent examination of the income distribution profiles of socialist, developed, and developing countries, see Hollis Chenery et al., *Redistribution with Growth*, published for the World Bank and the Institute of Development Studies, University of Sussex (Oxford: Oxford University Press, 1974), Chapter I.

in international society. It has no decision-making center, no authoritative allocator of values. Indeed, it is its very decentralized political nature—its "anarchy"—that for centuries has been used to distinguish international from civil society.

Yet from approximately 1947 to the early 1970s, there existed a set of international economic institutions that established and to some degree enforced the "rules of the game" in the international economic arena. Within the past two or three years, however, these institutions and their norms have been increasingly abused, and it is highly questionable at the moment how long and in what form they will continue to operate.[1]

How did a decentralized ("subsystem dominant") political system manage to develop a complex and fairly comprehensive set of institutions and rules covering international economic relations? How have those institutions and rules managed to endure for a quarter-century before facing major challenge? And where do the seeds of the present crisis lie? Although an examination of these questions focuses on a broad range of issues, it leads of necessity to a detailed delineation of present and potential North-South conflicts in the international economic and political spheres. The degree to which North-South conflict in varying forms may become a predominant aspect of the international political economy of the coming decade remains highly uncertain, but on both normative and empirical grounds the topic would seem to merit an examination.

The Rise of the Bretton Woods World

In reconsidering the emergence of the International Monetary Fund (IMF), the International Bank for Reconstruction and Development (IBRD), and the General Agreement on Tariffs and Trade (GATT), it is worth remembering that they all came into existence when the international system was probably less "decentralized" politically than at any other time since the Congress of Vienna, if not earlier. The international political system contained but a single "superpower," the cold war was in its earliest stages, and the so-called Third World, or South, had not yet emerged as a force to be contended with at either the economic or the political level. The Southern states that did partake as observers and actors during the construction of the new international economic order for the most part acted as allies of their Northern counterparts that had led the fight against the Axis powers. And since the North itself was basically at the mercy of its own hegemonial power, the United States, international political power—defined as the capacity to influence the actions of others—was highly centralized in the late 1940s and for most of the 1950s.

Inevitably, the emerging international economic system was in essence a U.S. design, although it was altered to a certain degree to achieve a general acceptability within the non-Communist developed countries of the world. Many of the small compromises that the U.S. did make were forced on it by Great Britain, whose limited bargaining strength resided in the role of sterling in the international monetary system and in the existence of the British Imperial Preference system of tariff protection. The role of sterling lent the British a greater weight in the Bretton Woods discussions than would otherwise have been the case; the Imperial Preference System was an element that the United States was willing to pay a price for to exorcise it from the world's trading system.[2]

It would be inaccurate to leave the impression, as does much revisionist literature on U.S. foreign economic policy, that the United States dictated the system of international trade, monetary and investment institutions, and norms and practices. There was too much basic agreement among the Western allies on the major goals of the new system–i.e., to prevent the reappearance of the international economic policies of the 1930s and to support the universally shared desire to maintain full employment–for the United States to have to "dictate" the terms of agreement. What the new left's scholarship does reveal prominently is the degree to which the United States was willing to use almost ruthless tactics to achieve certain specific approaches to the resolution of problems of general concern to all Western countries. Perhaps the best example was the U.S.'s insistence on the multilateralist policy of nondiscriminatory trade liberalization.

As the basic ground rules for international economic relations were hammered out and began to operate, little was heard from or done for the underdeveloped countries of the world (except of course for those states on the periphery of the "Communist bloc" that began to receive special attention as early as 1947). As Susan Strange has noted, the United Nations' preamble speaks of "economic advancement" and the charter itself contained the seeds of an egalitarian approach to international economic issues; as she concludes, the egalitarian premise was soon revealed "in practice to be unfounded."[3]

Countries of the South wasted little time in asking for more from the system. They desired commodity agreements to raise and stabilize prices of their major export products; they requested greater access to the markets of the North for those exports; and they wanted more foreign aid to assist their own domestic efforts to increase the pace of economic development. With rare exception these appeals were ignored, and the bulk of what foreign aid was forthcoming during the 1950s was allocated to countries whose pro-Western orientation was viewed as essential in the context of an expanding cold war. It was not until the 1960s that the issue of North-South income transfers in one guise or another forced its way onto the agendas of organizations and North-South meetings other than those of the Economic and Social Council and the U.N. General Assembly.

Why did the Bretton Woods system (I use the term to refer to all major aspects of the international economic system established between 1945 and 1947) last for a quarter-century without major challenge? The answers can be grouped under four general headings.

Pg. 223

Early Deviations from the Rules

The points to be made under this general rubric are well known and need not be spelled out in any detail. All involve instances of deviations from the established rules required by the exigencies of postwar reconstruction in Europe and by the emergence of the cold war. The Marshall Plan, not the IMF or the IBRD, banked the recovery of Western Europe. As Richard Cooper has noted of the IMF, "the period of 'normalcy' in which the Bretton Woods system was supposed to function efficiently was not formally acknowledged until 1961, fourteen years after the IMF began operations, and was nearly three times longer than the transition period anticipated."[4] Likewise, during the early postwar period of the "dollar shortage," trade discrimination against U.S. exports was severe; the degree of European restriction on U.S. imports was relaxed very slowly.[c]

Two other deviations bear mention. The first concerned financial aid for the process of economic development. As the spread of the cold war turned the attention of the superpowers toward the South, both began to develop and expand bilateral aid programs. Thus the World Bank's role in "development" even in the South was constricted in its early years. Second, the United States aided and abetted the process of trade discrimination of a type in its support of Western Europe's cautious moves toward economic integration. Trade discrimination that resulted from the formation of free trade areas and customs unions was not barred by the postwar trade regime; the GATT explicitly sanctioned such forms of discrimination. The point worthy of note is not that the formation of a discriminatory trading bloc in Western Europe was legal, but rather that it was generally encouraged and applauded by U.S. policy-makers throughout the 1950s and early 1960s.

The Opportunities Created for the Dynamic Growth of the Western European and Japanese Economies

A second major factor in the success of the Bretton Woods system was that it allowed the major developed countries of the non-Communist world—the world to which its rules applied—to achieve remarkable recoveries from World War II. For approximately twenty years, Japan experienced an annual growth rate of 10 percent or better; the corresponding rate in Western Europe was significantly lower but still well above its historical average. I am not arguing that a causal relationship existed; any serious attempt to causally relate these exceptional growth rates with the international economic system would face serious conceptual difficulties. And even if the attempt managed to surmount these

[c]Cooper notes that in 1953 only 11 percent of total "dollar area" imports were free of quantitative restrictions as compared with a 71-percent figure for intra-European trade. By 1961 these figures had risen to 89 percent and 94 percent respectively. Richard N. Cooper, *The Economics of Interdependence* (New York: McGraw-Hill, 1968), p. 39.

difficulties, the degree of "explained" growth would probably be small. What can be said is that the system, the deviations from it discussed above, and the embellishments added to it during the 1960s contributed to an international economic setting that was conducive to rapid growth in developed countries.

The conclusion to be drawn is simple: for at least twenty years after its inception, the Bretton Woods system created a benign international atmosphere for economic growth in the world's leading industrial nations. Therefore they had little reason to press for major changes until the issue of U.S. deficits became a major problem in the mid- to late 1960s. And even in this instance, the problem was more "political" than it was "economic."[5]

The Relative Unimportance of the South During the Bretton Woods Years

For many reasons, some grounded in empirical evidence, some in normative frameworks, and some in pure emotion, the developing world had severe doubts about the Bretton Woods system's impact on their growth potential. Their complaints ranged from the general—the workings of the international markets for goods, capital, and technology—to the specific. This is not the place to analyze once again the validity of the developing countries' views of the system's injustices, but it is important for following argumentation to understand the South's perceptions of the system's failings. For collectives as for individuals, it is always easier to place the blame for one's problems on others than it is to shoulder them oneself. And countries, like individuals, can always find elements of truth in that characterization of problems that does the least damage to their self-esteem. Thus the less developed countries of the world were quick to identify aspects of the system that seemed to limit their capacity to close the widening gap between their own levels of income and industrialization and those of the developed world. Generally overlooked in the developing countries' critique of the system was the fact that some of the most intractable bottlenecks to more rapid growth were of their own making, through sins of commission as well as omission. Nevertheless, given their generally limited levels of domestic savings and available foreign exchange and the sociopolitical constraints on attempts to raise those levels dramatically, the developing countries naturally looked to the international political economy in search of increased resources from abroad to speed the process of development. In that search, they perceived the following biases in the system:

1. Efforts at international trade liberalization through the instrumentality of the GATT have been singularly biased in favor of products of interest to developed country exporters, and the developing countries have therefore gained little from the six rounds of tariff-cutting negotiations that took place between 1947 and 1967. Few economists disputed this perception, and most attempts to

measure the extent of the problem have suggested that high levels of protection (through quota restrictions, health and safety regulations, nominal and effective tariff structures, variable levies, internal taxes and price supports, etc.) were costing the South several billion dollars per year in foregone exports during the mid-1960s, the most significant portion stemming from agricultural protectionism.[6]

2. The volume and value of foreign aid flowing from North to South were unjustifiably low whether measured by "absorptive capacity" of aid funds in Southern development projects or by proclaimed Northern commitments to assist Southern development efforts. Again, there was little Northern disagreement with either premise except by those who felt that most aid merely served to support Southern elite groups who were not really committed to the development process. As Table 10-1 illustrates, the North has never approached its oft-enunciated target of transferring 0.7 percent of its annual GNP to the South in the form of official development assistance, and the trend has moved steadily downward throughout the past decade. Additionally, the increased "tying" of aid during the 1960s substantially lowered the value of most Northern aid transfers.

3. The North has systematically rejected or stalled for lengthy periods before accepting Southern proposals to increase resource transfers to the developing countries. The South suggests international commodity agreements to raise and stabilize the prices for its major exports; the North responds by cataloguing the (generally genuine) problems that commodity agreements raise and by effectively rejecting the approach except in a very few cases. The South suggests a "supplementary financing" mechanism as part of the IBRD's efforts to increase North-South resource flows; the North quietly inters the proposal each time it is reintroduced. The South requested a system of generalized tariff preferences to increase the access of Southern manufactured products to the markets of the North in 1964; in 1974 the United States Congress finally enacted legislation granting the president the power to implement a scheme that is but a shadow of that requested a decade earlier.

The point is made without the recitation of further examples. The Southern perception is that each request for resource transfers—whether via aid, trade, or a combination of the two (e.g., schemes for "compensatory" or "supplementary" finance)—is met with a negative response from the world's developed countries in general and the United States in particular.[d]

4. Northern multinational corporations have in general restricted their potential contribution to the development process in one or all of the following ways: by limiting tax contributions through certain patterns of transfer pricing;

Perhaps this

[d]The *soundness* of the schemes suggested varies widely, as do Northern responses to them. For one of the most comprehensive and rigorous discussions of the various Southern schemes as presented through UNCTAD, see Harry Johnson, *Economic Policies Toward Less Developed Countries* (Washington, D.C.: Brookings Institution, 1967).

Table 10-1
Net Flow of Official Development Assistance from DAC Countries as a Percentage of Gross National Product, 1960, 1965, 1970-1975

	1960	*1965*	*1970*	*1971*	*1972*	*1973*	*1974*	*1975*
Australia	.38	.53	.59	.53	.59	.44	.53	.54
Austria	n.a.	.11	.07	.07	.08	.13	.13	.13
Belgium	.88	.60	.46	.50	.55	.51	.56	.62
Canada	.19	.19	.42	.42	.47	.43	.51	.51
Denmark	.09	.13	.38	.43	.45	.47	.49	.50
France	1.38	.76	.66	.66	.67	.58	.55	.51
Germany	.31	.40	.32	.34	.31	.32	.30	.28
Italy	.22	.10	.16	.18	.09	.14	.10	.08
Japan	.24	.27	.23	.23	.21	.25	.24	.24
Netherlands	.31	.36	.61	.58	.67	.54	.61	.65
New Zealand	n.a.[a]	n.a.[a]	n.a.[a]	n.a.[a]	.23	.27	.36	.47
Norway	.11	.16	.32	.33	.41	.45	.63	.65
Portugal	1.45	.59	.67	1.42	1.79	.71	.47	.42
Sweden	.05	.19	.38	.44	.48	.56	.69	.70
Switzerland	.04	.09	.15	.11	.21	.15	.15	.15
United Kingdom	.56	.47	.37	.41	.39	.35	.34	.32
United States[b]	.53	.49	.31	.32	.29	.23	.21	.20
DAC Total								
ODA ($ millions)								
current prices	4,665	5,895	6,832	7,762	8,671	9,415	10,706	11,948
1973 prices	7,660	9,069	9,346	9,976	10,059	9,415	9,391	9,452
GNP ($ billions)								
current prices	898	1,340	2,010	2,218	2,550	3,100	3,530	4,100
ODA as % of GNP	.52	.44	.34	.35	.34	.30	.30	.29
ODA deflator	60.9	65.0	73.1	77.8	86.2	100.0	114.0	126.4

Source: Robert S. McNamara, *Addresss to the Board of Governors of the World Bank Group*, Washington, D.C., September 30, 1974 (Washington, D.C.: World Bank, 1974).

Note: Countries included are members of OECD Development Assistance Committee, accounting for more than 95 percent of total Official Development Assistance. Figures for 1973 and earlier years are actual data. The projections for 1974 and 1975 are based on World Bank estimates of growth of GNP, on information on budget appropriations for aid, and on aid policy statements made by governments. Because of the relatively long period of time required to translate legislative authorizations first into commitments and later into disbursements, it is possible to project today, with reasonable accuracy, ODA flows (which by definition represent disbursements) through 1975.

[a]New Zealand became a member of DAC in 1973. ODA figures for New Zealand are not available for 1960-1971.

[b]In 1949, at the beginning of the Marshall Plan, U.S. Official Development Assistance amounted to 2.79% of GNP.

by limiting job creation through capital-intensive production methods and artificial limitations on exports; by limiting capital inflows through borrowing in host country money markets; by exacting monopoly rents on their technology, and so forth. In addition, these companies have often interfered in the internal politics of host countries, with or without the encouragement of their home governments. Finally, they and their home governments have been able to limit if not altogether halt other international capital flows to host governments in situations involving serious corporation-host government conflict.[7,e]

5. The terms of trade have moved consistently against the typical developing country export basket, and they have done so for reasons integral to the operation of the Bretton Woods system. This particular perception continued to exist until the commodity price boom of the early 1970s despite considerable evidence to the contrary.

The five general perceptions noted above are *not* universally shared within the developing world. Indeed, the Bretton Woods years witnessed significant progress within many individual countries of the South as well as within the South as an aggregate. It is often forgotten that the growth target for the first Development Decade—5 percent per year—was actually exceeded; and that per capita goals were disappointing for the most part due to the rapid rate of Southern population growth. What the previous paragraphs have tried to capture is not an analytical assessment of Southern complaints about the Bretton Woods system, but rather a developing country feeling about the equity aspects of North-South economic relations in the Bretton Woods era.[8]

The conclusion, again obvious, is that the South found the system severely wanting. To caricature the period, the South raised questions concerning equity (encompassing the redistribution of both income and economic opportunity) and the North responded with answers concerning efficiency.[f] Therefore the two sides talked past each other for much of the time, but until 1973 without any significant consequences for the international economic system itself. The reason: neither the North nor the South perceived that the South could damage the system if its requests—or demands—were not met.

The Role of the United States

The final reason that the Bretton Woods system lasted for over twenty years without major challenge was that it served the political and economic purposes

[e] Richard J. Barnet and Ronald E. Müller argue that the *net* effect of foreign direct investment on the development process is negative; this conclusion follows at least in part from their definition of development that focuses on better living standards for the poorest 60 percent of developing country populations rather than on aggregate growth rates. [*Global Reach: The Power of the Multinational Corporations* (New York: Simon and Schuster, 1974).]

[f] The North's responses, or lack of them, were obviously not consistently concerned with efficiency. If they had been, many of the Northern tariff and quota barriers most constraining on developing country exports would have been dismantled years ago.

of the one superpower that designed and nourished it—the United States. The system matched the blend of "idealism" and "realism" implicit in U.S. postwar foreign policy, and it placed few if any constraints on that policy until the mid-1960s. As for the idealistic strains, the system captured the essence of Cordell Hull's vision of world peace through minimum restraints on international commercial intercourse. Hull's concept was not all that different from that of the Manchester School in England a century or so earlier or that of Woodrow Wilson during the World War I period.

The "realism" was there as well—the avid desire for access to markets, to raw materials, and to new outlets for foreign direct investment. To the extent that concerns about the need for high levels of domestic employment motivated these policies, it should be noted that answers were available in policies other than those advocated by the United States—thus the major differences of opinion between Great Britain (and Lord Keynes) on the one hand and the Americans (and Harry Dexter White) on the other. Nevertheless, the system that was eventually established did suit the needs of the world's leading industrial-military power admirably. It helped to open and keep open much of the world to U.S. goods, investments, and influence during several decades in which U.S. policy-makers viewed such access as essential to both their immediate security goals and to their more nebulous range of "milieu" goals.

The System in Crisis

The successful operation of the Bretton Woods system has been attributed to four major factors: (1) the willingness and ability to deviate from it and improvise new processes of international economic relations when and where necessary; (2) the latitude that the system granted to Western Europe and Japan to recover quickly from wartime destruction and sustain rapid rates of growth; (3) the lack of power on the part of the world's developing nations to challenge effectively the system whose equity they questioned; and (4) the close fit between the system's norms and flexibility and the domestic and foreign policies of the hegemonial power of the Bretton Woods system. In attempting to understand the forces behind the present challenge to the system, one is forced to look beyond simple changes in these factors to a much broader and more complex array of changes in the international system that have occurred over the past twenty years and have symbolically culminated in the actions of the OPEC countries in 1973 and the Northern response to those actions.

During the course of the 1960s, a series of structural changes in the postwar international system slowly became apparent. They included the movement from a sharply divided bipolar world into one characterized by what Stanley Hoffmann several years ago labeled "muted bipolarity," "polycentrism," and "multipolarity."[9]

The muted bipolarity of the 1960s was a product of the "consecration of the nation-state, and new conditions in the use of force."[10] In Asia and Africa the drive to terminate colonial status and to develop new nation-states was perhaps the most prominent of all integrating forces in such transitional societies.[11] And in the old nation-states of Europe, the resurgence of what has often been called the "new nationalism" accompanied the growth of the Common Market and the economic regeneration of Europe.[12]

The growth of nationalist sentiments in new states and their somewhat altered reappearance in old ones were in part a reflection of the growing restraints on the use of force (at the least, the *perception* of growing restraints) by the world's two superpowers. Almost a decade ago Hoffmann, referring to the nuclear balance and its upgrading of the capacity to deter but downgrading of the capacity to compel, concluded that "Damocles' sword has become a boomerang, the ideological legitimacy of the nation-state is protected by the relative and forced tameness of the world jungle."[13]

The devaluation of coercive power was directly linked to the appearance of a de facto polycentrism in world politics. In a system where great powers are relatively cautious in their use of military power, states lacking the traditional coinage of the realm but possessing other factors capable of influencing the behavior of foreign states become more plausible players in the game. Their credentials remain questionable in standard balance-of-power terms, but as the OPEC example suggests, an Iran and even a Libya can act as a player on the largest stage unless and until its credentials are questioned; by the time the credentials are questioned, they may prove to be legitimate as the rules of the game and the asymmetries of power are altered.

Multipolarity has accompanied the emergence of muted bipolarity and polycentrism. If the concept of polycentrism seemed somewhat amorphous in the 1960s, multipolarity—the spread of nuclear weapons—suggested a more concrete trend in traditional terms away from the sharply bipolar world of the 1950s. With India's recent nuclear explosion and the incipient spread of various forms of "peaceful" nuclear technology throughout the Middle East, the process of multipolarization has been given an entirely new impetus; changing subsystemic balances of power on the Indian subcontinent and the Middle East, together with billions of dollars in oil profits throughout the latter region, literally guarantee the emergence of several new nuclear powers within the next decade in that region of the world alone. Events in South America, not entirely unrelated to the unfolding scenario in the Middle East, suggest a further increase in the number of nuclear powers by the 1980s.[g]

Beyond these major changes in the structure of the international system two

[g]Shortly after India's first nuclear detonation of May 1974, an Indian-Argentine agreement for the peaceful utilization of nuclear energy was announced. A spokesman for the South American government noted that the agreement could speed the construction of Argentina's third nuclear power plant. Brazil's first nuclear reactor is scheduled to commence operation in 1977. Neither Argentina nor Brazil has signed the 1968 Non-Proliferation Treaty.

other process factors—or transnational forces for change in the system's structure—have been growing in importance throughout the past two decades. They are the growing economic integration at the global level and the impact of "transnational actors" on the international system.[14]

Listing the more obvious changes in the international system is a far easier task than comprehending their likely impact on patterns of international behavior. Keohane and Nye have recently put forward some of the most thought-provoking generalizations along these lines. Accepting the view that a growing disutility has been attached to the use of force (compellance) over a broad range of international conflicts and that the old consensus supporting the basic structure of the Bretton Woods scheme of international economic relations has broken down, they posited three major propositions: (1) that threats to state autonomy have generally shifted from the security area to the area of *economic* interdependence; (2) that international "power" will therefore increasingly derive from patterns of asymmetrical interdependence between actors in issue areas in which they find themselves mutually engaged; and (3) that states suffering from unfavorable asymmetries in one issue area will seek to link that area to another in which they hold a preponderance of usable power.[15]

All the changes in the international system noted above have in varying degree contributed to the destabilization if not the demise of the Bretton Woods system. This point is best made by examining the strained relations between the system's major beneficiaries—the industrialized countries—and some recent actions of the system's major critics—the developing countries.

At the empirical level the years since the mid-1960s have been characterized by increasing dissension and fragmentation within the OECD countries, and the most significant sets of Northern relationships have been left in a state of relative disarray. None of the major relationships—U.S.-European Community; U.S.-Japan; U.S.-Canada; and European Community-Japan—can be expected from this generalization. The frictions preceded and were an integral part of the collapse of the Bretton Woods monetary system in 1971-1972; they have contributed directly to the increasing use of trade-restricting mechanisms that have damaged the GATT's remaining capacity for the exercise of moral suasion.

At a more analytical level, Northern fragmentation has resulted directly from the changes in the international system since the late 1950s. The muting of bipolarity, the appearance of the forces of the new nationalism, and the rapid economic growth rates in Japan and Western Europe created a situation that loosed the forces of national diversity rather than sustaining Northern unity. Japan, seeking a nonmilitary identity and an enhanced degree of economic security in the new system, put intolerable pressures on the world's trade and monetary mechanisms in its drive for export expansion. The members of the European Communities, unable to resolve their own identity crisis internally, externalized the process of regional integration to the point where some seventy-odd countries, many of them Southern, have now become members or associates of the Common Market. And each additional round of enlargement strained the bases of U.S. support for the EC and for further steps toward European union. The results of such processes and the equally nationalistic U.S. responses to them were highlighted by (1) the "Nixon Shock" of August 15, 1971; (2) a search for détente with the Soviet Union and China pushed with such singlemindedness that it left old allies concerned and suspicious; and (3) that comic opera entitled "The Year of Europe" in which Secretary of State Henry Kissinger's efforts to revitalize the rhetoric if not the reality of Atlantic "partnership" only revealed the state of disarray into which that relationship had fallen.

Then came the OPEC shock, and with it the desperate rush on the part of many Northern countries to arrange bilateral deals with a host of oil-rich countries of the Middle East to assure access to oil supplies. The French and the British made little pretense of Northern unity—for that matter, even Common Market unity—in the face of oil crisis; the United States publicly preached unity while attempting more silently to establish its own net of bilateral relations with Saudi Arabia, the country with the world's largest proven oil reserves.

Until very recently, the developing country response to the growing disunity within the OECD countries has been relatively consistent with the changes in the international system noted above. Southern countries have used a wide variety of mechanisms and institutions to capitalize on the growth of polycentrism and disunity within the OECD states to increase the value of North-South resource transfers. At the global level, they have used UNCTAD as a sounding board for their demands that the international markets for the exchange of goods, capital, and technology be altered in various ways in their favor; at the regional level, they have used a considerable number of integration schemes in attempts to increase growth potential and bargaining strength vis-à-vis existing global trade and investment structures and foreign direct investors; and at the product level, various developing country producers have attempted to institute arrangements to control the production and marketing of certain commodities to increase and stabilize their export earnings. In addition, individual countries of the South have sought to diversify their export markets and the sources of their long-term investment inflows, particularly in the area of foreign direct investment. Finally, as the sources of foreign direct investment broadened to include Europe and Japan, many developing countries have found themselves in a better position to impose conditions of entry that promised greater host-country benefits from multinational corporation activity than previous investments had produced.[16]

On the whole, these changes have until recently been marginal and undramatic in their implementation and results. With the success of the OPEC actions in quintupling the price of oil, the rhetoric—and to an as yet unmeasurable degree, the reality—of North-South political economy issues experienced a profound change.

Within the twelve-month period following the Arab actions of late 1973,

Southern movements on the commodity front confirmed the view that new and more aggressive bargaining tactics would become increasingly widespread. The seven leading bauxite producers formed the International Bauxite Association, and Jamaica thereafter unilaterally raised its earnings on bauxite production sixfold. The six leading phosphate producers tripled their prices. Developing country consultations on six or eight other commodities were begun or continued with increased effort, and over two dozen less developed countries had established ministries of national resources by the end of 1974. The measures they employed maximize their "economic power" included decreed prices, production cutbacks, increased royalty payments, negotiated price increases, direct market intervention, stockpiling, and export taxes.[17]

As these actions of individual Southern countries and groups of countries to challenge old trading norms through new efforts at monopoly and oligopoly pricing spread rapidly, the developing countries as a group produced a dramatic declaration in favor of a "New International Economic Order" at the Spring 1974 Special Session of the U.N. General Assembly. Reading like the quintessential UNCTAD document, the declaration accepted by the General Assembly on May 2 included support for all efforts "to facilitate the functioning, and to further the aims, of producers associations, including their joint marketing arrangements." Later, the developing countries held another special session of the U.N. General Assembly in September 1975 on the "New International Economic Order" to press for measures of implementation.

These activities took place at the end of the most inflationary spiral in recent history. During 1972 and 1973, the global demand for most raw materials had skyrocketed and was reflected in exceedingly large relative price increases. The degree to which such commodity activities and arrangements in general can survive several years of low, if not negative, growth rates is as yet untested and makes any generalization based on the events of 1973-1974 tenuous at best.

Prospects for Significant Alteration in the Political Economy of North-South Relations

Will we one day look back on the 1973-1975 efforts of the developing countries to alter the international economic payoff matrix as a turning point in the political economy of North-South relations, or merely as a temporary deviation from much less dramatic trends in the evolution of present international political and economic systems?[18] So far the outcome is uncertain, though a greater probability would have to be attached to the "temporary deviation" scenario if only because the major slowdown in global economic activity that began in 1974 (featuring negative growth rates in several OECD countries) and the potential discontinuities in capital markets likely to accompany the "petrodollar" crisis will be felt most severely in the world's developing countries. In short, developing country dependence on the industrialized countries for export sales, commercial capital flows, technology, and foreign aid is likely to weaken their bargaining position in the aggregate over the next several years if not longer (see Tables 10-2 and 10-3).

Nevertheless, there is one scenario worth exploring that could make the events of 1973-1975 memorable as a turning point in North-South economic relations. It is worth examining not because a high degree of probability attaches to it, but rather because it reveals the degree of uncertainty that currently characterizes international political and economic relations and the resulting potential for change inherent in present North-South relationships.

This scenario involves the possibility that the developing countries of the world can sustain the minimum degree of solidarity necessary to bargain successfully for significant structural changes in the present international economic "rules of the game." It draws whatever credence it contains from four major parameters of the present North-South bargaining setting.

The first involves developed and developing country perceptions concerning the international equity issue as it is affected by North-South economic relationships. In an article published in 1973, Zbigniew Brzezinski offered the following observation on this issue:

> It is to be expected that in the next two or three decades we will witness an intensified crisis in the developing world brought about by the twin impacts of demographic growth and the spread of education. Both will make global inequality even more intolerable at a time when equality is becoming the most powerful moral imperative of our time, thus paralleling the appeal of the concept of liberty during the nineteenth century.
>
> This quest for equality is already being felt both within societies and on a global scale; it is, therefore, essential that the richer nations develop more comprehensive, more cooperative and more planned policies toward the poorer parts of the world.[19]

If Brzezinski is even half correct in identifying equality as "the most powerful moral imperative of our time," more than likely we are in for a period of highly politicized international economic relations, to say nothing of their domestic counterparts.[20] The distribution of the world's wealth and annual income is so skewed, both globally and nationally, and the demonstrated capacity of the developed countries to partake responsively in efforts at redistribution is so meager thus far, that it is difficult to imagine anything but a further politicization of North-South economic relationships in the near to medium-term future.[21]

How will industrialized states respond to growing developing country efforts, both rhetorical and programmatic, to gradually redistribute global income and/or opportunities for socioeconomic advancement through a restructuring of the international economic system? Undoubtedly, the answer will depend to a considerable degree on the accuracy of Brzezinski's prediction. Is a

Table 10-2
World Exports by Origin and Destination, 1961-1972
($ billions and percentages)

Exports to: / Exports from:	*Developed Market Economy Countries*		*Developing Market Economy Countries*		*Centrally Planned Economy Countries*		*World Total*[a]	
	% of Total	*Growth Rate*	*% of Total*	*Growth Rate*	*% of Total*	*Growth Rate*	*Value*	*Growth Rate*
Developed market economy countries[b,c,g]								
1961-66 average	73.8%	10.8%	22.0%	6.3%	3.8%	13.0%	$112.6	9.8%
1967-72 average	76.7	15.3	19.1	12.2	3.8	12.9	213.4	14.6
Developing market economy countries[d,e]								
1961-66 average	71.9	7.5	21.3	5.7	5.7	11.1	33.0	7.2
1967-72 average	73.6	11.2	19.8	10.3	5.4	11.7	52.7	11.0
Western Hemisphere								
1961-66 average	74.7	5.2	18.1	8.8	7.1	10.0	10.2	6.2
1967-72 average	73.8	11.9	19.9	11.4	5.7	7.6	15.8	11.7
Africa[a]								
1961-66 average	80.7	9.4	11.9	8.8	6.4	14.6	6.7	9.7
1967-72 average	81.6	12.8	10.3	11.0	6.8	15.5	11.8	12.6
Middle East[d,f]								
1961-66 average	73.4	10.9	21.1	7.4	2.2	12.4	5.7	10.1
1967-72 average	76.5	11.9	19.0	12.5	2.3	18.2	10.4	12.4
Other Asia								
1961-66 average	58.7	6.8	33.5	3.5	7.3	9.7	8.6	5.6
1967-72 average	63.9	13.5	29.4	10.4	6.1	11.1	13.5	12.4
Centrally planned economy countries[g,h]								
1961-66 average	20.5	13.7	14.4	11.8	64.6	5.4	19.5	8.0
1967-72 average	24.1	13.2	15.0	9.9	60.7	11.1	32.3	11.2
World								
1961-66 average	67.1	10.2	21.0	6.6	11.4	7.7	165.2	9.1
1967-72 average	70.5	14.5	18.8	11.6	10.2	11.6	298.2	13.6

Source: Based on World Bank/IDA, *Annual Report, 1973*, pp. 84-85.

[a]Includes items not broken down by destination.

[b]Includes developing countries of southern Europe.

[c]For 1969-72, includes Israel.

[d]For 1969-72, includes Turkey.

[e]For 1969-72, excludes exports of Rhodesia.

[f]Includes Cyprus and Iran.

[g]Excludes the transactions between Federal Republic of Germany and Democratic Republic of Germany.

[h]Includes exports of U.S.S.R. not shown by destination.

Table 10-3
Net Flow of Total Official and Private Financial Resources[a] from Developed (DAC) Countries to Developing Countries and Multilateral Agencies, Disbursements, 1962-1972
($ Millions)

	1962	*1963*	*1964*	*1965*	*1966*	*1967*	*1968*	*1969*	*1970*[b]	*1971*[b]	*1972*[b]
Official development assistance	5,438	5,772	5,952	5,895	5,984	6,536	6,309	6,621	6,832	7,759	8,654
bilateral grants and grantlike flows	4,020	3,940	3,806	3,714	3,701	3,578	3,344	3,251	3,323	3,634	4,360
(technical assistance)	(747)	(871)	(954)	(1,063)	(1,233)	(1,314)	(1,467)	(1,528)	(1,532)	(1,655)	(1,839)
bilateral loans at concessional terms	907	1,465	1,740	1,833	1,947	2,222	2,282	2,320	2,384	2,786	2,395
contributions to multilateral institutions	511	367	405	348	336	736	683	1,050	1,124	1,339	1,898
Other official flows	546	243	−36	304	447	518	738	571	1,152	1,271	1,541
bilateral	531	246	−28	299	394	499	748	586	879	1,004	1,169
multilateral	15	−3	−7	5	53	19	−10	−15	273	267	372
Private flows	2,453	2,557	3,729	4,121	3,959	4,381	6,462	6,586	6,949	8,215	8,430
direct investment	1,495	1,603	1,572	2,468	2,179	2,105	3,151	2,919	3,563	3,877	4,306
bilateral portfolio and other	147	327	837	655	480	800	948	1,201	726	757	2,030
multilateral portfolio[c]	239	−33	461	247	175	469	767	419	474	771	667
export credits[d]	572	660	859	751	1,124	1,007	1,596	2,047	2,185	2,810	1,427
Grants by private voluntary agencies	–	–	–	–	–	–	–	–	858	913	1,026
Total net flow	8,437	8,572	9,645	10,320	10,390	11,435	13,509	13,778	15,791	18,158	19,653

Source: Report by the Chairman of the Development Assistance Committee, *Development Co-operation, 1973 Review* (Paris: OECD, 1973), p. 42.

[a]Gross disbursements minus amortization receipts on earlier lending.

[b]Including grants by private voluntary agencies.

[c]These funds of private origin are mingled with those provided under "ODA Contributions to Multilateral Institutions," "Other Official Flows (Multilateral)," and other funds from non-DAC sources, in programs governed by criteria similar to those applied in bilateral ODA programs.

[d]Measured by some countries as change in outstanding amounts guaranteed, by others as change in outstanding amounts due on disbursed credits. Interest is included in the sums recorded as outstanding, so that the net flow tends to be overstated if gross new guarantees are rising, and vice versa.

growing number of Northern elite groups sharing a novel perception about the moral imperative of attacking existing global inequalities? Much evidence suggests that the issue is being given a good deal of thought even if no consensus exists. It works its way onto an increasing number of Northern elite group agendas—the Trilateral Commission on which Brzezinski serves is no exception—even when it was not initially included.

An increased willingness on the part of Northern elite groups to consider a gradually altering structure of payoffs in international economic relations (trade, aid, and investment) need not rest on changing equity perceptions alone. Indeed, prudent self-interest as perceived by many influential groups is gradually dictating the same course of action. There is a growing belief within the North that certain global problems cannot be resolved without the active cooperation of the developing countries—the population explosion and ecological damage are but two of the most obvious: thus the sudden interest in and discussion of "global compacts," some presented straightforwardly and others allegorically.[22]

More specifically, most multinational corporations, looking for that minimum "stability" necessary for their continued access to supplies, markets, and so forth, will generally endorse changes that minimize North-South frictions (specific cases, e.g., expropriation issues, excepted) and attempt to influence their home governments accordingly. Everything we know, both analytically and empirically, concerning the process of oligopolistic competition suggests that multinational corporations will continue to expand their operations in developing countries as rapidly as possible. As Barnet and Müller have recently demonstrated, such companies will continue to do so despite changing conditions of entry and operation that increasingly tend to meet growing LDC demands for a far greater host-country return on such investment.[23] Given the corporate community's demonstrated capacity to influence governmental policy in capitalist societies, multinational corporation desires to keep the door open to Southern markets and materials may prove to be more influential than any generalized Northern *crise de conscience* regarding the international equity issue in altering the present pattern of North-South political economy. In sum, both an incipient crisis of conscience (of admittedly unknown dimensions) and a recalculation of longer-term self-interest would seem to be at work slowly altering Northern elite group perceptions about "doing more" to aid the process of development in the South. Whether there is enough in this trend to affect governmental policies of the industrial states in the next several years is impossible to predict.

It is readily apparent that Southern perceptions of the international equity issue are both shared and salient. Southern solidarity on this issue has been vividly demonstrated recently in developing country reaction to increased oil prices and in the outcome of the 1974 U.N. Special Session on raw materials. The quintupling of oil prices will probably have a devastating impact upon the Fourth World, may push several Third World aspirants back one space, and conceivably could undermine the medium-term growth prospects of such Third World giants as Brazil, if existing international financial mechanisms are unable to keep international capital markets open to large Third World borrowers. Despite all these threats to developing country economic health, the only public statements emanating from the South through early 1975 have praised the OPEC actions for reversing years of "Northern injustice."

Has this lack of public criticism been based on the fear of OPEC retaliation, on the hope that substantial OPEC aid flows will ease the burden on the most affected Southern countries, or on a latent hostility toward the world's rich countries that enables the South to place a premium on the psychic rewards of seeing Europe and Japan in periods of panic that outweigh their own suffering? If it is one or a combination of the first two reasons—fear and/or hope—Southern solidarity may prove to be a function of the degree to which OPEC aid flows ease the financial problems of the developing countries. If the third explanation—hostility toward the North keyed to the equity issue—is salient, Southern criticism of OPEC may be withheld indefinitely.

The second parameter of the North-South bargaining setting that will influence the capacity for Southern cohesion concerns the growth of an institutional structure and an elite group socialization process shared to some degree by all developing countries over the past two decades. Between the years of the Bandung Conference (1955) and the first meeting of UNCTAD (1964), a capability emerged for certain forms of Southern bloc activity in confronting the industrialized countries with agendas of both general and specific demands. At the Geneva meeting of UNCTAD in 1964, this capability was institutionalized in the so-called Group of 77.

Major ingredients in the development of the bloc represented by the 77 have been the various regional groupings that constitute its overwhelming membership [the Latin American group, now coordinated through the Special Coordinating Committee for Latin America (CECLA); the African group, coordinated through the Economic Commission for Africa and the Organization of African Unity; and the Asian group, the least homogeneous and almost without an organizational focus]. The scores of meetings that such groups have had throughout the past decade alone to prepare first regional then global positions for three UNCTAD Conferences, a series of nonaligned state meetings, and U.N. sessions of one form or another have clearly created in participants and their governments certain norms of behavior and patterns of action that by today dictate to a considerable degree the rituals of North-South confrontation. They can be seen in operation when environmental issues are discussed at Stockholm, when population problems are discussed at Bucharest, and when "the heritage of mankind" is discussed and distributed at the ongoing U.N. Law of the Sea Conference. The rules of the game are always the same: develop and hold as long as possible to a united front strategy that minimizes Southern costs and maximizes Southern benefits.

An intriguing example of this strategy was evident in the 1974 session of the Third U.N. Law of the Sea Conference. It can be argued that there is no "rational" reason for the developing states to hold together in this particular bargaining setting because the issues at stake should fragment rather than solidify the Southern group. What interests do the landlocked and shelflocked states of the South share with their coastal neighbors who are pressing for a 200-mile "patrimonial sea" regime? In effect, the latter regime would reduce the "common heritage of mankind" approach to the wealth of the seas to an empty phrase. Additionally, what interests are shared between resource-poor developing countries that would like to see the resources of the deep seabed mined immediately and the resource-rich developing countries that desire a deep seabed regime that will not depress price levels of their own natural resources?

Despite these and many other major and minor differences, the developing countries at the Law of the Sea Conference have thus far refused to negotiate seriously with the developed states of the world until they arrive at a consensus Southern position. As one long-time observer of developing country bargaining tactics summarized the issue, any final agreement emerging from the current Law of the Sea debate "implies that an agreement has to be reached beforehand within the Latin American group, the African group, and the Asian group, and that all of it will be combined in a position acceptable to all developing countries."[24]

When one examines the stakes at issue in the present Law of the Sea Conference, it is almost impossible to imagine that the developing countries can hold out much longer against the pressures that divide them internally. Yet their efforts at internal conciliation continue, as they do in so many areas where short-term "national interest" arguments would seem to foreclose Southern unity as a viable bargaining option. How long can such "irrational" behavior last? Certainly as long as its practitioners *perceive* it as rational behavior. That period is likely to vary with each issue and with the environmental factors encompassing each negotiation.

A leading student of the Group of 77, Branislav Gosovic, observing its performance at UNCTAD II in New Delhi, concluded as follows:

> Although the developing countries maintained a common front in UNCTAD, they failed to achieve the true behavior of a "trade union." The stronger bargaining posture for the 77 could not be attained for two basic reasons among others. First, individual developing countries were weak and susceptible to bilateral deals and the manipulation of the West, thus weakening the unity and thrust of their group. Secondly, the developing countries could not as yet agree to act as a group forcefully and systematically in other international organizations but UNCTAD. Assuming that these factors will continue to be valid for the time being, what, then, is the crucial ingredient in the bargaining stance of the 77? Apparently, it is the application of a skillful and persistent group pressure on the developed countries, grounded in an elaborate program, plus solid and rational arguments. . . . This approach imposes itself in a situation where there is

no possibility for barter between negotiating sides, or where the demanding side cannot induce "fear" in the opponent.[25]

Like the first parameter of the North-South bargaining setting examined—perceptions concerning the equity issue and Northern self-interest in developing a positive response to the issue—this one is not easy to evaluate. The same elites socialized in the Group-of-77 processes deal constantly and directly with developed countries on a broad range of regional and bilateral issues. Overlapping socialization processes are at work. And as the record demonstrates, until recently the degree of "solidarity" produced through the mechanisms of the Group of 77 has not been terribly impressive beyond the level of rhetoric.

Nevertheless, the machinery and the experience is there, and a change in any of the other parameters at play could alter the South's willingness and capacity to use them. It should be noted that Gosovic's conclusion quoted above was based on the premise that "the demanding side cannot induce 'fear' in the opponent." The OPEC example has since demonstrated that a demanding "South" may occasionally be able to induce Northern fear. How much difference will such an experience make in North-South relations in general, and in Southern capacity for "solidarity" in particular?

The third parameter of the problem involves precisely this issue—the potential in the present international context for radically altered perceptions of developing country power. Within the North, the crucial perception revolves around the issue of the growing dependence of Northern industries on Southern sources of raw materials coupled with developing country capacity to withhold those raw materials to increase the Southern share of global income. The perception would seem to be a distortion of reality as we have always understood it. In the first place, resources are a function of price; higher prices will lead to alternative sources of raw materials, product substitution, or some combination thereof. At least these are the perceptions of the economist.[26]

In the second place, the developing countries' ability to withhold access to raw materials in a period of slow global growth or recession would seem to be minimal. Aggregate OECD country real growth rates for 1975 are projected at less than 1 percent. Nevertheless, if corporations and governments in the industrialized countries *perceive* a world of increasing raw material scarcities and view access to the raw materials of developing countries as a crucial goal, then Northern perceptions will add to Southern bargaining strength despite the generally soothing words of resource economists. This argument is particularly applicable to multinational corporations that have little if any trouble passing on higher costs in the form of higher product prices. Their major concern has always been *assured* access to supplies; raw material price has and continues to be a far lesser concern. Oligopolists have little trouble passing on price increases to the ultimate consumer.

Developing country perceptions should also increase Southern bargaining strength. The rapidity with which other producer cartels attempted to follow the

OPEC example has already been noted. Not all attempts have succeeded, and immediate global economic conditions are not promising for attempts in the near future. Nevertheless, Northern insecurities have been revealed at both the nation-state and corporate level. When one adds to this the potential for unregulated developed country and multinational corporation competition to achieve *assured* access to supplies of resources, the conditions for changing perceptions of strength are evident even in an economic downturn. At the very least, aggregate levels of global demand may be less determinative of prices than bilateral agreements between countries, groups of countries, or specific developing country suppliers and Northern purchasers.

The final parameter of the Southern solidarity issue concerns Southern perceptions of the decreasing costs of North-South confrontations. Two essential ingredients are involved: (1) the growing perceptions in the North of the disutility of force in North-South conflicts; and (2) the growing economic capacity of the South to absorb the strictly economic costs that such confrontations may entail.

The literature on the disutility of force in North-South conflicts is far too lengthy to review here.[27] Reduced to its barest essentials it contains three elements. First, in the postcolonial era of emergent nations and strong anti-Western feelings, the costs of Northern military interventions are likely to outweigh the benefits in most instances. This conclusion follows from the enhanced capacity and willingness of Southern countries to resist Northern use of force.

Second, industrial countries, more sophisticated in their understanding of economics and their capacity to manage their economies, feel far less inclined to stake exclusive claims to resources or markets in the South. Again, the result is to undermine most traditional arguments for the use of force in less developed countries.

Finally, and most difficult to calculate, there is the *normative* devaluation of the use of force in such "unequal" struggles. Has the world moved close enough to that of the so-called global humanists so that in a normative sense, Northern policy-makers would find it possible to use overt force in a conflict with a country or region of the less developed world only in those limited instances thought to have a significantly destabilizing impact on East-West relationships? The cases of Vietnam and Chile suggest both that overt force may still be used when "internal wars" have been joined (or has the Vietnam backlash foreclosed this option for the future?) and that covert interventions remain possibilities in certain cases. Furthermore, statements by President Gerald Ford and Secretary of State Kissinger in the winter of 1974-1975 concerning the possibility of using force to avoid "economic strangulation" further emphasized the need to consider whether the devaluation of force in North-South conflicts should not be conceptualized as a dependent variable.

In fact, OPEC's actions have served to raise a host of questions concerning the general issue of the use of force in the present era of international relations.

The OPEC embargo served as a reminder that most analyses of the use of force question have posited the growing disutility of force—especially in the North-South context—upon implicit or explicit assumptions that include the existence of a liberal trading system and no resource scarcities. If, as the Bretton Woods system decays, access to raw materials is significantly impeded and international market uncertainties—for both goods and markets—increase rapidly, many of the factors that seemed to be increasingly constraining the use of force between "strong" and "weak" states may prove to be less formidable than once suggested.

OPEC aside, it is still probable that most Southern elites, observing the general post-World War II Northern restraints on the use of force in North-South conflicts, perceive a decreasing cost to themselves of North-South confrontations. These perceptions are strengthened to the degree that the South is also developing a greater capacity to absorb the potential costs of such conflicts in an economic sense. Several indicators suggest that such capacity is expanding. Throughout the Third World, domestic economies have been rapidly growing and diversifying. In many of these same countries, stronger governments employing well-trained *técnicos* are effectively strengthening their bargaining power with multinational corporations, adding to their own technological capabilities, export earnings, and potential for further diversification. The sudden appearance of new aid donors can only add to these general trends.

To repeat once again, a significant global slowdown in growth could sorely test this new strength found in many parts of the developing world. On the other hand, any OPEC actions to allocate even a modest portion of their increased earnings to developing countries could ease this burden. By early 1975 it was impossible to judge the likely magnitude of such flows. One of the major reasons was that the figures on OPEC aid flows were very difficult to aggregate. Much funding was involved in vaguely reported bilateral arrangements, the terms of such lending were often too imprecise to allow a differentiation between commercial and concessional financing, and it was often difficult to distinguish between vague promises concerning future flows on the one hand and concrete obligations on the other. The state of confusion was characterized by the range of estimates of OPEC lending to the developing countries, a range that started at about $2 billion and ran as high as $20 billion.

Nevertheless, by early 1975 it began to appear that the OPEC countries were moving, generally on an individual basis but occasionally in groups, to disburse a very considerable volume of funds throughout the developing world. An OECD attempt to measure the flows concluded that between January and September 1974, the commitments from OPEC countries amounted to $8.6 billion, not counting the $3.1 billion made available to the International Monetary Fund's oil facility and the more than $1 billion loaned to the World Bank (disbursements for the entire year apparently exceeded $2 billion). Of the total, $6.2 billion consisted of bilateral commitments and $2.4 billion consisted of multilateral aid. Of the total, it was further estimated that approximately one-third (over $2 billion) of bilateral OPEC aid had been committed to the U.N.'s category of "most seriously affected" nations, essentially the Fourth World countries.

The largest bilateral donors have been Iran (over $3 billion) and Saudi Arabia (over $2.5 billion). While a very large percentage of aid from the Middle East OPEC members has undoubtedly flowed to other Arab states and much of it has taken the form of military and "support" assistance, some major flows have been directed to non-Arab countries. To consider but one example, Iran is now believed to have committed close to $1 billion to India and approximately $640 million to Pakistan. Iran's agreement with India calls for the shipment of $500 million of crude oil to India over five years, to be repaid over five years at an interest rate of 2.5 percent with a grant element of 40 percent. Additionally, Iran has agreed in principle to provide approximately $400 million in untied credit to India on concessional terms. Finally, the loans to Pakistan are calculated to contain a grant element of 30 percent.[28]

In the Western Hemisphere, Venezuela's assumption of the role of an aid-donor is already intriguingly suggestive of the economic and political power that the OPEC countries might generate in defense of "Third World solidarity" at a very marginal cost given the size of their increased oil revenues. First, Venezuela has loaned $500 million to the Inter-American Development Bank under terms that are expected to support Latin America's effort to achieve greater technological sophistication and autonomy vis-à-vis developed country corporations. Second, it has initialed agreements to lend $60 million to the Central American Bank for Regional Integration (CABEI) and to spend another $60 million to $80 million to finance the stockpiling of Central American coffee beans. Finally, it has agreed to sell its oil at $6 per barrel to the Central American countries—about 50 percent of the December 1974 world price. The difference is to be deposited in local currencies in interest-bearing accounts at Venezuela's disposal in each country. Those funds will be used for local development loans approved by the new Venezuelan Investment Fund.

All these actions are initial steps in Venezuela's announced policy to use its oil profits (now in excess of $10 billion per year) to underwrite the economic development of Latin America. It is much too early to predict how large such flows will become, their degrees of concessionality, or the degree to which they may underwrite a "solid South" as North-South conflict over the changing global political economy is played out over the next several years. Already Venezuela has failed to meet the initial hopes of many Central American and Caribbean countries to share in the Venezuelan bonanza, just as Middle Eastern OPEC members have failed to fulfill similar expectations on the part of many of the poorer black African countries. Nevertheless, OPEC's first post-price-rise year efforts in the aid field are by no means unimpressive, and their experiences in this role are just beginning.

Conclusion

Can the world's developing countries sustain the minimum degree of solidarity needed to bargain successfully for significant structural changes in the present rules of the international economic game? After examining the foundations on which such solidarity might be built and maintained, the probabilities still do not seem very high. The more probable outcome is one involving specific bilateral, regional, and individual commodity arrangements as single developing countries or groupings of them attempt to surmount the difficulties of the years immediately ahead. Food, fuel, and fertilizer price increases in 1974 added over $15 billion to the import bill of the developing countries, and there is little reason to expect much easing in the new price levels in the near future. With import bills rising, export earnings and Northern foreign aid flows doing well to avoid decreases (in real terms), and commercial capital terms tightening for most Southern countries, international market forces could hardly be less propitious for united Southern efforts to restructure the remains of the Bretton Woods world in their favor. Under such conditions Nye and Keohane's 1973 prediction might well prove the most accurate portent of the future: "policies in rich countries will continue to influence economic development in poor countries, but poor countries will have very little political influence over them. . . . The danger is not that the rich will depend on the poor in the next decade, but that they may ignore them."[29]

Market conditions aside, what is the South anyway? As noted at the beginning of this chapter, the South is at a minimum several worlds. It is the OPEC world that has grabbed the brass ring and is currently earning $60 billion per year more than it can spend internally. It is the Third World, potentially the world's middle class if it can survive the present oil-induced international economic crisis. In the Third World, growth rates have recently been averaging 6 percent or better, per capita income generally exceeds $500 in nominal terms and may be higher in real terms, export capacity has been rapidly expanding, and a respectable international credit reputation has enabled it to borrow abroad on commercial terms as necessary to help finance further development. And the South is also the Fourth World, a world presently on the edge of desperation. As Robert McNamara noted at the joint Bank-Fund meeting in Washington in 1974:

> The rising prices of imported petroleum, fertilizer, and cereals, the slack demand for their exports to developed countries, and the erosion of the real value of development assistance, all have dealt severe blows to the growth aspirations of the poorest. . . . These nations, with a population of one billion [close to one-third of the world's population] and incomes average less than $200 per capita, on the most likely set of assumptions regarding commodity prices, capital flows, and growth rates in the OECD countries [will between now and 1980] suffer an actual decline in their per capita incomes. The effect of this on the already marginal condition of life of the poorest 40% within these countries is an appalling prospect.[30]

There is little on the historical record to suggest that Southern solidarity will withstand the centrifugal forces that are likely to prevail in the next several years. Exhibiting widely differing stages of development, national situations and degrees of internal integration, what is to hold developing countries together? The fivefold oil price increases since late 1973 instituted by one part of the South have become a matter of life or death to tens of thousands in other parts. Regional integration schemes within various areas of the South have faltered time and again essentially because of failures to develop mechanisms to assure a distribution of benefits whose equity was acceptable to all members.[h] The countries of the South are occasionally at war with each other (e.g., Honduras and El Salvador; India and Pakistan) more generally in arms races (e.g., in Latin America, the Middle East, and the Indian subcontinent), and they are quite often involved in attempts at subverting neighboring governments.

In all, the degree of heterogeneity encompassed by the term "South," the Group of 77, the Non-Aligned Countries or whatever other label is applied to the developing countries of the world, would almost seem a priori to defy the capacity for cohesive confrontation with the developed countries of the world at all but the rhetorical level. Their internal and occasionally external striving for national identity (Asia and Africa) or regional hegemony (the Middle East, the Indian subcontinent, and Latin America), their asymmetrical sources of power—not only with each other but with the North as well—and their symbiotic relationships with many transnational actors would seem of necessity to make them open to a lengthy series of cross-cutting coalitions that would range well beyond the constraints implied by Southern "solidarity."

Why should the Shah of Iran pour funds into India and Bangladesh when he has his own empire to build, his own vision to create in his own country? Why should Venezuela and Brazil contribute funds indiscriminately to the Fourth World when they have their own (perhaps clashing) destinies to meet in the heartland of South America? In other words, isn't the *embourgeoisement* of the Third World in the present international system a more likely outcome than a system transformation based on a North-South relationship of major tension (at first normative and economic, then increasingly strategic-diplomatic)? Even if some Southern elite groups favored the latter alternative, do the political elites of the major Third World countries in general have the will, and do their political systems have the capacity, to maintain Southern cohesion in a bid to significantly restructure the present pattern of international political economy?

On balance, the answer would seem to remain negative, that the capacity for such cohesion is still somewhat beyond the South's grasp. Domestic developmental and regional hierarchical issues (within the South, that is) will most

[h]The failures have not been due to any lack of paper schemes addressed to the distribution problem, but rather to the lack of political capacity to implement them. See Roger D. Hansen, "Regional Integration: Reflections on a Decade of Theoretical Efforts," *World Politics* 21, no. 2 (January 1969): 242-271.

probably lead LDC agendas, with Southern solidarity running third except where certan North-South issues make Southern solidarity almost a "free good." Domestic problems for developing countries continue to be staggering in the Fourth World and significant for the Third World. Furthermore, the very process of structural change created by development initiates a series of sociopolitical demands that must be managed by political systems in one way or another, absorbing the time, concern, and resources available to governing elites.

Directly behind domestic problems one is likely to see precedence given to issues of regional hierarchy. Development is an uneven process both within countries and within regions. Its potential for producing destabilizing effects at the regional level is well documented in the growth of the European state system, and it is likely to be a characteristic of present patterns of development in Asia, Africa, the Middle East, and Latin America.[i] The diminished utility of force (compellance as opposed to deterrence) in great power relationships has not been demonstrated logically or empirically to apply to the use of non-nuclear force by emerging powers within the developing world. Furthermore, the growing potential for the rapid spread of nuclear weapons following India's 1974 nuclear explosion and a series of related and unrelated events in the Middle East will undoubtedly give impetus to an increased allocation of domestic resources in the South to the struggles for regional hierarchy.

These considerations suggest that the probabilities are still somewhat unlikely that the period 1973-1975 will be remembered as one in which the developing countries reshuffled the payoff matrix of the international economic system and significantly altered the political economy of North-South relations. Nevertheless, these probabilities are too significant to be easily dismissed. And at the very least, the years 1973-1975 are likely to be remembered as the period in which developing countries first made a serious attempt, individually and in groups, to institute major changes. Prior efforts had been for the most part rhetorical; global supply and demand conditions together with the OPEC example coupled significant action with rhetoric for the first time.

Where the political economy of North-South relations goes from here is difficult to discern. Much will depend on two sets of formal and informal negotiations now in progress. The first concerns intra-OECD relations, and the second concerns the broad range of negotiations and institution-building efforts being undertaken between OPEC member countries on the one hand and much of the developing world on the other.

With regard to the Northern countries, a crucial issue will be the degree to which the OECD countries can overcome internal conflicts and control the "beggar-thy-neighbor" potential inherent in the group's $40 billion oil-induced

[i]Indeed the one reason that the Shah of Iran might pour substantial funds into India and Pakistan would be intimately related to the continued subtle and not-so-subtle game of regional hierarchy in the Middle East. Venezuela's concentration on Central America and the Caribbean region seems explicable in similar terms.

trade deficit. If the industrialized countries are induced by the oil crisis to overcome present differences over trade, monetary, and other international economic and political issues and to bind the wounds of the GATT, the IMF, and other institutions in the process, then an international economic system that continues to make incremental but steady progress toward assisting Southern development efforts is a plausible projection.[j]

However, the obstacles to achieving the necessary degree of industrialized country cooperation in the present international system have been noted above. They are essentially political obstacles, and as I have noted, they are *systemic*, not superficial. This point is amply demonstrated by continuing intra-OECD conflicts over strategies to deal with the petrodollar crisis in particular and with OPEC more generally. The establishment of the U.S.-sponsored International Energy Agency in December 1974 has not resolved these developed country conflicts. If they prove insurmountable, we may be headed toward a world of international economic relationships that combine a few quasi-universal norms—perhaps most notably in the monetary sphere—with stronger regional (and therefore discriminatory) trade and investment groupings and a host of de facto bilateral arrangements. The bilateral accords reached between France and Iran and the U.S. and Saudi Arabia during 1974 suggest the outlines of what such arrangements might entail.[k] In such a world there would be little left of Bretton Woods, Northern unity, or Southern cohesion. The political economy of North-South relations would be significantly altered but not in any systematic manner.

The other crucial issue concerns the evolution of the OPEC countries' relations with the OECD countries on the one hand and the developing world on the other. Will the "new rich" defy the "laws" of history and forego *embourgeoisement*, choosing rather to link themselves much more closely to the political economy and the goals of the developing world? Obviously this is not an either/or choice; the issue is one of degree. The more the OPEC countries, individually and collectively, do develop institutional links with and provide resource transfers to the South, the greater the opportunity for the present period to be remembered as one in which the global political economy did undergo a major structural change. The forces pulling OPEC countries and all other developing countries in this direction have been analyzed above. To those already mentioned should be added one other—the dangers to certain oil-rich

[j]This outcome would be even more likely if the OECD countries arrive at a consensus that invites OPEC cooperation rather than conflict. An OECD-OPEC *entente cordiale* would tend to limit the prospects for successful Southern attempts at major system change (i.e., structural change); it could at the same time increase the pace of North-South resource transfers within the present framework (i.e., process change).

[k]These two bilateral accords still appear to be devoid of much substance. This is probably due to the very uncertainty of events and trends in the present international atmosphere. If there is to be a system change such as that projected in this paragraph, however, one would expect to see such accords move from paper to the implementation stage.

states in abandoning ties to the developing world too quickly. The nature and degree of danger vary from state to state. For some of the smallest and richest, the threats are likely to be from outside their borders and may come in such disparate forms as a radically oriented struggle for Arab unity or straightforward regional hierarchical struggles. For other OPEC states, the dangers may take the form of radical domestic political challenges to leadership that appears to be joining the "old rich" of the world too rapidly.

But the OPEC countries will also be pulled the other way. In addition to the factors listed above suggesting their eventual *embourgeoisement*, there are two further reasons worth mention. The first involves their growing investments in the OECD countries and reliance on Northern industrial and military technology. With the passage of each year, the oil-rich countries will increasingly depend on the old rich for their future economic security. In effect, they will slowly become hostage to their own portfolios and development programs.

Second, and obviously, those less-than-radical regimes within the OPEC countries have little to gain and a great deal to lose from carrying a "Southern unity" strategy too far. By doing so they could jeopardize the beneficial aspects of their present political and economic relations with certain OECD countries; such an OPEC strategy could also raise developing country expectations regarding OPEC transfers of resources to the developing world that would most likely eventuate in disillusionment.

The OPEC countries will undoubtedly increase their political, economic, and military power by sizable increments each year for at least another five to ten years. How the major actors among them choose to commit that power will very probably determine the outcome of the fundamental issue raised in this chapter: the degree of change to be expected in present North-South political and economic relationships. Given the risks to these countries—especially those located in the Middle East—of opting unambiguously for *either* the North or the South, the most likely goal of OPEC country policies will be to keep both bridges open. The Southern connection can purchase a great deal of international "legitimacy" at a very small marginal cost; the Northern connection guarantees access to weapons, technology, investment opportunities, and, for some regimes, an added measure of support for domestic stability.

Given all the factors at play (save the Arab-Israeli conflict, the analysis of which would require another essay), the gradual *embourgeoisement* of the OPEC and other regional contenders for political and economic hegemony within the developing world seems the most probable outcome. But it would be *embourgeoisement* with one significant difference: the OPEC states, goaded by Algeria for its own ideological reasons, will have every reason to keep their bridge to the South in good order until they are convinced that their acceptance in Northern circles is genuine.[1] And this suggests a period of at least several years during

[1]The performance of the OPEC countries at the April 1975 Paris meeting to discuss an agenda for a summer conference on energy problems confirms the view that they intend to

which developing country bargaining power within such institutions as the International Monetary Fund and the World Bank and in the present round of GATT trade negotiations will be strengthened. While major structural changes in the international political economy are unlikely to result, altered bargaining power at the process level may produce some significant gains for the South. They can be sought in altered approaches to commodity arrangements, technology transfer, and world food reserves, and in increased bilateral and multilateral aid flows. And if OPEC aid levels remain significant, they may provide a major impetus to developing country regional arrangements designed to permanently strengthen bargaining power vis-à-vis Northern states and corporations.

Least likely to benefit from such changes will be the so-called Fourth World, generally poor in everything except population. That this unfortunate circumstance would distinguish this particular form of system evolution from any plausible alternative, however, is highly unlikely.

Notes

1. See Chapter 1.

2. For a more detailed exposition, see Richard N. Gardner, *Sterling–Dollar Diplomacy* (Oxford: Oxford University Press, 1956); and Richard N. Cooper, *The Economics of Interdependence* (New York: McGraw-Hill, 1968).

3. Susan Strange, "The United Nations and International Economic Relations," in *The Evolving United Nations: a Prospect for Peace?* (New York: St. Martin's Press, 1971), p. 114.

4. Cooper, *Economics of Interdependence*, p. 36.

5. The literature on the European–particularly the French–reaction to growing U.S. deficits during the 1960s is enormous. For divergent views on the issue, see the essays written by some distinguished international economists in Benjamin J. Cohen, ed., *American Foreign Economic Policy: Essays and Comments* (New York: Harper & Row, 1968), Part II. For an engaging presentation of the "European" case from a political point of view, see David P. Calleo and Benjamin M. Rowland, *America and the World Political Economy: Atlantic Dreams and National Realities* (Bloomington: Indiana University Press, 1973).

---

retain their "Southern connection" for some time. The Paris meeting ended in a deadlock when the OPEC members insisted that *all* commodity issues be placed on the agenda; the OECD countries refused to accept this point. However, it should be noted that the oil-producing countries may have had reasons of their own–for example, the supply and demand conditions for oil at that time–for allowing the Paris meeting to end in deadlock. Only time will reveal their real motives. Meanwhile, with Algeria serving as the lynchpin, OPEC's Southern connection remains intact.

6. See, for example, Harry G. Johnson, *Economic Policies Toward Less Developed Countries* (Washington, D.C.: Brookings Institution, 1967), Chap. III.

7. For the latest and most comprehensive analysis of the *negative* aspects of foreign direct investment on the development process in the South, see Richard J. Barnet and Ronald E. Müller, *Global Reach: The Power of the Multinational Corporations* (New York: Simon and Schuster, 1974), especially Part II and the studies cited therein. For a broader spectrum of views on this issue, see Robert O. Keohane and Van Dorn Ooms, "The Multinational Firm and International Regulation" in C. Fred Bergsten and Lawrence B. Krause, ed., *World Politics and International Economics* (Washington, D.C.: Brookings Institution, 1975), pp. 169-209; Keohane and Ooms, "The Multinational Enterprise and World Political Economy," *International Organization* 26 (Winter 1972): 84-120; Raymond Vernon, *Sovereignty at Bay: The Multinational Spread of U.S. Enterprises* (New York: Basic Books, 1971); Charles Kindleberger, ed., *The International Corporation: a Symposium* (Cambridge, Mass.: MIT Press, 1970), and the articles by C. Fred Bergsten and Joseph S. Nye, Jr., in *Foreign Affairs* 53, no. 1 (October 1974): 135-175.

8. For such an analytical assessment, see Johnson, *Economic Policies*, and John Pincus, *Trade, Aid and Development: the Rich and Poor Nations* (New York: McGraw-Hill, 1967).

9. Stanley Hoffmann, *Gulliver's Troubles, or the Setting of American Foreign Policy* (New York: McGraw-Hill, 1968), Chap. II.

10. Ibid., p. 21.

11. See Theodore Geiger, *The Conflicted Relationship: The West and the Transformation of Asia, Africa and Latin America* (New York: McGraw-Hill, 1967), Chaps. III and IV.

12. See Theodore Geiger, *The Fortunes of the West: The Future of the Atlantic Nations* (Bloomington: Indiana University Press, 1973), Chap. II.

13. Stanley Hoffmann, "The Fate of the Nation-State," *Daedalus* (Summer 1966): 865.

14. For a discussion of the impact of these forces on nation-state behavior, see Cooper, *Economics of Interdependence*, and Robert O. Keohane and Joseph S. Nye, Jr., eds., *Transnational Relations and World Politics, Special issue of International Organization* 25, no. 3 (Summer 1971), particularly the opening and closing essays of the volume.

15. Robert O. Keohane and Joseph S. Nye, Jr., "World Politics and the International Economic System" in C. Fred Bergsten, ed., *The Future of the International Economic Order: An Agenda for Research* (Lexington, Mass.: Lexington Books, D.C. Heath and Company, 1973), pp. 118 ff.

16. For some impressive evidence on this point, see Barnet and Müller, *Global Reach*, Chap. 8, and C. Fred Bergsten, "Coming Investment Wars?", *Foreign Affairs* (October 1974): 135-152.

17. See C. Fred Bergsten, "The New Era in World Commodity Markets," *Challenge* (September/October 1974): 34-42.

18. This section draws heavily on my essay, "The Political Economy of North-South Relations: How Much Change?" *International Organization* (Autumn 1975): 921-948.

19. Zbigniew Brzezinski, "U.S. Foreign Policy: The Search for Focus," *Foreign Affairs* 51, no. 4 (July 1973): 726.

20. On the renewed potential for serious confrontation over the issue of income distribution within the United States, see Alice M. Rivlin's 1974 Richard T. Ely Lecture presented to the American Economic Association, "Income Distribution–Can Economists Help?" (mimeo).

21. See Roger D. Hansen, "Agenda for Thought: The Global Distribution of Income and Economic Opportunity" in James Howe et al., *The U.S. and World Development: Agenda for Action 1975* (New York: Praeger, 1975) for a discussion of present profiles of global and domestic income distribution.

22. For an example of the former, see *The World Food and Energy Crises: The Role of International Organizations*, Proceedings of an International Conference with a Report by Richard N. Gardner (Rensselaerville, N.Y.: The Institute on Man and Science, 1974), p. 65; for an example of the latter, see McGeorge Bundy, "After the Deluge, the Covenant," *The Saturday Review*, August 24, 1974, pp. 18 ff.

23. Barnet and Müller, *Global Reach*, Chap. 8.

24. Francisco Orrego Vicuña, "Latin American Policies on the Law of the Sea: The Prospects of a World Compromise Agreement," paper presented to the Conference on Conflict and Order in Ocean Relations, Airlie House, Airlie, Virginia, October 21-24, 1974.

25. Branislav Gosovic, *UNCTAD: Conflict and Compromise* (Holland: A.W. Sijthoff-Leiden, 1972), p. 272.

26. On the "resource scarcity" issue in general, see William D. Nordhaus, "Resources as a Constraint on Growth," *American Economic Review, Papers and Proceedings* (May 1974) 64: 22-26 and the literature cited therein, particularly Nordhaus's other works.

27. One of the best and most succinct analyses remains Klaus Knorr's *The Uses of Military Power in the Nuclear Age* (Princeton, N.J.: Princeton University Press, 1966).

28. For a summary discussion of the OECD findings, see "OPEC Members Lift Aid Outflows to New Peak of Nearly $9 Billion," *IMF Survey*, November 18, 1974, pp. 357 ff.

29. Keohane and Nye, "World Politics and the International Economic System," p. 156.

30. Address by Robert S. McNamara to the Board of Governors of the World Bank Group, 1974.

About the Contributors

C. Fred Bergsten is Assistant Secretary for International Affairs, U.S. Treasury Department. He was formerly a senior fellow at the Brookings Institution, where the work here was performed, and assistant for International Economic Affairs to Dr. Henry Kissinger, on the senior staff of the National Security Council. Dr. Bergsten has written and edited numerous books in the field of international economics, most recently *American Multinationals and American Interests; The Dilemmas of the Dollar: The Economics and Politics of United States International Monetary Policy; World Politics and International Economics;* and *Toward A New International Economic Order: Selected Papers of C. Fred Bergsten, 1972-1974.*

Marcello de Cecco is professor of monetary economics at the University of Siena and visiting professor of international economics at the Johns Hopkins University Bologna Center. He has also been a research fellow of the Royal Institute of International Affairs, London; visiting professor at St. Antony's College, Oxford; visiting lecturer at the London School of Economics; and, visiting professor at the Ecole National d'Administration, Paris. His publications include *Money and Empire* and articles on international financial markets and European economic integration.

Benjamin J. Cohen is associate professor of international economic relations at the Fletcher School of Law and Diplomacy, Tufts University. He has worked at the Federal Reserve Bank of New York and taught at Princeton University. His publications include *The Future of Sterling as an International Currency* and *The Question of Imperialism.* In 1975-1976 he was visiting research associate at the Atlantic Institute for International Affairs (Paris), and in 1976-1977 was full-time consultant to the Secretary General of the Organization for Economic Cooperation and Development.

Geoffrey Denton is a reader in economics at the University of Reading in the United Kingdom and is director of the Federal Trust for Education and Research in London. Professor Denton's publications include *Growth in the British Economy; Economic Planning and Policies in Britain, France and Germany* with M. MacLennan and M. Forsyth; *Trade Effects of Public Subsidies to Private Industry* with S. O'Claireacain and S. Ash; and *Economic Integration in Europe* (edited).

H. Edward English is professor and director of the Center of Canadian Studies at the Johns Hopkins School of Advanced International Studies. From 1949 to 1973 he taught economics at Carleton University, Ottawa, where he also served as director of the School of International Affairs. He has also served as Assistant

Deputy Minister of the Department of Commerce and Corporate Affairs of the government of Canada, and in various other economic research and advisory capacities. His publications include *Transatlantic Economic Community: Canadian Perspectives* and *Canada in a Wider Economic Community* with Bruce W. Wilkinson and Harry C. Eastman. He is also editor and contributor to *Canada-United States Relations;* and *Telecommunications for Canada.*

Wilhelm Hankel, formerly a banker and an official of the Ministry of Economics of the Federal Republic of Germany, is a professor of economics at the Johann-Wolfgang-Goethe University in Frankfurt. During 1974-1976 he was a John F. Kennedy Fellow at Harvard University and a visiting professor of German and International Affairs at Georgetown University. His publications include *Währungspolitik–Geldwertstabilisierung, Währungsintegration und Sparerschutz, Der Ausweg aus der Krise, Wirtschaft ohne Grenzen: eine Weltwirtschaftslehre.*

Roger D. Hansen is a senior fellow at the Overseas Development Council and the Council on Foreign Relations. In 1972-1973 he served as Special Assistant to the Special Representative for Trade Negotiations. Previously, he worked as an international economic and project director at the National Planning Association. He is also visiting Blaustein Professor of International Organization at the Johns Hopkins School of Advanced International Studies. His publications include *A Central American Common Market* and articles on the political economy of the developing countries.

Harold B. Malmgren, formerly United States Deputy Special Representative for Trade Negotiations, a professor of international business at George Washington University and an economic consultant in Washington, D.C. During 1975-1976 he was a fellow of the Woodrow Wilson International Center for Scholars, Smithsonian Institution. His publications include *International Economic Peace Keeping in Phase II, Pacific Basin Development: The American Interests*, and numerous articles on United States foreign economic policy.

Edward L. Morse is a senior fellow associated with the 1980's Project at the Council on Foreign Relations and visiting associate Blaustein Professor of International Organization at the Johns Hopkins School of Advanced International Studies. From 1969-1975 he was associate professor of politics and international affairs at the Woodrow Wilson School, Princeton University. His publications include *Modernization and the Transformation of International Relations, Foreign Policy and Interdependence in Gaullist France,* and numerous articles on interdependence and international political economy.

Theo Peeters is professor of economics at the University of Louvain where he is also associated with the Center for Economic Studies. He has also taught at the Facultés Université Notre Dame de la Paix at Namour, at the College of Europe, and has been a consultant to the Belgian Ministry of Foreign Affairs and the European Community. He is the author of numerous articles on international trade and monetary affairs, and on European economic integration.

Philip H. Trezise is a senior fellow in Foreign Policy studies at the Brookings Institution. From 1946-1971 he served in numerous posts with the United States Department of State, his last position being Assistant Secretary of State for Economic Affairs. He is the author of *The Atlantic Connection, Rebuilding Grain Reserves: Toward an International System,* and coauthor of *Asia's New Giant: How the Japanese Economy Works.*

About the Editor

Wilfrid L. Kohl is associate professor of political science and director of the Johns Hopkins University Bologna Center. From 1972-1976, he taught at Columbia University where he was also associate director of the Institute on Western Europe. Previously he served on the staffs of the National Security Council and the Ford Foundation. He is the author of *French Nuclear Diplomacy* and of articles on foreign policy and U.S.-European relations in *World Politics, Journal of International Affairs, Orbis, Political Science Quarterly,* and others.